AF519763

Entrepreneurship in Developing and Emerging Economies

Ali J. Ahmad
Punita Bhatt
Iain Acton

ATLANTIC
PUBLISHERS & DISTRIBUTORS (P) LTD

ATLANTIC
PUBLISHERS & DISTRIBUTORS (P) LTD

7/22, Ansari Road, Darya Ganj, New Delhi
Tel.: +91-11-4077 5252, 2327 3880
E-mail: orders@atlanticbooks.com
Web: www.atlanticbooks.com

All rights reserved. No part of this publication may be reproduced, stored in a retrieval system, transmitted or utilized in any form or by any means, electronic, mechanical, photocopying, recording or otherwise, without the prior permission of the copyright owner. Application for such permission should be addressed to the publisher.

Published by Atlantic Publishers & Distributors (P) Ltd 2024

Copyright © Ali J. Ahmad, Punita Bhatt and Iain Acton, 2019

Previously Published by SAGE Publications in 2019

Disclaimer

- The author and the publisher have taken every effort to the maximum of their skill, expertise and knowledge to provide correct material in the book. Even then if some mistakes persist in the content of the book, the publisher does not take responsibility for the same. The publisher shall have no liability to any person or entity with respect to any loss or damage caused, or alleged to have been caused directly or indirectly, by the information contained in this book.
- The author has fully tried to follow the copyright law. However, if any work is found to be similar, it is unintentional and the same should not be used as defamatory or to file legal suit against the author.
- If the readers find any mistakes, we shall be grateful to them for pointing out those to us so that these can be corrected in the next edition.
- All disputes are subject to the jurisdiction of Delhi courts only.

Printed & bound in India by Atlantic Print Services

Advance Praise

This book is for entrepreneurship educators who believe that their students can learn more by 'doing' entrepreneurship than just 'learning' about entrepreneurship. It is a powerful guide for faculty and students keen to understand the process of entrepreneurship. Moreover, it doesn't matter which domain expert you are, the content here is relevant to all.

Abha Rishi
CEO, AIC-BIMTECH and Chairperson,
Centre for Innovation and Entrepreneurship Development,
Birla Institute of Management Technology, Greater Noida

This is an easy-to-read book with many descriptions, illustrations and exercises dealing with basic concepts in entrepreneurship. The book will prove relevant and useful to students seeking an introduction to entrepreneurship issues in developing countries.

Alnoor Bhimani
Honorary Dean,
LUMS Business School, Lahore

Academics and practitioners seem to have different ways of looking at life. Through extensive research, academic grit and personal entrepreneurial experiences, the authors effectively built interweaving bridges between these two worlds. The book is not just helpful with its exercises and framework but is also a lot of fun to read. Emerging economies, changing times and paradigm shifts in technology will require astute understanding of the past and courage to embrace the future keeping cultural connotations in mind; the authors, through wonderful real-life experiences, anecdotes, metaphors and engaging storytelling, have been able to create a wonderful piece of work. This book can prove invaluable not only to entrepreneurs in the developing world but also to ones in the West who may want to understand cultural nuances and help prepare for opportunities in tomorrow's world.

Kaustav Majumdar
Head, Start-ups & Incubation,
S. P. Jain Institute of Management & Research (SPJIMR), Mumbai

A very well-researched book with amazing examples of the entrepreneurial mindset from all over the world. To complete the learning process, the book also suggests exercises at the end of each chapter. Aspiring entrepreneurs from diverse backgrounds will find this a very practical guide to understand the fundamentals of entrepreneurship.

Priyank Narayan
Director, Centre for Entrepreneurship,
Ashoka University, Sonepat, Haryana

Entrepreneurship has become a source of hope of millions of youth in the emerging and developing economies. Entrepreneurship has enabled people to create new ventures with the least amount of resources and solve emerging problems and needs. A textbook on entrepreneurship in the emerging and developing economies was long awaited. I hope that this book will be a great resource for faculty and students.

Shahid Qureshi
Associate Professor and Program Director,
IBA AMAN Centre for Entrepreneurial Development, Karachi

Teaching entrepreneurship requires a fine blend of theory and practice, with relevant case studies that could create interest among learners. I am glad to find all these in this textbook which adds to the existing knowledge, more so from the perspectives of developing economies. The book not only covers 'the practices of entrepreneurship' and 'enterprise design' but also does justice to the relatively newer critical issues related to 'start-up enterprise management'. I hope both students and educators will find it immensely useful.

Sunil Shukla
Director,
Entrepreneurship Development Institute of India, Gandhinagar

This work is dedicated to all my students who have taught me much.

—Ali J. Ahmad

I would like to dedicate this book to my son Shubhro, who has endured my focus on writing projects over most holidays.

—Punita Bhatt

For Imogen and my three wonderful shadows, Oscar, Pearl and Flora.

—Iain Acton

Contents

Detailed Contents

SECTION B
ENTERPRISE DESIGN

SECTION C
START-UP ENTERPRISE MANAGEMENT

List of Figures

List of Tables

List of Abbreviations

CAC	customer acquisition cost
CREME	Centre for Research in Ethnic Minority Entrepreneurship
CSR	corporate social responsibility
DCM	digital content management
DIY	do-it-yourself
DJI	Da Jiang Innovations
E&E	enterprise and entrepreneurship
EVs	electric vehicles
GIAN	Grassroots Innovation Augmentation Network
GMW	Gayam Motor Works
GST	general sales tax
HPS	Husk Power Systems
IM	inventory management
IP	intellectual property
J2BD	jobs-to-be-done
MFIs	microfinance institutions
MMI	Modern Montessori International
MMORPG	massively multiplayer online role-playing game
MUDRA Bank	Micro Units Development and Refinance Agency Bank
MVP	minimum viable product
NGOs	non-governmental organizations
O2O	online to offline
OP	original post
P2P	peer-to-peer
PPC	pay-per-click advertising
R&D	research and development
SEAB	Singapore Examinations and Assessment Board
SEO	search engine optimization
SEWA	Self Employed Women's Association
SMEs	small and medium enterprises
SVC	social venture capital
UNHCR	United Nations High Commissioner for Refugees
VAT	value added tax
VCs	venture capitalists
VP	value proposition
WC	working capital
WOM	word-of-mouth
WTP	willingness to pay

Foreword

Entrepreneurship and innovation are imperative for developing countries. Our experience at the Centre for Research in Ethnic Minority Entrepreneurship (CREME) demonstrates the importance of these processes time and again in the case of migrants who make their way in new societies by being creative, resilient and entrepreneurial.

New ventures that commercialize home-grown technological innovations out of local institutes of higher learning and research can bring great prosperity in developing countries. Taking the 'high road' to development through innovation-led new venture creation is undoubtedly more demanding than low value-added enterprise. But it is likely to be more personally rewarding, scalable and generative. To make this happen, we need to nurture the leaders, the change-makers, the creative sparks, who will drive developing countries' next transformation. This is the ability to develop and exploit new ideas that will produce something—whether a product or a service is better than anywhere else in the world. In turn, this ability to create newness and value drives growth and attracts investment, creating a positive cycle. The foundation for this ability is *education*.

This teaching text encourages progressive entrepreneurship and innovation and aims to help higher education institutes develop the next generation of pioneers. The authors Ali and Iain teach at Warwick Manufacturing Group (WMG) and Punita works at Aston University's CREME. They are accomplished academicians and practitioners who share my vision. Their research and association with students from around the world who enrol for our programmes at Aston Business School have meant that they have considered the 'teaching and learning', as well as the 'doing business' environments of developing countries. The authors have helped hundreds of students from around the world to develop their business ideas, think about link-ups with science and technology research from their own countries and step into the exciting world of entrepreneurship.

Students and educators will find that the range of topics covered and the example case studies are well written with good explanatory scope. Reading through some of the cases, I found the achievements of unsung hero entrepreneurs from developing countries building a sense of pride and confidence in me. You will find familiar names and some new ones, and can easily follow the text because it is practically orientated. What I also appreciate is that the authors have not assumed *any* prior learning for students—you do not have to be taking a course in business disciplines to benefit from this text. You could be studying musicology, mathematics or medicine; irrespective of that, an education in entrepreneurship would benefit you tremendously.

I wish you all the success in your entrepreneurial careers.

Professor Monder Ram

OBE, Director of CREME,

Aston Business School, UK

Preface

We were motivated to write this textbook because the development of conceptual and empirical understanding on the subject of enterprise and entrepreneurship (E&E) has primarily been from a Western and developed country perspective. This is not to say that what we know about the phenomenon is inaccurate; however, our understanding in the area is certainly incomplete. E&E tools and techniques often taught at American and European business schools, if not adequately modified to the starting and doing business context in emerging and developing countries, can yield meaningless and counterproductive results.

We find that existing E&E teaching texts have not taken into account the unique problems of new venture creation in parts of the world where cultural norms of doing business have no semblance with what constitutes professional practice in nations categorized as 'developed'. Emerging and developing countries have unique entrepreneurial ecosystems, and they significantly differ from their developed/industrialized counterparts. In such countries, the environment for doing business is often earmarked by high levels of income inequality, institutional decay and problems of regulation and transparency—which increases the level of complexity and uncertainty many folds for would-be entrepreneurs. Hence, the role of E&E education in emerging and developing countries would, therefore, be to adequately equip students for navigating the entrepreneurial process in a manner that is adequately embedded in their own socio-politico-cultural contexts.

NOTE TO EDUCATORS

If you already teach E&E, we laud your choice and through this textbook aim to revitalize your teaching work with new content. If you are new to E&E education, we offer our *congratulations* on a number of fronts. First, on taking a step towards becoming an educator in arguably the most important phenomenon of the modern era. Entrepreneurship drives innovation and creates new markets, which generates employment and new wealth. Second, on the privilege of planting seeds in students' minds that might one day germinate into history-making action on their part—the creation of new enterprises that could transform lives. Third, with the aid of this textbook, on the surety that you will be teaching the most colourful, compelling and rewarding course of your academic career.

Our primary aim is to enable educators, irrespective of their academic specializations, to deliver a high-impact E&E course to 18+ students undertaking any programme of study at an institution of higher learning. Whether you already teach within the broad area of business and management studies or are an educator in any other discipline—chemistry, law, phlebotomy—this textbook and its accompanying resources will make your task of delivering an E&E course more stimulating and intellectually rewarding.

Teaching E&E, where you wish to cultivate within your students the skills necessary for 'doing' entrepreneurship (as opposed to learning 'about' entrepreneurship), though rewarding, is not an easy task. You, the educator, and not the content, will be the centrepiece of the delivery equation, and this will require the cultivation of an entrepreneurial orientation within yourself first. If you were fortunate enough to have started a business and succeeded (or even failed), then know this—you will bring tremendous credibility to your teaching style. If you have not met the right conditions yet to begin your own entrepreneurial journey, then reflect on your past personal and professional experiences, and recollect instances where you were able to demonstrate entrepreneurial skills—it may have been original thinking when renovating your house, negotiating a good deal for the purchase of your car or winning a research bid. Not much can substitute the value of personal experience when teaching a subject like E&E. Unlike heavily technical or conceptual business subjects, such as accounting, marketing and operations management, E&E teaching is required to be personally reflective, experiential and kinaesthetic or tactile in mode. This makes learning a lot more playful and compelling for students and fun for educators.

Your role in the course ought to be one of a steward, facilitator and broker of knowledge and experience—not a lecturer or tutor. In our design of an E&E curriculum and teaching methodology, you will have an opportunity to absorb new ideas from your students and students will have an opportunity to learn from not only you but also one another. The wonderful news is—*no prior learning in any business discipline is needed for either you—the educator—or your students.*

TEACHING *NON-BUSINESS* STUDENTS E&E

Considerable sums are invested by students in their education, and particularly in emerging and developing countries, a return on investment is expected—meaningful employment upon graduation. Youth unemployment and underemployment are on the rise in such economies, and even the most well-trained and dedicated students find it difficult to secure jobs upon graduation. Student employability can be positively impacted if they are equipped to systematically consider self-employment and entrepreneurship as a viable career option. Moreover, existing employers benefit from new staff with an entrepreneurial skill set. Intrapreneurs have shown to add value to organizations by identifying new opportunities for growth, work with resources available to bring innovative ideas to market and take on new challenges through affirmative action.

We advocate that students undertaking higher education qualifications in any discipline would immensely benefit from a taught component in E&E. Quite often, teaching programmes in the area are housed within business and management faculties or departments. Although such arrangements may appear to be the most 'natural' for deploying E&E teaching and learning programmes, experience shows that doing so is fraught with a number of difficulties. These difficulties arise due to a number of inaccurate assumptions about the role and recipients of E&E education, including the following.

First, would be an assumption often made about the nature and purposes of E&E education, that it primarily deals with infusing students with the kind of technical business knowledge that enables the efficient *running* of new enterprises. Indeed, a reasonable level of technical expertise in accounting, sales, marketing, intellectual property management, information systems and human resource management is highly desirable in new entrepreneurs who are actively looking to set up new enterprises. However, such expertise usually comes into play when managing enterprises grow and *not* during the time when their foundations are being laid. 'Set-up' and 'growth' are distinct phases within the start-up lifecycle of any enterprise, demanding entirely different types of expertise. Hence, it would be important to cultivate, alongside technical business skills, those important skills which would help students deal with the initial opportunity framing, uncertainty and risk-related problems inherent in any new venture-creation exercise—skills that students do not automatically acquire when studying for business and management qualifications.

Second, would be the erroneous assumption that business and management students are the best candidates for undertaking E&E education because it is they who are most likely to embark on entrepreneurial journeys leading to new venture creation. Both experience and research data negate this assumption. Depriving students from other disciplines such as medicine, law, engineering, information technology, the pure sciences and other disciplines is unfair and short-sighted. Research shows that most new enterprises are in fact set up by individuals who undertake non-business studies at the higher education level, disciplines where 'creation of newness' or solving meaningful problems is a central focus. Such entrepreneurs often complain about the manner in which the university education system ill-prepared them for the trials of new venture creation. Hence, students in any discipline and arguably at any level can benefit from E&E education.

Finally, and allied to the above, the third contestable assumption would be that business and management academicians are best qualified to design and deliver programmes in E&E. If teaching and learning programmes are designed keeping in view the above two assumptions, then it could certainly be argued that business and management faculty would be best qualified to teach students with suitable prior knowledge on the 'technical' aspects of E&E activity. However, our understanding of what constitutes learning within the area has moved beyond mere technical learning outcomes. Hence, the focus alongside technical knowledge must also be on practice-based skills and internalizing the principles through which entrepreneurial decision-making occurs. Aspects which subject tutors in any discipline and *without* business and management experience and training would be able to infuse through the aid of this textbook.

We hope you are now convinced that teaching E&E to non-business students is exceedingly important. Not only are such skills valued by existing employers, but they also equip students to steer an alternative career choice—self-employment and new venture creation—if not immediately upon graduation then at some stage during their careers.

ABOUT THIS BOOK: ITS STRUCTURE AND HOW TO USE IT

For developing this textbook, we assessed numerous other popular texts for facilitating the teaching of E&E. We also looked at the peer-reviewed literature and UK's Quality Assurance Agency's guidelines on what constitutes a good E&E curriculum and teaching approach. Combined with our own experience of teaching the subject in UK, Nigeria, India, Saudi Arabia and Pakistan, a much more nuanced understanding around the design and delivery of E&E education in an emerging and developing country perspective came forth.

In this book, we have brought together the most valuable elements of three predominant 'programmes' that have been used to cultivate E&E skills in students. These *programmes*, singly, have been normatively the entire focus of E&E textbooks. Valuable in their own right, such *programmes* on their own remain incomplete schemes for meeting what we believe to be the one fundamental requirement of E&E education in an emerging and developing economy context—to calibrate students with the skills and behaviours that prompt, at some stage in their careers, affirmative action towards self-employment and new venture creation.

Hence, this book, drawing on the valuable contributions of earlier entrepreneurship textbook authors, is divided into three sections, each of which constitutes a *programme* of study to help students realize their entrepreneurial potential. These include the following:

1. **The Practices of Entrepreneurship:** Students are introduced to fundamental practices of enterprise including creation, experimentation, reflection and decision-making.
2. **Enterprise Design:** Students build the skills to engage in pre-start-up activity including value proposition design, lean start-up principles, jobs-to-be-done thinking and undertaking customer research.
3. **Start-up Enterprise Management:** Students learn the fundamentals of start-up financial management, sales techniques, pitching for investment and about ethics and professional practice.

Most delivery within our scheme relies on learning by doing, storytelling with case study analyses and self-reflection exercises. All chapters follow a more or less standardized format to build familiarity and accompanying case studies, photos and illustrations aid in improving the book's readability for both instructors and students.

For course facilitators, comprehensive accompanying resources are provided for executing engaging sessions on 13 topics. Such resources include slide decks, multimedia content and relevant preparatory materials.

About the Authors

From left to right: Punita Bhatt, Ali J. Ahmad and Iain Acton

Ali J. Ahmad teaches innovation at WMG, University of Warwick, UK, as a senior teaching fellow. He was born and schooled in Karachi, Pakistan. He has an MSc in information systems awarded by the London School of Economics and Political Science, another MSc in management research awarded by the University of Oxford's Said Business School and a PhD in entrepreneurship from Dublin City University. He has a decade of experience in teaching and scholarship in the areas of entrepreneurship and innovation; his articles on technology and business incubation and social innovation and entrepreneurship are regularly published in reputable international journals. His teaching, research and consulting activity is spread across Nigeria, Saudi Arabia, Pakistan and India. He has supervised over 100 projects of final-year students and co-supervised a number of PhDs in the area of entrepreneurship. He also started up three ventures in Pakistan as CEO and prides himself on having first-hand experience of doing entrepreneurship in a developing country context. Ali has wide-ranging interests, but most of all he enjoys motorcycling and practising Muay Thai.

Punita Bhatt is a research fellow at Aston University's Centre for Research in Ethnic Minority Entrepreneurship. She has a PhD in business from Oxford Brookes University, an MA in economics and an MBA in finance from India.

She was born in Allahabad, India, and did her schooling from Indian School, Muscat. She has over a decade of teaching experience in entrepreneurship and innovation in leading business schools in UK. She has supervised hundreds of master's dissertations and entrepreneurship projects at both undergraduate and postgraduate levels. Before joining academia, she headed Sony Corporation's treasury in India and founded a start-up IT firm delivering multimedia solutions to schools.

Iain Acton is co-founder and partner at Disruptive Lemonade, which builds innovation and entrepreneurial capabilities by providing coaching and training programmes for individuals, teams and organizations. Over the last 15 years, he has worked fluidly between academia and business consulting, specializing in customer-led innovation projects, designing management practice, marketing strategy and entrepreneurship. He supervises students on University of Warwick's MSc Innovation and Entrepreneurship programme and teaches the innovation module internationally for WMG, University of Warwick. He has a significant track record of delivering entrepreneurship programmes in collaboration with UK universities, business consulting services and strategic customer research programmes at multinational companies (such as Jaguar Land Rover), UK-based start-ups and small and medium enterprises (SMEs). His key strength is his multidisciplinary knowledge of design, marketing and business innovation strategy.

SECTION A

THE PRACTICES OF ENTREPRENEURSHIP

1

An Introduction to Enterprise and Entrepreneurship

LEARNING OUTCOMES

- Identify the differences between enterprise and entrepreneurship
- Become familiar with enterprise skills and the means to practise them
- Understand the requirements for practising entrepreneurship by becoming familiar with entrepreneurship skills
- Be able to create a personal entrepreneurial road map

1.1. WHAT IS ENTERPRISE?

Spotlight on Farhan Masood, an 'Entrepreneur Extraordinaire' from Pakistan: Part 1

Farhan was born in Lahore, Pakistan, where his father owned an offset printing business. He loved technology, and this love was unknowingly kindled by his father who would buy the trendiest gadgets but would not allow Farhan to play with them. Once his father brought home an IBM XT computer; although he was not allowed to play with the new machine, he would watch his father, peeking through the room's key-hole, whenever he played 'Digger'. One day he got his chance. When his father went away on a business trip, seizing the opportunity, Farhan mimicking his father's key strikes was able to get the XT booted and became a natural at playing 'Digger'. Upon return, his father was not too happy, but he began to admire Farhan's natural skill with the computer. This seminal incident laid the foundation for Farhan's entrepreneurial career in the world of computing technology.

Farhan recalls being a rebellious teenager. As a young boy, not enjoying regular studies, he would skip his classes at a local Urdu-medium school to spend his days at a book store in Hafeez Centre—Lahore's hub for computing equipment. He was interested in the computer books and luckily the store owner let Farhan read as many as he wanted and to also use his computer to practise. It was there that Farhan created his first computer program—a drawing of a Volkswagen in the BASIC language. He had found his passion—something he enjoyed and was getting good at—computer graphics programming.

At the age of 14, he set about to put his newly found skills to work and created software for textile design, which, through a friend, he was able to sell to a manufacturer. However, by the time he turned 19, tensions arose at home because Farhan's father wanted him to pursue a traditional academic career. His tenacity though was unwavering, rather than studying for college entrance exams, Farhan's father found him programming and designing the website of Brain Net—the country's first internet service provider. Instead of making him appear for exams, his enraged father dropped him off to the Brain Net office where he was able to create enough of a ruckus so as to secure a meeting with its CEO. His reimagining of the Brain Net website impressed the CEO and when Farhan was asked what he wanted in exchange for his services, he did not ask for money; instead, he demanded something a lot more valuable and that which Brain Net could easily provide—unlimited and totally free-to-use internet when the cost of a dial-up internet connection was exorbitant. With unlimited free internet, Farhan could now fully immerse himself into web technologies and design.

Farhan's story continues later in this chapter.

Source: Rizvi (2017).

Note: The authors acknowledge Mr Azhar Rizvi for introducing to us the case of Farhan Masood through his book *Entrepreneuring Pakistan: 27 stories of struggle, failure and success.*

Enterprise is the application of ideas to practical situations for the purpose of solving problems. To be enterprising requires the application of creativity to develop ideas that offer practical solutions. Once an idea evolves into a good 'solution', an enterprising individual like Farhan (above) uses expression, communication and practical action to take his/her solution to implementation. The twin abilities of being able (a) to creatively think about problems and their solutions and (b) to take affirmative action to realize such thinking's potential come together in an enterprising individual.

Indeed, both the above sets of abilities are needed, and Farhan's case (above) is a useful example to prove this rule; he used his computer graphic programming skills to think creatively about the problem of textile design that manufacturers in Pakistan faced and came up with a solution—a piece of software. He could have stopped there or at an earlier point. His goal was not merely to develop the software but to also see it used commercially. Using his friend's connection and plunging into action, he set up his software at a manufacturer and was duly compensated for his endeavour. The combination of 'thinking' and 'doing' forms the basis for enterprise, in other words, conjuring an idea and making it happen.

Enterprise skills are a mix of emotional, intellectual, social and practical learned behaviours (like whistling or cycling) which cannot be easily taught in the classroom; they need to be practised in the real world. The following in equal order of importance represent the seven most significant skills enterprising individuals possess; you can hone these by undertaking their proposed application.

1. **Taking Initiative to Make Things Happen**
   This skill is about being able to take affirmative action even if that means going against the status quo, facing daunting challenges and being pioneering. Taking initiative is not an easy prospect, especially if you have not had the experience of taking up an issue seriously or championing a cause in the past. It does require a degree of courage and self-belief, behaviours you can infuse your personality with through systematic practice. A majority of people wait for others to take initiative due to a mixture of fear of consequences, inertia, cognitive dissonance and apathy. For some of us, becoming comfortable with taking initiative requires baby steps, and the first of those at times proves to be the biggest challenge. Starting with something menial like making our beds the first thing in the morning, a first step which gives structure to the day and creates impetus to take further more serious and purposeful initiative.
2. **Intuitive Decision-making**
   Making sense of rapidly changing situations without the need to labour through complex reasoning is an important enterprise skill. Think about this skill through the analogy of competitive sport—footballers in a typical game make rapid decisions in real time about their field placement and game strategy, without pausing for analysis. It simply becomes known to them and they act. Sometimes they make mistakes, but expert players make fewer of these than novices. To be a good intuitive decision-maker, you will need to train your brain to become good at recognizing patterns. Look within yourself and dig out a passion, if you do not have one now, you will need to keep on trying different things till you settle on one. Once you discover it, then begins the no-shortcuts journey of practising your passion. Remember, it is an established rule, to be an 'expert' at doing anything you will need to put in about 10,000 hours of practice.
3. **Connecting with People**
   Enterprising individuals are able to make bonds quickly with all manner of people while keeping their biases in check. Connecting also requires investment in time and energy for building relationships, especially with individuals who are outside of your personal network. It is nearly impossible to make things happen on your own, you will need to work with others. Getting buy-in and winning people's trust are personal skills that can be honed with practice. It is well known that people relate with others much better face to face and when they are treated as equals. This will require the demonstration of vulnerability and an attitude that acknowledges their importance.

   To connect with people for the purpose of getting buy-in for a new venture, prepare stories with familiar characters. Complex information can be conveniently encoded in story-like narratives, and telling it well with flair can be a very useful technique for securing buy-in and winning trust.

4. **Identifying Opportunities**
   Enterprising individuals are constantly on the lookout for or creating a set of circumstances that can lead to personal growth. Developing a mindset that is *opportunity open* requires that you internalize a number of beliefs: 'I am valuable', 'my growth is my own responsibility' and 'it is okay to fail but not okay to not try'. Looking at the world through the above beliefs filter will show you sets of favourable circumstances which you could use to initiate personal growth. The 'opportunity open', as opposed to 'opportunistic', mindset will also necessitate the creation of personal growth conditions. At times a long and fruitful chain of events can be created by taking a small first step: making a phone call to an old school friend, responding to an advertisement, introducing yourself to a stranger on the bus or visiting an unfamiliar place purposefully to explore.
5. **Creative Problem-solving**
   It is the ability to conjure up non-traditional solutions for 'solvable' problems. It is one of the most difficult-to-master enterprise skills as it relies on techniques learned through a considerable amount of practice. Combating a host of mental biases which trigger familiar and patterned behaviour requires a good understanding of the limits of human cognition and the techniques used to circumvent these. The practice of out-of-the-box or creative thinking requires that we challenge assumptions about problems with the knowledge that our brains 'jump to the easiest conclusions'—conclusions which can be grossly inaccurate. A useful method to train your brain for creative thinking is solving riddles and other numerical problems often seen in IQ exams, taking apart gadgets and putting them back together, asking more 'why' and 'how' type questions to elicit in-depth details and providing detailed explanations of problems to interested participants.
6. **Strategic Thinking**
   An important enterprise skill is the ability to set goals and develop accompanying plans to achieve these. Being one step ahead of developing situations and ushering events in a manner which leads to intended outcomes is what strategists are able to manoeuver. Strategic thinking starts with the following clear premises: 'I know what I want', 'I am willing to be patient', 'I know what I will need' and 'I can anticipate intended and unintended consequences of my actions'. Exercising strategic thinking requires a good understanding of human motivation and micro-norms that inhibit or enable action. At times it becomes exceedingly difficult to accurately predict outcomes of action because hidden risks may not have been adequately accounted for. Hence, the ability to exercise patience and to internalize learning resulting from strategy failure is equally important within the range of skills that influence one's ability to do strategic thinking.
7. **Personal Effectiveness**
   Being intellectually and emotionally equipped to thrive in environments marred by complexity and uncertainty is a skill that all enterprising individuals equip themselves with. To exercise other enterprise skills, a great deal of personal effectiveness or self-management must be learned. The premise of such learning is neither optimism nor extroversion, but rather an attitude that puts a tangible value on your time. The realization that we can only be effective in a small and finite amount of time available to us during a typical day is the

cornerstone of self-management. Planning for spending that time meaningfully, in a manner that influences personal growth, and then following through with such plans will lead to enterprising outcomes. Being personally effective for those who are not self-motivated or are trapped in a state of inertia is necessarily difficult. The realization that the only person who can help you is 'you' is also not readily acceptable for those who have typically relied on others, like their parents, teachers or siblings, to get jobs done for them. A weaning off period for such individuals is thus a requirement.

In addition to the seven enterprise skills explained above, a number of personal *behavioural* traits that Farhan possessed, which he acquired through real-world experience in enterprise and entrepreneurship (E&E) activity, are also fundamentally important. Six of such personal traits include the following:

- Integrity
- Grit or determination to succeed
- Self-belief or -confidence
- The ability to learn from failure
- The need for achievement
- Strong desire to be independent

Just like Farhan, you too can develop these behaviours by doing enterprise activities as described in Table 1.1; they cannot be 'taught' in a classroom. The more you *do* enterprise activity, just like continually practising a musical instrument, the greater the chances that you will acquire the traits highlighted above.

1.2. WHAT IS ENTREPRENEURSHIP?

Spotlight on Farhan Masood, an 'Entrepreneur Extraordinaire' from Pakistan: Part 2

Farhan did go to college honouring his father's wishes, but he chose to drop out from the bachelor's programme he was enrolled in. Balancing work alongside education meant making substantial sacrifices—not something he was prepared to do. He felt at the time that his education was holding him back from what he really wanted to pursue—an entrepreneurial career. After his abilities as a software and IT technician were acknowledged by high-profile political and government functionaries and his work on local IT projects added to his fame in professional circles, he felt it was time to venture overseas.

Between 2000 and 2005, Farhan worked in Dubai—occupying senior positions on e-government projects as an expert consultant for the United Arab Emirates government. He put together an expert team and was able to design facial and iris recognition algorithms and systems and an analytics engine to monitor employee productivity. This experience built up his expertise to a level where he felt confident that the time was right to set up his own venture—Quick Fix Advertising Technologies, operating out of Dubai.

Unfortunately, work–life balance problems once again created hurdles for growth. His dysfunctional marriage, which led to divorce and becoming a single parent to a baby girl, and betrayal and intellectual property (IP) theft by his key staff at Quick Fix created immense emotional pressure. Farhan dealt with it by making radical changes—he returned back to Pakistan. The best opportunity he saw was extending his family's printing business to include a plastic bank card manufacturing facility to ride the ongoing boom in consumer finance. Unfortunately though the timing was not right, inadequate research and a lack of clarity around the new business's strategy led to the failure of the venture.

After this setback, Farhan tapped into his grit and soldiered on. He knew he had built up expertise in security technologies, and that is where his true interests remained. Combined with the imagery in the then popular sci-fi film *Minority Report*, Farhan believed he could create advanced and new-to-the-world facial and iris scanning technologies using 2D and 3D recognition tools. Hence, in 2006 he set up a company SoloTech, which is now prominent worldwide in security technology circles via its name SoloInsight Inc—developers of sophisticated and accurate 3D facial, iris and retina recognition and Internet of Things technologies.

Source: Rizvi (2017).

Note: The authors acknowledge Mr Azhar Rizvi for introducing to us the case of Farhan Masood through his book *Entrepreneuring Pakistan: 27 stories of struggle, failure and success.*

Entrepreneurship is the application of enterprise skills for creating and growing new ventures. However, our understanding of entrepreneurship should not be limited to new venture creation. The demonstration of entrepreneurial behaviours and skills within existing organizations is also important for economic growth and innovation, such as the launch of new products and services which create new lines of business. Very simply, when individuals set up new ventures by working with other people, they are being entrepreneurial; when they demonstrate entrepreneurial skills and behaviours within an existing organization, they are being intrapreneurial.

From the above case description, it becomes clear that Farhan Masood put into action the entire range of enterprise *behaviours* and *skills* he fostered over the years as both an *entrepreneur* and *intrapreneur* to create a new organization—SoloTech. Farhan grew up within a socio-economic, cultural and family context, which no doubt instilled within him enterprise and entrepreneurial tendencies. One may ask the questions: Why did not Farhan's siblings become entrepreneurs like him too; after all, they experienced similar conditions? Was there something special about Farhan, perhaps some innate physiological or genetic advantages that gave him an edge? If Farhan had innate (or naturally endowed) abilities or qualities which facilitated his entrepreneurial journey, then is there any purpose in studying E&E?

The aforementioned would be important high-level questions that all students of E&E must have reasoned answers to. First, in response to the first hypothetical question, experiences, even within a closely-knit family unit like Farhan's, are fundamentally personal. No two individuals are alike. If Farhan went to a school with highly engaged teachers and students, who taught subjects in a manner that suited his individual learning style, it can be reasonably argued that Farhan would have taken to academic responsibilities at school and college more favourably and would not have had the need to exercise his enterprise skills outside of his academic life. This would mean that SoloTech would not have come into existence. Since experience is personal, every entrepreneur's journey is individual; however, we have a good understanding of common skill sets and behaviours that underpin the success behind a majority of entrepreneurs' routes into new venture creation. Learning these skills and behaviours is likely to facilitate our own entrepreneurial journeys.

Second, in response to the second question, although research has attempted to link entrepreneurial behaviours with particular genetic markers, there is no evidence that an 'entrepreneur gene' exists. Most likely a combination of genes creates entrepreneurial behaviour traits like the six discussed in the previous section. This being said, we do know that heredity has a good deal to do with personality and behaviour, and certain personality traits acquired through genetic transmission via parents do facilitate entrepreneurship. Studies at Kings College, London, have highlighted that between 37 and 48 per cent of an individual's tendency to become an entrepreneur is genetic, especially the tendency to identify new business opportunities and to perform entrepreneurial tasks. On the other hand, we have research which suggests that although genetics or heredity factors may have a role in promoting entrepreneurial tendencies, their role must be seen in combination with other important entrepreneurship influencers such as personal experiences, the environment with which one interacts with and upbringing by parents. While one may not be able to control their genetic make-up or change their upbringing, they can certainly influence the type and quality of their personal experiences and the environment they operate in.

Third, in response to the final hypothetical question, we can say with confidence that any individual who pays attention to their own development by participating in E&E education with an engaged mindset and then takes positive steps towards new venture creation, it is likely, despite their genetic make-up and upbringing, that they will in time achieve success. In time, because learning from failure and the other five traits described in the previous section are important dimensions of entrepreneurship, which can be acquired through the right personal experiences. Experiences that can be gained during or after undertaking a programme of entrepreneurship education.

Entrepreneurs in training, like yourself, need to master a number of technical skills to excel in environments where rapid technological and social changes will become the norm. The emergence of social and technological trends facilitated by globalization and the 'democratization of technology' (or technology becoming affordable for all) mean that interesting opportunities to start new businesses will come forth. In this exciting new time, entrepreneurs will have the ability to benefit from low-cost early-stage failure, quickly pick up the pieces and move on to their next new venture—repeating the process with less personal risk than they would otherwise have taken in the past. The world of tomorrow for the new entrepreneur holds considerable promise: better access to customers, the ability to find likeminded partners, good access to investment finance and favourable economic conditions and government policy to do business.

Entrepreneurship skills, though still personal, are somewhat technical in nature and should be worked on once there is a reasonable amount of mastery over enterprise skills. Seven of the most important such skills are explained as follows, along with techniques to acquire them.

1. **Estimation**
   Entrepreneurs need to develop the ability to judge potential outcomes of a chosen course of action or decision. Estimation is a fundamental aspect of starting a new business. Entrepreneurs need to develop fairly realistic and believable estimates for time to completion of key business start-up tasks, their associated costs, the level of effort and external help needed, what might be the hidden dangers that could stall or put a stop to work. Interestingly, seasoned entrepreneurs do not tend to estimate potential earnings at the early stage of their start-up. However, they do tend to develop estimates of potential earnings to attract investment.

   It is difficult to develop accurate estimates or forecasts, which require peering into the future for which there is no data. Data is only available for the past, and using past data to try and look into the future is fraught with problems that philosophers of science have long struggled with and have been unable to resolve. However, successful entrepreneurs have been able to cultivate good estimation skills by using various devices (separately or together), such as mental reference points (e.g., Richard Branson's famous test 'if it is simple enough for my mother to understand, then it is worth doing'), relying on gut feeling or instinct and by talking to a wide variety of people.
2. **Vetting Partners**
   This is the ability to find and include individuals into a new venture who will best fill in your knowledge and skill gaps. The start-up histories of a large proportion of businesses will highlight that it takes usually two or more individuals to get the new venture off the ground. It is nearly impossible for a single individual to possess the entire range of technical knowledge and personal skills needed and to bear the tremendous workload involved in the creation and growth of new businesses. In instances where one finds a prominent and charismatic front person leading a new firm, upon digging into the venture's start-up history, one would find that there are a few key individuals in the background, the silent heroes or entrepreneurs in the shadows, without whose involvement the entire start-up operation would have folded in on itself.
3. **Selling**
   To be able to sell is perhaps the single most important skill any successful entrepreneur could possess. Sales activity is responsible for generating new revenue for an enterprise. Selling not only includes the ability to acquire new customers but also to inspire confidence in the general public of the new enterprise's vision. Selling yourself—as in presenting yourself in the best possible light—is also important for attracting investors, partners and potential stakeholders to further the interests of the new enterprise.

A minority of individuals have an innate ability to almost effortlessly inspire trust and confidence in others with their speech and mannerisms, and they can channel this ability to generate new sales activity. Such individuals are often referred to as 'natural salesmen'. The clear majority, however, can learn the techniques associated with selling to hone their skills to acquire new customers. It does take a lot of perseverance and grit to close a deal, often requiring patience and tact, because there is only a fine line to cross into 'hard or aggressive selling'. Hard or aggressive selling may yield some returns in the short term, but in the medium to long terms it can negatively impact your reputation and ability to attract referrals. In most businesses, word-of-mouth (WOM) customers or referrals contribute the largest proportion of revenue. To increase chances of a prospect converted into a customer through sales to make a positive referral to your enterprise, it is crucial to adopt the right attitude during the sales process.

4. **Communication**

Being able to articulate ideas and relay well-formed arguments that attract value for your enterprise would be a key skill contributing to entrepreneurial success. Enterprise creation requires a degree of mastery over communication techniques, in not just English but also in one's mother tongue. There are various aspects of communication which the would-be entrepreneur must practice; these include active listening, public speaking, writing succinctly and non-verbal behavioural cues. Effective communication's importance cannot be stated enough, and its link to the other entrepreneurship skills in this table is quite pronounced.

Active listening requires the practitioner to adopt a demeanour where listening and responding to another person improves mutual understanding. This requires that one's mind is tuned to block out distractions when engaging in a dialogue with any individual. To be avoided is the usual half-listening and half-thinking demeanour, where the mind might be occupied in formulating a response and not tuned into what is being said. Watch expert debaters on YouTube (like Hamza Tzortzis) or in real life, observe the manner in which they focus their undivided attention to what their opponent is saying, nodding, taking written notes, waiting for their opponent to finish and then systematically responding to their opponent's arguments. Although debating is about winning an argument and not usually about creating mutual understanding, absorb what you learn and to practise choose any contemporary topic and set up a debate with someone who has experience. Active listening is difficult and by putting yourself in a debate scenario, your mind will have no choice but to adopt the active listening demeanour.

5. **Trial and Error**

Entrepreneurs use their ability to solve problems by repeatedly trying out one solution after another iteratively, while eliminating errors or causes of failure. It is important to internalize that the very first iteration of any new enterprise will be a failure. On average, entrepreneurs, irrespective of background or geography, fail at least twice before succeeding in business. With this understanding, new entrepreneurs can 'prepare to fail', through enlightened trial and error. The crucial element would be to protect from very large potential losses—to have a clear maximum and known potential loss, which would be bearable, so as to allow further trials.

Trial and error relies on several assumptions about the nature of defining 'problems' and 'solutions'. First, that no solution is ever perfect; the solution can be optimized to only deliver a certain number of potential outcomes whilst deoptimized for others. For example, it is quite difficult to achieve both low cost and high quality or high speed and high accuracy in any solution. Second, in every failed trail there are important clues about making the subsequent trial more successful. Third, being prepared to accept the unexpected, because it is nearly impossible to predict the outcomes of any trial.

Trial and error can be exhausting and demotivating for some individuals; it requires patience and grit to take a proposed solution through successive trial after trial in the search of the best optimized outcome(s).

6. **Research**

Being able to put together a well thought through, convincing, reliable and verifiable case for new manoeuvers to grow your enterprise is an important skill for you to master. Market research is less useful in the early stages of starting up a new enterprise—entrepreneurs tend to rely on intuition guided by trial and error to define the problem and then to design a deliverable and commercially viable solution. Once the enterprise is set up, however, and a certain period has elapsed—say a year or maximum two—then the new enterprise is no longer a start-up; it has morphed into a 'going concern'. At this stage, if the entrepreneur has had early success or signs of it, then it would be crucial to take the next steps to grow the business on only robust and well-reasoned grounds which are linked to undertaking and presenting findings from research. Being able to undertake such research is especially important when it comes to attracting new investment or to gain access from 'gatekeepers', like a license from a government agency. Without adequate backing up of the viability of growth options, manoeuverers made to grow the business would carry too much risk, and potential losses from taking the wrong steps might lead to irrecoverable failure.

There are two broad categories of market research: primary and secondary. Secondary research relies on already published materials—reports, newspaper articles, books, journal papers and so on. Primary research is based on wholly new and original data collected by the researcher through traditional or non-traditional approaches (interviews, observations, surveys, focus groups, important blogs online or netnography). In both cases, there is a need to develop a set of objectives or research questions. The entrepreneur-manager needs to realize a few important things about market research; first, it is time-consuming and expensive, second, it could produce unintended or wrong results if not done following proper protocols or the data not analysed properly, third, it will have limitations as the conclusions of the research will only be valid when a certain number of conditions are met. Finally, the quality of the research's outcome(s) will depend on the experience of the researcher.

7. **Technological Prowess**

The final entrepreneurship skill requires that you develop the ability to assess the impact and use of science and engineering for commercial problem-solving. Solutions to most commercial problems have a science and engineering dimension. The role of the new entrepreneur is to devise solutions that bring about efficiencies which ultimately upends the 'status quo'. Such efficiencies could make ways of doing things either less expensive, more accessible, less complicated or better in some other way. Think about online ordering, applying for passports through e-government sites, new types of genetically modified seed varieties which improve crops' yields and resistance to pests—all these 'technologies' rely on science and engineering to deliver efficiencies or conveniences to various kinds to end users.

Access to technology is constantly improving due to the availability of digital search and other media platforms— think about how finding the latest technological solutions has become easier due to tools such as mobile broadband and smartphones, web search engines, social media platforms, online communities, crowd sourcing platforms and IP registers.

The best way to develop technological prowess is by first identifying the broad spheres of commercial or even social activity that most interests you, for example, adult education, child health or culinary art. The next step would be keeping abreast with technological advancements by reading about advances in your interest area(s) on specialist websites, watching expert talks or attending relevant events such as trade shows and conferences. Knowing what is possible or the state of the art from an engineering and science dimension can give you the mental space of possibility to exercise your creativity for devising solutions.

Another often overlooked way of developing technological prowess is to become comfortable with searching IP registers. Many amazing new inventions developed by your home country's scientists and engineers go unnoticed and are never put to real-world use. This is because scientists and engineers are good at science and engineering and not usually E&E—two very different skill sets. Plan a visit to the local patent or IP office and seek their assistance to search for IP filed in your areas of interest (going back 15–20 years), for instance, new types of fertilizers, renewable energy-based mini power units and so on. Ignore patents or design rights filed by large multinational corporations; focus instead on IP filed by local inventors. If you believe that some of the search results might be relevant solutions, then acquire the contact details of the inventors and approach them for negotiating the use of their IP. You will need their help in setting up the solution from a technical standpoint; and for their assistance you could either license-in their technology by paying them a yearly fee, make them an equity partner in your new venture or pay them a royalty on the income you generate as a result of using their technology.

Sometimes inventive individuals do not file for IP protection because they might be unaware, or the process might be too cumbersome and expensive. If you cannot find registered IP then do not give up, search for relevant departments or individual researchers at higher education institutions and get in touch with them. They would be, in most instances, willing to help you design and develop your technological solution(s).

1.3. SUMMARY AND APPLICATION

Farhan Masood's case captures the broad outlines of any individual's entrepreneurial journey in a developing country context: family values which push towards stable professions, navigating an education system that does not wholly recognize or reward enterprise talent, little access to expertise, the need to direct one's own learning and accumulating experience at any expense, even if it means working for free. Using his E&E skills, Farhan attracted a $3.5 million investment to transform SoloTech to SoloInsight—a pioneer of a cloud-based global recognition platform called the 'Internet of People', employing 67 employees working out of China, the USA and Pakistan.

E&E are intertwined concepts, while all entrepreneurs are enterprising, not all enterprising individuals become entrepreneurs. We have covered the seven most important E&E skills and the manners in which you could practise them. Remember, research suggests that in order to become an 'expert' at anything—playing a guitar, computer programming, sport, painting—about 10,000 hours of practice are needed. The average age of the successful entrepreneur lies in the early 40s; but do not feel dejected by that number, you will have time to enjoy the fruits of your success considering the rising life expectancy rates in developing countries. This also means that entrepreneurship is a difficult vocation with accompanying risks and rewards; only you can decide whether you have mastered all the 14 skills and acquired the accompanying six behavioural traits to a level where you feel confident in yourself. Tables 1.1 and 1.2 present the skills again along with techniques to practise them.

Think carefully about the skills highlighted in Tables 1.1 and 1.2. Then reflect on which of these you enjoy putting into practice the most. Take mental notes and try and justify your choices. You are also encouraged to ask peers and mentors for feedback on what you believe, when it comes to both E&E skills, you are best at. Look for discrepancies between your mental notes and the external feedback you are given. There are most likely differences between what you believe you are good at and what people who regularly interact with you feel on the same point. This will be because it is nearly impossible for an individual to be objectively self-critical; and we do tend to rely on external feedback for validation. Your task is to fill in your skills gaps over time through practice.

TABLE 1.1 Enterprise Skills and How to Practise Them

Enterprise Skill	Exercise
Taking initiative to make things happen	Look around in your neighbourhood or the wider community where you live, do you spot any socio-economic problems that are waiting to be solved but are not because of general apathy? It might simply be a case of graffiti vandalism or littering. Think about the most convenient ways to solve it. Pick any solvable local problem within your community—say access to water or stable electric supply—think of ways of solving it or reducing its impact. Create a personal plan of action to start to resolve this problem. Share this plan with your class.
Intuitive decision-making	Create a plan for learning something new like computer programming, a new language or welding, choose one or even two new things that will take you out of your 'comfort zone'. Give it your best effort and assess your progress weekly for six months.
Connecting with people	Conceptualize a programme to help alleviate the lives of the less fortunate or the vulnerable. The issues that create socio-economic problems are usually complex and multifaceted; consider for instance substance abuse or homelessness. Think about the individuals or

Enterprise Skill	Exercise
	organizations you would need to bring on board. Take a few moments and visualize talking to them about your project, carefully noting their reactions. Now start to draft a narrative, make it personal, reveal some of your aspirations and embed in it a story about an affected individual who went through your programme and emerged much better off. Commit this narrative to memory and share it with your class.
Identifying opportunities	Think about the major or minor incidents that occurred in your life in the past few weeks—a chance meeting with someone important, or something you read about or overheard. Create a list of top three incidents/conditions/circumstances that you could turn into 'opportunities' alongside a 'next step' to initiate action.
Creative problem-solving	Find any commercial problem that is minor and 'solvable'; mull over it for at least five days; try coming up with non-traditional yet elegant solutions, for instance, 'how can we stop the loss of USB memory sticks' or 'how can we create a more fair system for paying for taxi and rickshaw journeys'. Try and spend time on those problems that annoy you the most and that you believe not only solvable but also worth your time solving. Recollect it at odd hours of the day to think of solutions. Share what you have come up with your class.
Strategic thinking	Becoming familiar with what master strategists used in the past to 'get what they wanted' would be a good starting point in building your own strategic thinking skill set. Look at books published by influential entrepreneurs, politicians and other members of your country's intelligentsia—read through these and prepare concise summaries to share with your class.
Personal effectiveness	Develop a plan to become physically and financially independent spanning over a period of one year. Detail down to the individual tasks to be achieved for each milestone you set for yourself.

TABLE 1.2 Entrepreneurship Skills and How to Practise Them

Entrepreneurship Skill	Practice Technique
Estimation	Run an experiment for a week; carry a small diary and take down observations that catch your attention—an interesting news story, a comment that a friend or a parent made that seemed intuitively appealing, any behavioural quirks you observed in a member of the public, and anything else that your mind conjures up which you believe is worthwhile.

(Continued)

TABLE 1.2 (Continued)

Entrepreneurship Skill	Practice Technique
	Once your week's diary is complete, pour over your notes and attempt to highlight at least three trends that might take a strong hold in your community/city/region in the near future. These could be related to changes in socially accepted behaviours, an increased demand for solutions to certain public problems and/or crises about to happen due to unaddressed problems. Finally, verify your developed trends through discussions with open-minded individuals and develop mental justifications for why and under what conditions would these trends develop traction.
Vetting partners	Look within or outside your immediate network or connections for a suitable partner. Draft and post an advertisement in the local press or online—roughly outlining your business idea and highlighting the qualities you seek in your prospective partner. Attract as many applicants as you can over a period of one month. Set up face-to-face meetings with the prospects and look for (a) shared vision and values, (b) credibility and experience, (c) professional connections, (d) good moral values, dedication, integrity and work habits. Even the most well-trained and experienced recruiters often make mistakes and end up hiring the wrong people. There is no magic formula that will point to the right prospect. Let your 'gut feeling' guide you—who do you see yourself working with over long hours, who makes you comfortable, who you feel will be the most trustworthy and reliable and who is most excited about your business idea?
Selling	Shadow a good salesperson and to observe and reflect on their sales tactics, observe them at work for at least two days. During your two-day observation period, take a diary with you to take notes on how your host manages the sales process, their conversation techniques and body language to close transactions. Reflect on your notes and draw out key learnings. Set up a debate with someone who has experience.
Communication	Set up a debate on any contemporary topic with a seasoned rival. Practise your arguments prior in front of a mirror or you could also film yourself. Take note of your facial expressions and voice modulation and the tone of your voice. You will intuitively know when you are best communicating through your speech the sort of qualities you wish your listeners to gauge. Presenting complex information in a succinct or easy to understand form is fundamental to attracting value for an enterprise. Find a mentor who is an expert business communicator. Prepare a brief 'concept paper' on any solution you have come up with to a social or commercial problem.

Entrepreneurship Skill	Practice Technique
	Use rich but just enough detail to describe the problem, its justification (is it enough of a problem), who the affected are, what the ideal solution might be and its justification and as to how you propose to implement the solution (who else will you need, any facilities or investment for instance). Use pictures, data visualization and diagrams as much as possible and cite your sources to add legibility and credibility. Request honest feedback and suggestions for improvement; make the recommended changes and produce a second draft for which you ought to seek another round of feedback. Keep repeating this exercise patiently (remember this is all a part of learning) till your mentor feels that the final draft is near perfect. Share this final draft with relevant stakeholders and see how they respond. If you sense engagement and encouragement, then your labour was fruitful; in the opposite scenario, try not to take matters personally, and re-attempt the exercise with a new concept paper and a new mentor.
Trial and error	Put a team together to develop proposals to solve any real-world problem, for example, long queuing times at your cafeteria, job-hunting success rates of new graduates, or raising money for charity. Carefully flesh out each proposal (or solution) and rate them on a scale of 1–5 along a number of criteria. Choose the proposal that attracts the best rating and implement it for a brief period of time. Take observations and note if the proposal has resolved the problem or made it worse. Use those notes to go back to the drawing board and repeat the process with new proposals to solve the problems that arose in the first trial, rate those proposals and then implement once again in a similar manner. Keep on repeating this process till you exhaust the process and come up with the most optimized solution.
Research	Create a market research project in alliance with an existing new enterprise. Choose a 'researchable' commercial problem that your chosen alliance partner might be facing—say a local small business. By 'researchable', it is meant that the topic ought to not exceed your personal time and monetary limits. You could focus on topics such as 'the potential for selling your partner's product in another town' or 'what would happen to their bottom-line if they were to hire five new employees and work double shifts'? Then choose an appropriate strategy—either primary or secondary research—it could also be both. Carefully formulate your data collection strategy—read about the potential problems of the various data collection approaches, none is perfect. Practise interviewing or running

(Continued)

TABLE 1.2 (Continued)

Entrepreneurship Skill	Practice Technique
	focus groups by watching YouTube videos with tips and tricks. Plunge into action and collect data; making sure that you carefully record all the data you collect systematically—because data is precious. After a few interviews or getting 10–15 responses to your survey for instance, pause, and take stock. You have your initial data collection done in a pilot study. Analyse the responses just by reading through them carefully. Do you see any patterns at all? Are the respondents answering the questions properly? Are you getting predictable answers or nothing interesting? If so, then this would be a good sign to revisit your data collection approach and to make suitable changes and try again. It is worth doing this because if you are not highly certain about the quality of your results, then the conclusions you will draw for your alliance partner will be dubious and not inspire confidence. Worse, if they took your wrong work seriously, it might lead them to make a wrong move, costing them time and money. The final element of the research process is the presentation of outcomes. Try and write up what you found out concisely and make a case for against, always on the balance of probabilities, the main research objective or question. Gauge the response of your alliance partner—the confidence they have on your outcomes is your most reliable indicator on whether your work was good quality.
Technological prowess	Identify the broad spheres of commercial or even social activity that most interests you. Keep abreast with technological advancements by reading about advances in your interest area(s) on specialist websites, watching expert talks or attending relevant events such as trade shows and conferences. Plan a visit to the local patent or IP office and seek their assistance to search for IP filed in your areas of interest. If you believe that some of the search results might be relevant solutions, then acquire the contact details of the inventors and approach them for negotiating the use of their IP. Search for relevant departments or individual researchers at higher education institutions working in your area(s) of interest; get in touch with them and bring them on board to work with you on your commercial solution.

2

Practising Creativity

LEARNING OUTCOMES

- Understand the nature and function of creativity
- Become familiar with creativity barriers and strategies to overcome these
- Learn to apply creative thinking techniques to solve commercial problems

2.1. WHAT IS CREATIVITY?

Spotlight on Professor Muhammad Yunus, 'World's Banker to the Poor' from Bangladesh

Muhammad Yunus has dedicated his life to eliminating poverty, creatively transforming a small experimental research project lending money to the poorest factions of Bangladeshi society into the large and thriving Grameen Bank. Grameen loans out small sums of money to millions of borrowers across Bangladesh. He created a brand new means for solving a pressing social problem—giving access to marginalized and exceedingly poor families, who have no credit history or access to regular banking services, to 'microcredit'. For this new model which brought banking to the world's poorest, Professor Yunus was awarded the Nobel Peace Prize in 2006.

GRAMEEN
Banking for the poor

In the 1970s, as Head of the Economics Department at Chittagong University, Professor Yunus had no intentions of becoming a banker. He was an inquisitive child, studious and a talented artist who had experience travelling to other countries as a boy scout. The faces of silently starving people in Bangladesh haunted him, and he wondered desperately how they could be helped. His training in economic theory did not resonate with on ground realities and the complex multifaceted issues surrounding poverty elimination in developing countries.

Deciding to take action, in the nearby village of Jobra, to solve the problem of low yields, he set up a cooperative with rice farmers and landowners to grow rice more efficiently. The yield at the end of the season was higher than before, however, to his surprise the farmers did not share profits with him. He wondered why the farmers turned to behaving in this manner, there had to be a root cause.

To understand poverty issues in a more nuanced manner, he began taking field trips to Jobra with students and colleagues. He discovered that access to credit was one of the most pressing problems for local farmers. One day, taking a small personal risk, he experimented by lending a small amount of money, less than 27 dollars in all, to 42 impoverished villagers. Surprisingly, they paid him back. This was his 'eureka' moment. He continued this experiment and discovered very quickly that not only do the poor pay back their loans even without any collateral, but they tend to pay back at rates far higher than the 60 per cent rate that was typical of commercial banks. This insight was Professor Yunus's defining moment.

Along with the profit motive, risk-taking, opportunity recognition and the creation of an enterprise, creativity and innovation are also fundamental aspects of entrepreneurship. Creativity is the ability to make sense of the world in new ways, to discover hidden patterns and make connections between seemingly unrelated phenomena. This is done for the purpose of generating solutions to problems, which is the main focus of the creative individual. Artists and musicians develop the skills and talent through long periods of practice to create fine works of art, using imagination or original thinking. 'Good' artists are creative because they are able to enact ideas from their imagination into tangible pieces of work. However, one does not need to be an artist to be creative. If you possess the experience, skill and talent to use your imagination to create newness and solve problems, you are being creative.

Creativity does not occur within a vacuum; exercising one's imagination requires the above three fundaments—experience, skill and talent. The greater the experience, skill and talent set, the greater the scope for creative thinking. To illustrate, do a quick thought experiment: close your eyes and try and imagine a colour you have never seen before. Is it even possible? Or, try and imagine a wholly original and fantastical alien world on another planet. I assure you, all you can conjure up in your imagination would be the sum total and various combinations of colours, textures and creatures you have already seen or have had experience with prior. In some ways, we remain prisoners or confined to what we already know and have experienced. Thus, the famous metaphor 'one cannot outgrow their own skin' then applies to creative ability also. The lesson is to be on the lookout to constantly increase your experience, skill and talent set to allow you greater creative scope.

Finally, it must be kept in mind that creativity is somewhat different to innovation—whilst creativity produces an original or unusual solution to a problem, innovation, which we will explore in the following chapter, is the implementation of that creative solution that creates new commercial value. Thus, creativity becomes the first necessary step in innovation.

Consider the case of Professor Yunus and the above discussion on creativity, his 'eureka' moment did not occur out of the blue one day magically; his life and work experience, training and skills in economics, insights from his experiments and field trips led to an imaginative new insight. The insight was possible because of his life experiences and learned skills. His insight was a creative solution for countering the problem of rural poverty in agricultural communities, which was original and undiscovered. This is often the pattern when one carefully studies the histories of good ideas, that they are not indivisible magical events occurring as a result of brain physiology or chemistry, but a long-term experiential process of applying creativity.

2.2. OVERCOMING BARRIERS TO CREATIVITY

NeoNurture, a Medical Device out of Car Spare Parts

In the developing world, the problem of infant mortality is quite pronounced. Every year over 4 million infants in the developing world die within a month of birth. Half of these newborns would survive if given a warm and clean environment in which to grow stronger, like a baby incubator. However, modern incubators are complex and quite expensive, up to US$40,000, which is prohibitively high for most hospitals or clinics in developing countries. Even if such devices are donated, they tend to have complicated equipment breakdowns, with spare parts not available and local technicians unable to repair them, they remain broken and unused. Studies suggest that as much as 95 per cent of medical technology donated to developing countries breaks within the first five years of use.

To counter this problem, an MIT professor Timothy Prestero, had been designing a solution for several years—a less expensive and more reliable incubator that would not break down in a catastrophic way. The problem they encountered was the lack of guarantee of a steady supply of spare parts or trained repair technicians. To overcome this hurdle, Prestero and his team looked into building an incubator out of parts that were readily available in the developing world. This idea had originated with a Boston doctor—Jonathan Rosen—who observed that even the smallest towns in the developing world seemed to be able to keep motor vehicles functioning with a good availability of car mechanics and spare parts available. So Rosen approached Prestero and suggested: What if you made an incubator out of car parts?

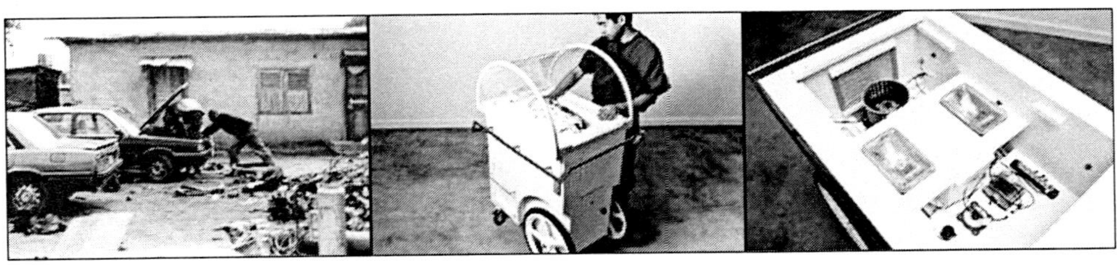

It took Prestero's team three years to introduce a device called the NeoNurture. It very much resembled a modern baby incubator, but its core technology comprised of used car parts. Sealed headlights supplied the warmth, dashboard fans facilitated filtration and air circulation and door chimes sounded alarms. The device could be powered via an adapted cigarette lighter or a standard motorcycle battery. NeoNurture, because it was built out of car parts, proved to be doubly efficient; it tapped the local supply of parts and the local knowledge of motor vehicle repair. Hence, you did not have to be a trained medical technician to fix the NeoNurture, you did not even have to read the manual, all you needed to know was how to replace a broken car headlight.

Two major barriers can inhibit or retard your creative ability. However, if you are mindful of these, then action can be taken to overcome them.

2.2.1. RULES AND TRADITIONS

These are guidelines for conducting ourselves with others in society—conforming to social ideals and depicting a socially acceptable personality and behavioural traits. Sometimes, rules and traditions like 'status hierarchy' (e.g., relative importance of a person in relation to their official title in a company) limits our ability to be creative. In a society with a pronounced status hierarchy, a low-status individual might be quite reluctant to share creative ideas with individuals of higher status because of insecurity and fear of judgement. Compare the USA with Taiwan and the notion of 'failure in businesses'. Whereas, in the USA, under the national ideal of the 'American Dream' failure is often viewed positively, a necessary stepping stone to success; in Taiwan the notion of failure is often seen as bringing upon oneself and their family immense shame.

Rules and traditions also affect training and education. When engineers, for example, are taught to think about design issues in a prescribed manner in educational institutions where the curriculum and teaching delivery have been 'perfected' over many years, such thinking and training often becomes an ingrained habit that might be performed mechanistically. Although habit makes the performance of tasks more efficient and effort economizing, it does make it difficult for us to see a new, perhaps even better, way of performing the same task. This then inhibits creative thinking and ability.

2.2.2. COGNITIVE BIASES

Creativity relies on thinking and thinking happens in our brains, therefore, it is important to understand the basics of how thinking occurs. Our brain occupies approximately 2–3 per cent of our body's mass but consumes about 20 per cent of its entire energy produced. It is an energy hungry yet very energy efficient organ.

Thinking requires the expenditure of precious energy, thus, the brain deploys two modes of thinking to economize on energy expenditure: Systems 1 and 2. System 1 is an automatic, fast and often unconscious way of thinking like computing 5 × 5 (most people instantaneously know the answer to be '25') or riding a bicycle or swimming. In effect, most of our thinking activity, typically in a day, relies on System 1. It is efficient, requires little energy or attention, but is prone to biases and systematic errors in judgement. There are hundreds of such errors documented by experimental psychologists that we make regularly. One of these, for example, is stereotyping or 'a notion widely adopted about specific types of individuals (like Arab or Chinese people) or certain ways of behaving (such as rowdiness or laziness) which is then used to represent the entire group of those individuals or behaviours as a whole (e.g., all X people will behave in a Y way)'.

System 2, on the other hand, is an effortful, slow and controlled way of thinking like computing the answer to 17 × 32. Creativity requires System 2 thinking which consumes more energy, and the brain being intrinsically an energy efficient organ, attempts to restrict its deployment as much as possible. Doing System 2 thinking is akin to fighting against yourself; it is somewhat hard to do. To reduce the need to deploy System 2 as much as possible, the brain uses cognitive heuristics and biases, which are mental shortcuts to quickly arrive at decisions, especially under conditions of uncertainty. In common parlance, heuristics and biases help us in 'jumping to conclusions'.

The documented and scientifically demonstrated list of heuristics and biases is quite long, the one which hampers creativity the most is the 'confirmation bias'. Individuals are used to perceiving things in their own ways, which often makes it difficult to see new meanings, relationships and ideas. To illustrate, try and solve this riddle as quickly as possible:

A father and son are going to a cricket game when their car breaks down on railroad tracks. The father cannot restart the car in time and an oncoming train collides with it. The father dies, and an ambulance rushes the boy to a nearby hospital. In the emergency room, the surgeon takes one look and says, 'I cannot operate on this child; he is my son'. How is this possible?

What prevents most people from seeing that the surgeon is the boy's mother is the reliance of the brain on the 'default assumption' that a surgeon must be a man. Such default assumptions are one of the strategies the brain uses to judge the most likely interpretation of an ambiguous situation via the 'confirmation bias'. The confirmation bias is helpful in some ways, it allows us to make quick judgements on a wide variety of confusing events to arrive at a 'most likely conclusion'. How far away is that cycle in the distance? Is that shape in the shadows a street light or a man with a gun? Yet, as this riddle demonstrates, these same assumptions can lead people—even the most broad-minded people—astray. Thus, the brain fools us into seeing what we expect to see and how it rejects any information that challenges our already established points of view can be a route to bias and discriminatory conclusions.

Prestero and his team (described in the case synopsis above) encountered both of the above described barriers; however, they were able to overcome them successfully and created a good solution in the form of the NeoNurture device. Initially, the team, consisting of individuals with similar backgrounds—mostly engineers with no direct experience of living or working in developing countries—attempted to design a more reliable and less expensive baby incubator for two years but failed. They were unable to create a usable device because the parts they were using were not readily available in developing countries and the fear was that should such parts break down or need replacing, there would be little possibility, due to shortage of skills and availability of local spares, for a repair or replacement. They were able to overcome the barrier of groupthink and 'confirmation bias' by giving credence to voices from outside the team to influence design—the Boston doctor, Jonathan Rosen for instance. Rosen's input forced the team to shed their preconceived notions and westernized design thinking leading to their 'eureka' moment. They challenged normative thinking and 'tradition' by asking fundamental 'why'-type questions, for example, why do modern baby incubators need to be hi-tech and expensive when the technology they employ is very similar to inexpensive chicken incubators?

2.3. THE CREATIVE MINDSET

Jack Ma: From English Teacher to the Warrior Spirited 'Super Entrepreneur'

Jack Ma is known to be a larger-than-life figure and a showman who has attracted the loyalty of employees and customers alike. He was born in 1964 in Shanghai, China. He somehow knew he had to master the English language to be able to succeed in life. To practise his English, for nine years he got up early every morning and rode his bike to the Hangzhou Hotel, where he befriended foreign tourists and worked for free as a tour guide. He got an opportunity to travel to the USA in 1995 as a translator in a business negotiation. This is when he understood the potential of the internet, which at the time was virtually non-present in China. Thinking about how he could use the internet to create new value, he set up a Chinese version of the famous yellow pages. This venture unfortunately failed. By chance, when working for the government after this setback, he was assigned to take an American visitor to see the Great Wall—this individual happened to be Yahoo co-founder Jerry Yang. Jack Ma struck up a lasting friendship with Yang. By 1999, he had enough know-how to set up Alibaba.

He states: 'Chinese brains are just as good as theirs, and this is the reason we dare compete with Americans. If we're a good team and we know what we want to do then one of us can defeat 10 of them'. This statement depicts a kind of warrior spirit. It is known that Ma gives his employees kung fu nicknames and refers to himself as 'Feng Qingyang'—a reclusive swordsman character in Chinese lore. He defeated eBay—the giant online auction in China by refusing to charge either sellers or buyers on his own website. Everyone thought that keeping his Chinese eBay competitor Taobao free was foolhardy, but Taobao grew into a giant revenue producer with its search and display ads. In Ma's own words: 'I had always wished that I was born in a period of war. I could have been a general. I thought about what I could have achieved in war'.

Jack Ma has also developed an ability for seeing every situation clearly, down to its fundamentals. For instance, he wanted a readily recognizable name for this business. While sitting in a coffee shop in San Francisco, he came up with Alibaba as a name. He checked with a waitress if she recognized the name, and when she did he simply knew it was globally recognizable. Jack Ma believes: 'Nothing is more powerful than taking a word with a strong, specific connotation, grabbing a slice of it, mapping that slice to a portion of your positioning, and therefore redefining it. This naming strategy is without question the most powerful one of all'.

The creative mindset requires 'making connections between things that others miss'. One of the three Apple founders, Steve Jobs, fervently believed in this notion. For example, his trip to India in the 1980s inspired him to think of a utilitarian device for personal home users—which became the PC. Jobs was also a famous practitioner of Zen meditation. He spoke openly about his experiences in meditation and how such experiences allowed him to make mental connections between disparate thoughts or ideas that influenced his later product designs. In this connection, Jobs told his biographer, Walter Isaacson:

> *If you just sit and observe, you will see how restless your mind is. If you try to calm it, it only makes it worse, but over time it does calm, and when it does, there's room to hear more subtle things—that's when your intuition starts to blossom and you start to see things more clearly and be in the present more. Your mind just slows down, and you see a tremendous expanse in the moment. You see so much more than you could see before. It's a discipline, you have to practice it. James (2015)*

The creative mindset also uses 'reasoning from first principle'. Reasoning from first principle is the process of taking existing concepts and theories and asking fundamental questions to design and fill gaps, essentially reinventing the wheel resulting in the creation of the 'new'. Elon Musk, the founder of Tesla, is an example of someone who uses this principle to create new concepts. He has stated that:

> *It is important to view knowledge as sort of a semantic tree. Make sure you understand the fundamental principles, i.e. the trunk and big branches, before you get into the leaves/details or there is nothing for them to hang on to. Bhattacharya (2015)*

This shows the importance of assessing the core attributes critical to an idea before attempting to expand on it, as it makes gaps and problems easier to identify (see Figure 2.1). For example, when he was developing the new Tesla truck, the first step was to ask an interesting question: What are the essential parts of a truck? This question is very different from 'how do I make a better truck than my competitors?' as it enabled him to start from scratch, without any preconceived ideas. The next step was to gather as much evidence as possible about the idea, by conducting interviews with experts and doing relevant research. The third step was to construct hypotheses based on the

FIGURE 2.1 Elon Musk's 'Reasoning from First Principle' Process

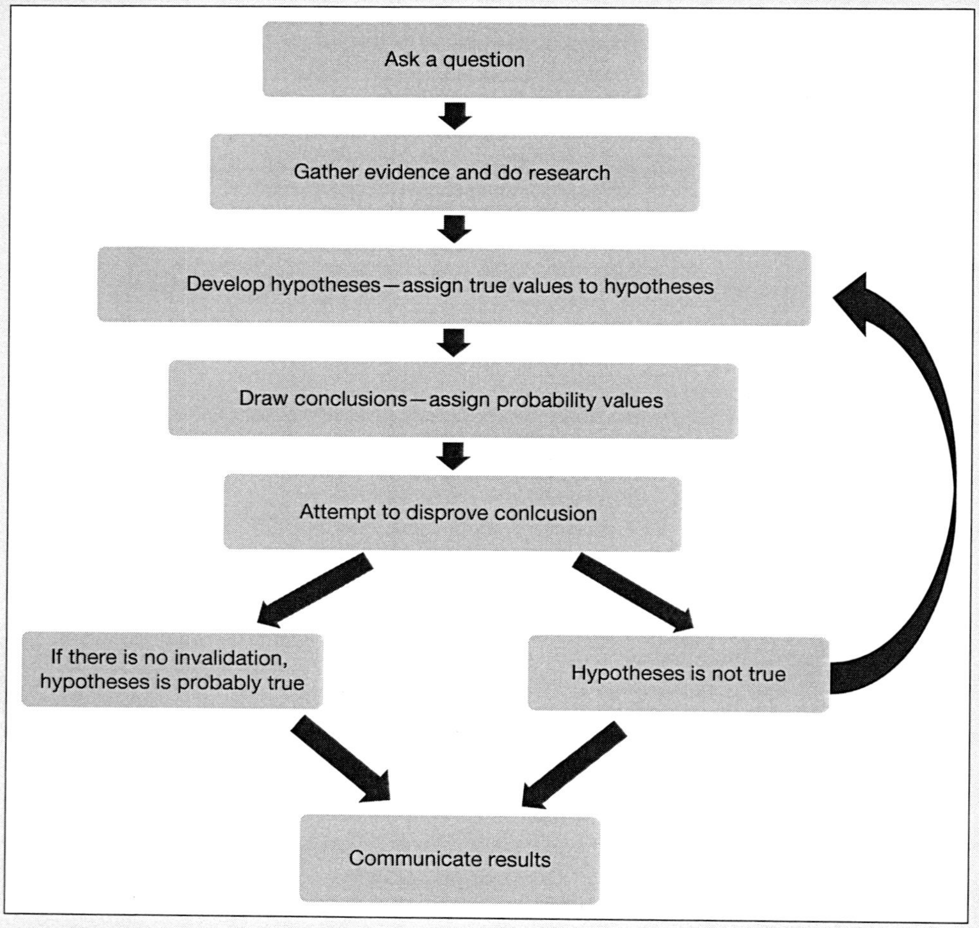

Source: Ali J. Ahmad.

evidence. His creative approach was to assign a probability of truth to each hypothesis in order to be aware of how likely it is to be correct. The fourth step dictates that for a conclusion to be drawn successfully the following questions need to be answered: Are these hypotheses correct? Are they relevant? Does the conclusion necessarily follow from these hypotheses? And how probable is this conclusion? The fifth stage is to apply the famous philosopher of science—Karl Popper's—model of falsifiability; in the case of Elon Musk, his approach was to try and refute the conclusion by asking others to think of counter arguments. This step is an essential part of the creative process as it helps avoid the trap of 'confirmation bias' (discussed in the previous section). This whole process leads to the last stage: if there is no refutation of the hypothesis, then it is most probably right, but not certainly right. This mindset allows creative individuals to modify and change their line of thinking if contrary evidence appears.

Jack Ma has introduced us to a new aspect of the creative mindset, the 'warrior spirit'. Warriors are heroes; and heroes make personal sacrifices for the overall good. They are also brave and determined to succeed. Skilled warriors are well-trained and can identify weaknesses in their opponents and exploit these to win. Warriors also make alliances and lead by example. Jack Ma's life history highlights the value of the warrior mindset: self-belief and pride in his heritage and culture, hard work and a witty and at times seemingly foolhardy tendency to pitch his new ideas against very well formed and previously successful ideas. He showed flexibility and adaptability in how he configured and transformed his ideas to the extent that it became impossible for giants such as eBay, Amazon and PayPal to compete and outperform his creation—Alibaba. The real lesson from Jack Ma is that one needs to have a degree of certainty in their minds that what they know about the world is valid, and the extent of what one knows cannot be known by anyone else, then taking this knowledge and transforming it into something valuable that solves a problem better than anything else that is available.

2.4. CREATIVITY TECHNIQUES

There are a wide variety of creativity techniques; discussed as follows are three of the most prominent ones with explanations on how they have been used to generate creativity.

1. **Storyboarding**
   Storyboarding is used in most creative industries, such as film and television, as means to depict ideas, allowing for a conceptual framework to emerge showing the manner in which the creative idea could become reality. A Storyboard, such as the one presented in Figure 2.2, consists of the use of images as well as annotations, bringing together both abstraction and verbalization to produce a clear roadmap of the ideation process.

   The use of storyboarding allows individuals the opportunity to visually represent their 'solution' (the idea) to a 'problem', which can be beneficial for ascertaining the manner in which the idea creates new value. The clear benefits of storyboarding lie in collecting feedback from potential users and an exploration of potential problems. An important aspect to consider when using storyboarding is to ensure that the subject idea is storyboard-able. It is possible that certain ideas may not be readily suited to visualization, for example, a complicated software fixed in a banking system to stop hackers. Other than this example and similar complicated technical solutions, most ideas can be fleshed out using diagrammatic representation which highlights the manner or process through which the solution will solve a problem and create new value for end users.
2. **Six Thinking Hats**
   Six Thinking Hats is a tool developed by Edward de Bono which can be used for facilitating more effective group discussions around specific problems. It involves using the analogy of six coloured hats (Figure 2.3). Thinking is the most important human resource, and the human brain thinks in a number of distinct ways. The Six Thinking Hats deliberately challenge these distinct ways through six different directions. In each of these directions the brain will identify and bring into conscious thought certain aspects of the issues being considered (e.g., gut instinct, pessimistic judgement and neutral facts).

FIGURE 2.2 **An Example Storyboard**

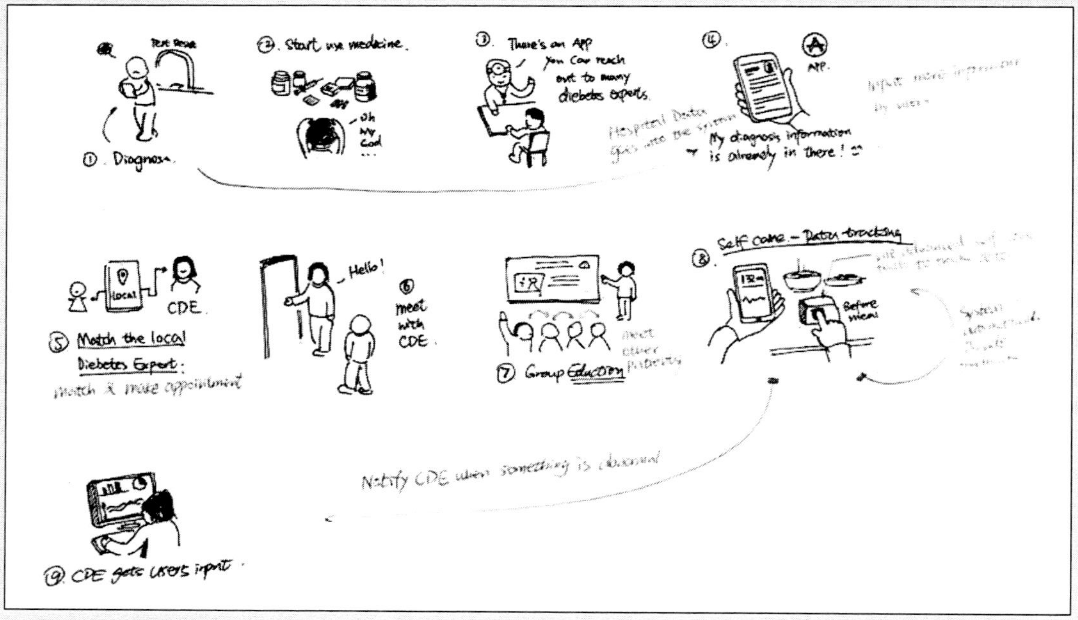

Note: This figure is for representative purposes only.

There are no specific guidelines for the sequencing of the hats, however, it is best for the group to decide the Hats' sequence ahead of time to aid coordination of thought. It is also important to clearly understand the meaning and purpose behind each Hat so that, for example, the group leader or facilitator could suggest 'let us have white thinking here' or 'we are now switching from yellow to black thinking'. The more the technique is practised, the better the results from its use are. Experimenting with alternative methods like skipping hats or rearranging the order have also been shown to be useful. Using real hats can also be helpful because these tend to provide tangible reminders to the group in the direction the thinking process ought to be taking.

IBM chief scientist, Dharmendra Modha, was charged with overseeing a highly ambitious government-funded project to develop a chip that could mimic the human brain. He was tasked with managing a team of 200 of the brightest scientists who were working out of eight different IBM labs, two government labs and five university campuses and had diverse areas of expertise. The team members struggled to find any form of consensus through their email or digital communications. Modha decided to use the Six Thinking Hats technique to approach this problem and asked his team members to characterize their arguments with colours, each representing a different way of thinking: white for facts, red for emotions, green for investigating an idea, black for discernment

FIGURE 2.3 Six Thinking Hats

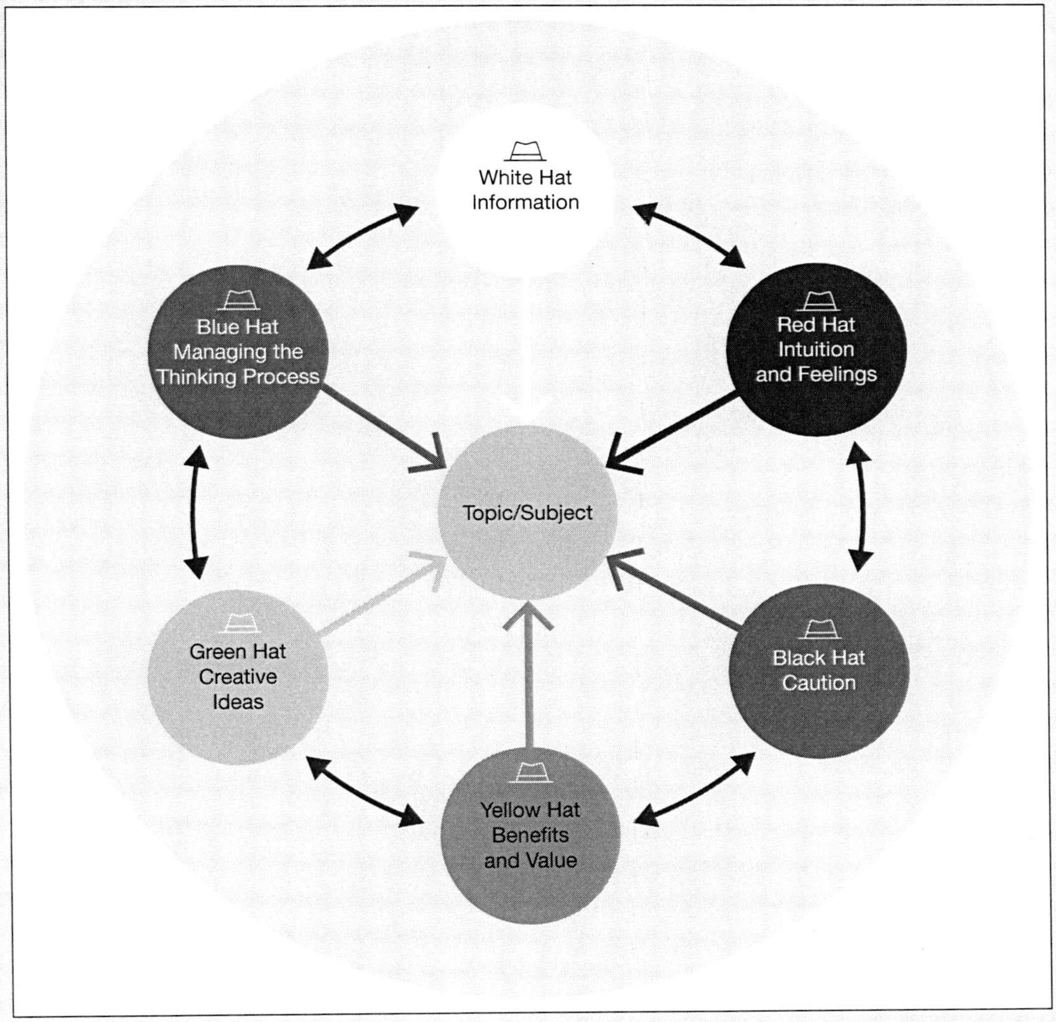

Source: Edward de Bono (1985).

and yellow for optimism. His goal was to separate emotion from facts, thereby driving objectivity in the team. According to Modha, the method helped quieter participants to speak up and helped everyone accept and discuss diverse thoughts.

3. **SCAMPER**
   The SCAMPER technique was developed by Bob Eberle to address problems that stifle creativity during typical brainstorming sessions for generating creative solutions. SCAMPER (Figure 2.4) is a mnemonic that stands for: S (substitute) is related to consider about the

FIGURE 2.4 **SCAMPER**

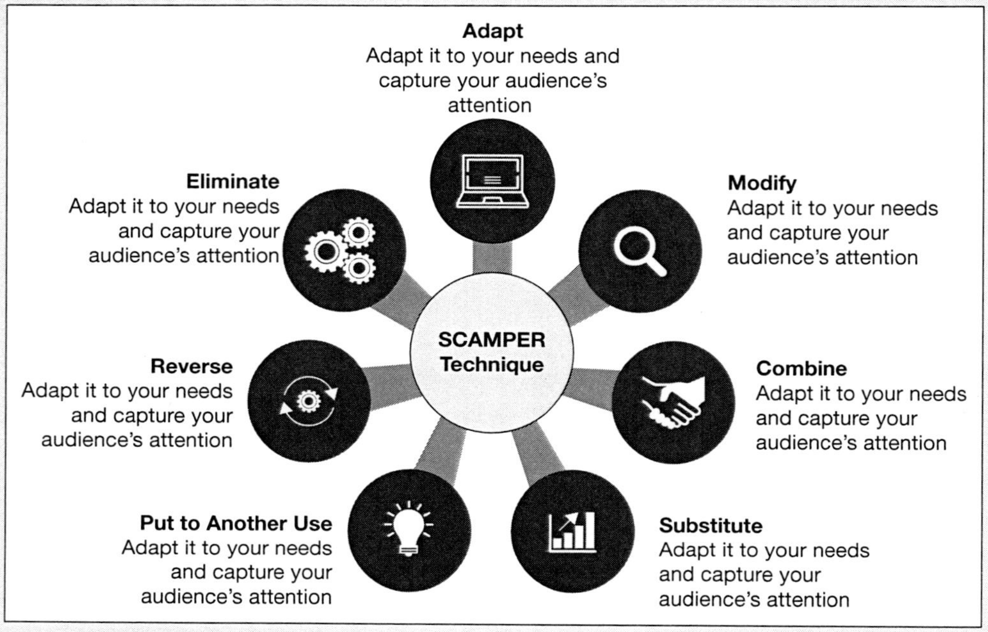

Source: Bob Eberle (1996).

substituting part(s) of a solution, which might be a product or process with something else; C (combine) is how to combine different parts of the solution, problem or process to create something new; A (adapt) to think about the different ways in which the solution could be adapted to address other foreseen or unforeseen issues; M (modify) is about changing a part or all of the current aspects of the solution such as its size, colour and shape to meet new needs; P (put to another use) is about exploring the possibility of putting the current idea or product into different uses; E (eliminate) is to thinking about ways to simplify, minimize or reduce part(s) of product or idea; R (reverse) is about considering what would happen if the sequencing of the various stages of the solution was set differently.

The McDonalds restaurant franchise's reconfigurations represent a good example of the SCAMPER technique used in practice. Using 'S' (substituting), they changed the way of serving food by substituting the delivery of food to the table for a self-service counter. You find the menu at the counter and order/pick up everything here. Using 'C' (combine), they collaborated with Disney to attract families with children to buy Happy Meals. The free gifts inside for children provided good promotion for Disney. Using 'A' (adapt), in catholic areas, where sales dropped on 'meat-free Fridays', they introduced a new burger, the Filet-O-Fish. Customers made it clear that they wanted to sit down and eat, so McDonalds installed indoor seating in all of their restaurants. In 2003, they adapted to the new health focus of society and started a global marketing campaign to promote a new healthier image. The campaign's slogan was 'I'm lovin' it', and this slogan is still used today.

2.5. SUMMARY AND APPLICATION

How 'good' ideas take form, resemble the story of the NeoNurture device. They are a sum total of the experience, talent and skills of the originator. We often believe that breakthrough ideas which became new creations, like radar or antibiotics, are separate from the context they were born in; somehow, a very gifted individual, born with special qualities, was able to look beyond the garbage pile of bad ideas and rise above norms and tradition to single-handedly deliver something new that changes everything. This would be a false belief; because, creativity requires bricolage or 'working with what you have' because 'something cannot come from nothing'. We take from existing ideas, those which we might have inherited or merely stumbled across by chance, what we find useful and recombine them together in some new shape.

Exercise 2.1. Choose a relatively new and interesting 'home grown' product or service in common use within your community—one which you feel creatively solves a problem. It could be a phone application, electronic device or personal hygiene product. Hold an interview with the creator of your chosen product or service—ascertain how specifically they came up with the idea. Delve into the history of the idea creation process and unearth the conditions and results of any trial and error that led to the final shape or form of the chosen produce/service. Depict your findings visually as a storyboard. Draw out major lessons.

No one is born creative; one might be born with a vivid imagination—but creativity requires that we are able to draw on what we imagine for creating something new, original and useful. Thus, creativity is a learned skill, the more you practise it the better you will become at it. To practise creativity, attempt the following.

Exercise 2.2. Put together a team of colleagues whose thinking and world views do not necessarily resonate with yours, but you could still work together effectively. Take anything familiar with a known outcome, for instance, socks sold in pairs to 'ensure uniformity', fizzy drinks tasting sweet to 'ensure pleasure through taste' or using a toothbrush and paste for brushing your teeth to 'ensure dental hygiene', and reimagine it. Think first about 'why do we always do it this way?' As a result of asking this question, your team will develop assumptions and explanations which might come across as quite convincing and practical. The creative mindset will require challenging each of these assumptions by turning them upside down. Use the SCAMPER technique for doing this and completely reimagine the process of delivering your chosen outcome. Share what you have come up with the class and generate feedback.

3 Understanding and Doing Innovation

LEARNING OUTCOMES

- Understand the special issues around managing innovation in developing countries
- Become familiar with the roles social and frugal innovations can play in socio-economic development
- Learn to use innovation management techniques in early-stage start-up companies

3.1. WHAT IS INNOVATION?

Spotlight on Dr Moses Kizza Musaazi, 'the Genius Fixer of Things' from Uganda

Dr Musaazi's innovations are examples of 'appropriate technology', which champion sustainable, low-cost, high-human-labour production methods that blend science with local knowledge. In Uganda, more than 50 per cent of the population survives on less than $1.25 a day and large-scale socio-economic problems cause immense disruption in people's day-to-day lives. As a holistic innovator, Musaazi attacks such problems systematically with inexpensive, dual-use and very low waste solutions.

He found that a large number of Ugandan girls abandon school when they reach puberty. This happened due to poor solutions for female hygiene; school girls could not afford sanitary napkins (and turned to using unsafe alternatives). To solve this problem, Musaazi developed the MakaPad in 2006, a sanitary napkin using natural and renewable materials at Makerere University with a US$78,000 grant from the Rockefeller Foundation. He experimented with various materials including water hyacinth (decays too quickly) and elephant grass (requires boiling to break down) before settling on papyrus. Papyrus is chopped from swamps, workers peel the thick green stalks and pound them into fibre, then mix them with wet paper waste, donated by non-governmental organizations (NGOs) and businesses, to create a slurry that is dried on frames laid on wooden racks in the sun. Other workers remove the stiff, dried sheets; slide them through softening machines (designed by Musaazi); cut them to size; and seal them in polyethylene imported from China, using an electric sealing machine (modified by Musaazi). Finally, the pads are sterilized in plastic buckets under ultraviolet lights.

Musaazi had counted on the Ugandan Ministry of Education buying MakaPads and distributing them to students. He had already piloted the product at 12 schools. But the ministry did not take interest. When the Rockefeller Foundation project came to an end, Musaazi started to market MakaPads as best he could. A local newspaper wrote about the pads which got the United Nations High Commissioner for Refugees (UNHCR) interested. In Uganda, the UNHCR is responsible for 40,000 girls and women living in Kampala and eight refugee settlements. They immediately ordered 50,000 packets of 10 pads each, an order Musaazi was unprepared to fulfil because he did not have mass production facilities. However, the UNHCR remained patient, and in time a very large proportion of girls and women in their target refugee settlements began to receive MakaPads.

Finally introduced in 2007, the product costed less than a third when compared to other global brands and accounted for roughly half the revenue of Musaazi's Kampala-based company, Technology for Tomorrow or T4T. To facilitate mass manufacturing, T4T runs factories which employ locally available and impoverished workers. For example, there is a factory at the Kyaka II refugee settlement in western Uganda which houses roughly 16,000 people in mud huts. Since 2007, the settlement's MakaPad plant employs 45 refugees earning as much as $200 a month. This makes the plant, by far, the settlement's most substantial employer.

Musaazi wants to find customers beyond the UNHCR. The consumer market though is more difficult because the perception in Uganda is that a product made by a local person cannot be as good as or better than something imported. To overcome this hurdle, he recently ordered more attractive packaging from China and plans to deploy three-wheeled motorcycles towing carts filled with pads in the cities and villages, as well as a team of door-to-door saleswomen.

Innovation is the transformation of a creative idea or an invention into a 'solution' that is 'better' than what was available in the past and generates new value. Innovation is different to invention; inventions represent a scientific or technological breakthrough which builds on the existing state of the art and can be protected using IP rights like patents. However, about 97 per cent of all awarded patents for new inventions do not generate any revenue stream. This is a startling statistic; the problem being that a vast proportion of inventions do not solve a 'problem' worth solving. To understand innovation, consider the light bulb—it is a creative advancement in science and technology—however, on its own it creates no value. When you insert the light bulb into a lamp and wire that lamp to electricity, you get light energy. The production of light energy through the method of electricity-lamp-light bulb is superior to the light energy kerosene lamps produced in the past. It is superior in terms of safety, cost, portability and durability; hence, the 'method' of producing light energy through electricity-lamp-light bulb is an innovation. Innovations can be such new methods, processes (like additive manufacturing using 3D printing), products (MakaPads described in the above case study) or services (DiDi Taxi in China).

It is often said that due to structural problems in developing countries such as access to finance, unavailability of science and technology infrastructure, government corruption and lack of skilled labour, doing innovation is too difficult, on the verge of being nearly impossible. Innovation is known to benefit from environmental volatility and stressors; in other words, developing countries' often thought to be unstable internal conditions, in a way, provide a fertile ground for innovation to take place. Dr Musaazi's case described above highlights that innovation is not always about making 'solutions' more technologically advanced and sophisticated, which is usually the norm in developing countries (to improve profit margins). At times taking features away and stripping the solution down to its bare essentials so that it is best aligned to 'user requirements' is the best way to innovate. The problem with most innovative solutions is that over time, with small refinements and improvements, they tend to become more and more feature laden, complicated and over engineered and as a result more expensive, eventually coming to a 'peak point' from which any further advance does not increase utility for the user. Consider the smartphone; after many successive generations, screen sizes, processing capabilities, camera quality and other features have improved to their 'peak' extent—any further increases, say in screen size, would mean losses in portability as users would not be able to fit any larger screened devices in their pockets.

It is important to note that the rate of innovative new product and service failure in developing vs. developed countries is similar—only the quantum or extent of failure is different, it is higher in developed countries because in aggregate more innovations are brought to market spaces therein. Therefore, there is no reason to doubt the innovative capacities of developing country innovators because the reasons for innovation failure in developing vs. developed economies are very much the same. These include lack of alignment with user requirements, wrong timing for market entry, not supported by an effective commercial model and/or weak supporting organization. If we look at the case of MakaPads in Uganda, the product satisfies the necessary requirements of being labelled an 'innovation'—it solves a problem in a much better way than existing and any previous solutions, it meets the target users' criteria in terms of features and affordability, the product is supported by a good commercial model and generates revenue for the innovator's (Dr Musaazi's) well-functioning organization, T4T.

The fact that MakaPads are manufactured using meagre locally available and renewable resources, provide employment to impoverished refugees, help improve girls' access to education and solve a pressing (and humiliating) social problem for women awards an elevated status to the product—as both a 'frugal' and 'social' innovation. These concepts are discussed in the following sections.

3.2. SOCIAL INNOVATION AND ENTREPRENEURSHIP

Social innovation is a process through which 'solutions' to pressing and often systemic social and environmental issues are developed and launched to promote socio-economic development.

Although 'solutions' developed out of the social innovation process often require multiple collaborators, most commonly though, social innovations are developed and launched by social entrepreneurs. Social entrepreneurs set up social enterprises to do social innovation, and they do earn a revenue stream from their innovative 'solution'—which may be a product, service or a hybrid of both. Hence, social enterprises are for-profit entities and not charities or NGOs. At times, but not always, social entrepreneurs reinvest their profits back into their social enterprise or the local community. In developing countries, where socio-economic problems are highly pronounced and government agencies are often unable to alleviate the lives of their adversely affected citizens, private capital in the form of social enterprise provides alternative 'solutions'—or social innovations—to replicate or augment the role of government. Provided further are a number of prominent examples of social innovations in developing countries.

Social Enterprise and Innovation Exemplars

Lijjat Papad: India

Lijjat is a for-profit social enterprise based out of Mumbai, India, established in 1959. The enterprise was started by seven semi-literate women and is to date solely run by women. The organization manufactures 'papad'—an Indian snack popularly known as Poppadum in Western nations. What makes them unique is not poppadum but an alternative model of running their business. It is based on 'Sarvodaya'—a Gandhian philosophy which teaches self-reliance, collective ownership, profit-sharing and cooperation.

M-KOPA Solar: Kenya

Founded in 2011, M-KOPA focuses on the provision of solar energy to Kenya's rural poor. The innovative social enterprise was set up by three individuals—Chad Larson, Nick Hughes and Jesse Moore and is headquartered in Nairobi. They sell solar power systems for home use in not just Kenya but also Uganda and Tanzania. One of the founders, Hughes, was responsible for the setting up and running of the M-Pesa—a mobile phone-based money transfer, financing and micro-financing platform.

Klong Dinsor: Thailand

Klong Dinsor is a Thai social enterprise established in 2013 that focuses on helping children with visual disabilities through the provision of innovative educational tools. The company was founded by Chatchai Aphibanpoonpon, a 30-year-old entrepreneur. Five years prior to start-up, Chatchai was a regular volunteer at a Bangkok school helping students with visual disabilities. During this work experience, he realized that the teaching and learning approaches for students with visual

The organization's aim is not profit maximization but to provide employment to women and empowering them to earn a decent and dignified livelihood. India is known to be a patriarchal society; to provide alternatives to women, Lijjat encourages self-employment among them. Through a system of small-scale, home-based distributed manufacturing, Lijjat members acquire ingredients for an agreed-to daily quota for papad every day in the early hours of the morning, swear an oath of sisterhood and integrity, and then proceed to their respective homes to make the product. Later in the day, they return back to Lijjat, and based on the amount of papad they were able to make, they are duly compensated. This model improves their economic status and helps their self-confidence. Today Lijjat is recognized as the world's largest women's only community-based social enterprise.

Social Innovation: A low-cost model for distributed manufacturing that aims to create self-employed and economically empowered women.

Since 2012, M-KOPA has been able to connect more than 300,000 homes in East Africa with solar powered energy. Household customers who are off-the-grid from the mains power usually pay a deposit to M-KOPA after which a solar system is installed in their homes. They are then expected to pay a pre-agreed amount to the company on a daily basis through M-Pesa for a year, after which ownership of the system is transferred to the customer. The uniqueness of the service is that in addition to immediately getting solar power on sign up, customers are able to offset the cost of the device over time, and at the end of their agreement, fully own it. The company estimates that most of their customers, about 80 per cent, live on $2 a day, and as such, energy costs take up a significant portion of this amount. The power system sold by the company costs $200 and includes a solar panel, two LED bulbs, a rechargeable radio, an LED flashlight and adaptors to enable phone charging. The system is also supplied with a two-year warranty.

Social Innovation: A supplied and fitted pay-as-you-go system with minimal running and maintenance costs for rural electrification.

disabilities were quite poor due to the lack of adequate teaching tools. Most teaching tools available were made by teachers, and were quite limited in scope due to their design, lack of investment and suitable production facilities. To solve this problem, he established 'Klong Dinsor', which means 'pencil box' in Thai. The first product launched was the Lensen Drawing Kit—an educational tool, followed by a specially designed pen which uses yarn instead of ink. Existing similar products are too complicated for visually impaired students to use and not readily available either. On the other hand, the Lensen Drawing Kit is designed via the help of special education experts, made out of good quality materials and preferred by target students over other available solutions.

Social Innovation: Educational aids for visually impaired students which reduce their writing and drawing learning curve.

3.3. FRUGAL INNOVATION

The idea of 'bricolage' or working with what you have got adequately captures the overriding focus in the frugal innovation process. First discovered to be occurring on a large-scale in India, it is referred to colloquially in Hindi as 'jugaad'. India, like other developing countries, is beginning to emerge as an ideal environment for frugal or 'jugaad' innovation owing to several factors, such as the political promotion of a sense of national pride in the 'made in India (or home country)' label, growing economies, a resource constrained environment that promotes bricoleur thinking and action, high price sensitivity and low purchasing power, a large proportion of aspiring youth in the population and the availability of new sources of social financing. These characteristics promote a 'jugaad culture'—a creative inventiveness due to limited resources and a 'can do' approach motivated by necessity. Such a culture allows the creation of 'solutions' which are able to deal with the lack of mains electric power, work despite users' lack of literacy and technology know-how, affordable for the most impoverished, solve a social problem, not be reliant on sophisticated mass manufacturing technology and easy to maintain and repair. Thus, as a result of 'jugaad', a new or improved product or service that uses the minimum amount of resources (both financial and material) is created which reduces purchasing cost.

At times, 'jugaad' is labelled as a 'low-cost fix' which solves a problem quickly, but the quick-fix is often not sustainable; such thinking goes against the essence of frugal and bricoleur thinking and can lead to 'dark innovation'. Dark innovation is innovation with negative consequences, usually executed by threat actors to break systems. Dark innovators or threat actors can depict high degrees of innovation by using technology frugally—in a simple and often straightforward manner. They include computer hackers, fake ID makers, currency counterfeiters, prisoners who make improvised weapons, terrorists, cheaters in sports and individuals who facilitate student cheating. Their purpose is to use vulnerabilities to exploit any system's configuration. Like frugal innovators, dark innovators also use bricolage, but their solutions are not necessarily simple (but can be) and the purpose is not solving a pressing social problem. The innovation process employed by both frugal and dark innovators though is similar—finding unexpected uses of commonly available items, using trial and error, relying on extreme simplicity, designing to solve a very specific problem, not as concerned about alternate uses or long-term sustainability and designing to deliver a self-contained solution. What differentiates frugal and dark innovators primarily is the fact that dark innovators are not concerned about solving pressing social problems, while frugal innovators are. The difference, thus, lies in their ethical and moral beliefs and their sense of 'right' and 'wrong'. However, this is not to say that there is nothing to learn from the dark innovator's 'mindset'; the more we understand such a mindset, the better we will become at designing solutions that will be able to withstand and fend off attacks from threat actors.

Dark Innovation Example: Cheating Technologies in Examinations

Singapore: A 32-year-old tuition teacher was convicted for helping at least six Chinese nationals cheat in their GCE O-Level exams in 2016. Tan Jia Yan pleaded guilty to 27 counts of cheating. Twenty-six charges were for conspiring with three others to cheat the Singapore Examinations and Assessment Board (SEAB), while the remaining charge was for abetting a 20-year-old student to cheat in an English exam on 24 October, 2016. The 'cheating operations' were 'highly sophisticated', said a deputy public prosecutor. On the day of each exam, tuition teachers attached Bluetooth devices to the students' clothing. The devices were linked to mobile phones which were also hidden under their clothes, and each student wore a skin-coloured ear piece. The teacher who had also registered for the GCE O-Levels as a private candidate, would sit for the exams as well. She had an iPhone attached to the front of her blouse with scotch tape and wore a jacket to hide it. Once the exam had started, Tan would connect via FaceTime with confederates, who were stationed outside, giving them a live feed of the exam questions. At the tuition centre, the trio would scramble to find answers to the questions, then call each of the six students and read the answers to them.

From left to right: Electromagnetic vest to beat metal detectors, a pair of glasses for recording and transmitting video, old cell phones set up as cheating devices and eraser with a hidden chamber.

In developing countries, jugaad innovators look for new ways to do more with less and deliver greater value to consumers at a lower cost, which is a conditioned response to the pervasive scarcity in their environments and at times a key to their very survival. While innovators in developing countries operate in resource-rich conditions, jugaad innovators must contend with the scarcity of financial resources and access to lines of credit for investment in research and development (R&D). They also face scarcities in the availability of natural resources, such as water and basic building materials, which might be expensive and hard to reliably obtain. A scarcity of talented individuals such as technicians and market development experts. Finally, poor quality infrastructure like roads and limited transportation networks make it difficult to distribute frugal goods and services to impoverished communities. In addition to all these scarcities, jugaad innovators must also contend with a demanding user base, who are value conscious, aspire to a better quality of life and are quick to reject offerings which do not deliver significantly higher value than existing 'solutions'. This user base is also usually very diverse in terms of language and other cultural differentiators.

Doing frugal innovation requires the application of 'frugal thinking' in every activity associated with the 'solution' design and delivery process. Hence, they are frugal in how they design products, how they build them, how they deliver them and how they perform after sales and maintenance. They are also frugal in how they use capital and the way they maximize the output from their time and energy reserves. They tend to rely on partners to perform various functions during design and delivery; they tend to reuse and recombine; do not tend to invest in specific assets that are difficult to dispose of should the product fail; remain flexible and adaptable—making refinements and changes through experimentation, trial and error and feedback; keep the solution basic; and include a profit margin to ensure the sustainability of their venture. The MittiCool fridge described further was developed using 'frugal thinking' by an individual embedded in a marginalized community. The device subscribes to the characteristics of jugaad or frugal innovations—low cost, uncomplicated and familiar, easy to maintain and repair, and most importantly, solves a problem for marginalized communities.

Frugal Innovation Example: MittiCool Fridge by Mansukhbhai Prajapati

Frugal innovator Mansukhbhai, from Gujarat, India, has a number of frugal innovations to his credit. He was exposed to traditional clay making since childhood; however, due to financial pressures, he had to leave studies early and take up various odd jobs to support the family. In 1988, he took a small loan to start his own factory of earthen plate manufacturing. He modified a roof tile making hand press and developed a hand press machine using which he could produce 700 earthen pans per day. He could sell these at very low prices and within two days was able to sell his entire batch. When he started getting negative feedback from customers regarding the durability of the pans, he experimented with varied proportions of clay to get a mix which was more heat resistant and durable. He also made earthen thermos flasks and water filter systems out of clay as well. Unfortunately, in the aftermath of the 2001 earthquake, Mansukhbhai suffered huge irreparable losses. His stock was decimated to a large extent, and whatever remained, he chose to distribute among earthquake victims in Kutch. Soon after, a local newspaper carried a photo feature on the earthquake where at one place a photo showed one of Mansukhbhai's water filters with the caption 'Fridge of the poor got broken'. Apparently, the writer-photographer mistook the water filter for a fridge. This caption gave him an idea—why not create a fridge that could be used by rural masses out of his favourite medium, clay.

Hence in 2002, he started working on his clay refrigerator design and came in contact with Grassroots Innovation Augmentation Network (GIAN), who assisted him in various stages of product development. The technology used in this simple device works on the same principles as earthen pots. It does not require electric power or any source of energy, therefore, has no recurring costs. The device also preserves the original taste of fruits and vegetables. GIAN facilitated design improvements in the device through the National Institute of Design (NID), Ahmedabad. During testing, the shelf life of coriander was extended by four days when compared to only one-and-a-half to two days at room temperature. Similarly, the shelf life of vegetables such as Aubergine, Chili and Okra increased on an average by 5–6 days.

Mansukhbhai finally launched the MittiCool fridge in 2005, after three years of testing different clay mixes and fridge designs. Priced very reasonably, the device cools water down by almost 10 degrees and keeps perishable items such as milk, fruits and vegetables, fresh for between four and five days. It works on the principle of evaporation. Water from the upper chambers drips down the side and gets evaporated taking away heat from the inside, leaving the chambers cool. By 2010, he was supplying his products across India and received orders from 41 countries.

3.4. DOING INNOVATION

Creativity, which we discussed in the previous chapter, is the starting point for doing innovation. The imaginative idea to solve a problem, born out of the creative process, jump-starts the innovation process. The process itself can be difficult to manoeuver—outcomes are usually uncertain, and things can go wrong without any overt mistakes having been made. Entrepreneurs need to innovate constantly to ensure that their venture remains competitive. Being innovative in a small new venture within a developing country context requires the following.

3.4.1. KNOWING YOUR CUSTOMERS VERY WELL

Innovation can be done via the technology-push or the customer-pull approach. Technology-push—which would be introducing new products based on original research is a difficult approach to take within a developing country context. As a result, to innovate, entrepreneurs therein must rely on the customer-pull approach, which is finding ways to solve customer 'problems' without relying on novel science. The key would be to understand the needs of less-affluent customers and using this knowledge to devise creative solutions to their problems. For example, employees of China's Haier (white goods manufacturer) visited rural customers and found that they were using their washing machines not only to launder clothes but also to wash vegetables. This led to the identification of new needs and a clear customer problem. By making modifications to their existing washing machine technology, Haier was able to market new machines to these customers which were versatile enough to wash both clothing and vegetables. This move led to them becoming the white goods market leader in rural areas of China.

Haier's (China) Dual-Purpose Washing Machine

3.4.2. INNOVATE AROUND THE TECHNOLOGY

Multinationals like Phillips or GlaxoSmithKline plc can drive innovation from their research laboratories turning scientific advances into new products. In a developing country context, the innovations come not from product technology but from all the elements of the business that enable the delivery of the core product technology, such as manufacturing, logistics, distribution and finance. These elements need to be carefully configured to deliver maximum value. Very often it is not the quality of the product or the efficacy of the core technology, but the manner in which it is delivered or the customer's need is serviced. For example, in Mexico, CEMEX—a cement maker, carefully looked at the issue of delivering ready-mix concrete to its local customers. Its customers are building contractors who would often change their orders at the last minute. This caused a number of back office administrative problems which led to delays in delivery. CEMEX could not expect its customers to moderate their ordering behaviour; frequent last minute order changes were the norm needed to undertake building work in developing country. CEMEX found that, on average, it would take three hours between the time when a change request was received from a customer and when the order could be delivered. This delay was a concern to customers, as it impacted their schedules. To decrease turnaround time, CEMEX equipped its fleet of concrete mixer trucks with tracking systems. They got this idea from a 911 call centre they saw in Houston. Their team saw the way emergency call operators quickly reacted to urgent requests, dispatching help rapidly within minutes despite traffic issues and unpredictable call patterns. By using a similar approach, dispatchers at CEMEX could dynamically re-route on-road trucks to the best possible delivery destinations without the need for them to return to the factory. As a result, deliveries became possible within a twenty-minute window, whereas, CEMEX's competitors still operated on the three-hour window. This tracking and dispatching system did not emerge from a science and technology lab, but out of internal innovation efforts. It has allowed CEMEX to increase its market share, charge a premium to time-conscious contractors and reduce costs resulting from unused concrete.

CEMEX's (Mexico) GPS Tracked Cement Mixer Trucks

3.4.3. LOOK AROUND THE WORLD FOR GOOD IDEAS

Due to increasing smartphone penetration rates and the availability of high speed mobile internet, developing country entrepreneurs can now search for potential solutions from around the world. The key would be to not simply copy something seen in use elsewhere. Rather, it would be important to adopt parts of a particular practice or technology that is found and to recombine these in new ways to solve customer problems. To illustrate, Natura—a Brazilian cosmetics company—understood that it could not compete on technical innovation with global competitors such as Procter & Gamble and Estée Lauder. These multinationals earmark hundreds of millions of dollars on science and technology research every year. Hence, Natura developed relationships with universities and research centres around the world and began to license-in their technology. Science and technology is available for licensing from around the world—entrepreneurs from developing countries need not worry about building indigenous research capability, which is very difficult. For Natura the hard part was knowing what they were looking for in the plethora of ready-to-license products and technologies available from universities and research centres around the world. This is where their conceptualization of new lines of beauty products which served local needs became very important. For example, Natura launched Chronos—a skin cream targeted to women in their 30s. This product was licensed-in and relied on combining several existing technologies into an integrated product that specifically served the needs of their target market. Their competitor Lancôme has three different products for wrinkles, each with either the vitamins A, C or D. These three products sell in Brazil on the basis of their brand recognition. Chronos incorporates the three vitamins into one cream because all the vitamins are beneficial for older skin, particularly in Brazil's sunny and humid climate.

Based on the above three precepts and the prior discussions on social and frugal innovations, in developing countries, the process of doing innovation would follow several stages as described in Figure 3.1.

Natura's (Brazil) Skin Cream

3.5. SUMMARY AND APPLICATION

The cases of Dr Moses Kizza Musaazi and Mansukhbhai Prajapati, highlight the approaches the entrepreneur-innovators take in doing innovation within a developing country perspective. MakaPads and the MittiCool 'solutions' are truly frugal in nature, using renewable resources, and locally available material and labour. The products' design and delivery rely on jugaad thinking—small amounts of investment with highest possible production output; reliance on partners for R&D, manufacturing and distribution; there is a novel use of a locally available raw material; the entire operation is quite flexible and can be scaled according to demand; there are small refinements constantly made to appeal to new customers; there is a profit margin; and the operation is run like a business, not a charity.

Exercise 3.1. Plan a field trip as a group with your other classmates to an irregular settlement or a locality where marginalized/poor communities make their home. Spend your day talking to people and taking observations about their day-to-day lives. Remember to take down notes on aspects which you believe are major negative contributors to their quality of living. Develop a few clear problem statements, for example, 'water available to locals should subscribe to legal potable water standards, however, tests through portable testing kits show a high degree of contamination. These contaminants are the major contributor for disease in women and children'. Choose a particular problem statement and discuss potential 'solutions' with your group. Think about the frugal innovation process discussed in this chapter and create a plan to solve your chosen problem via jugaad thinking—ensuring participation from the target community. Finally, go back to the settlement and present your idea to the settlement's representatives. Request feedback and see how your plan might need modifications to be practical.

FIGURE 3.1 **Innovation Process in Developing Countries**

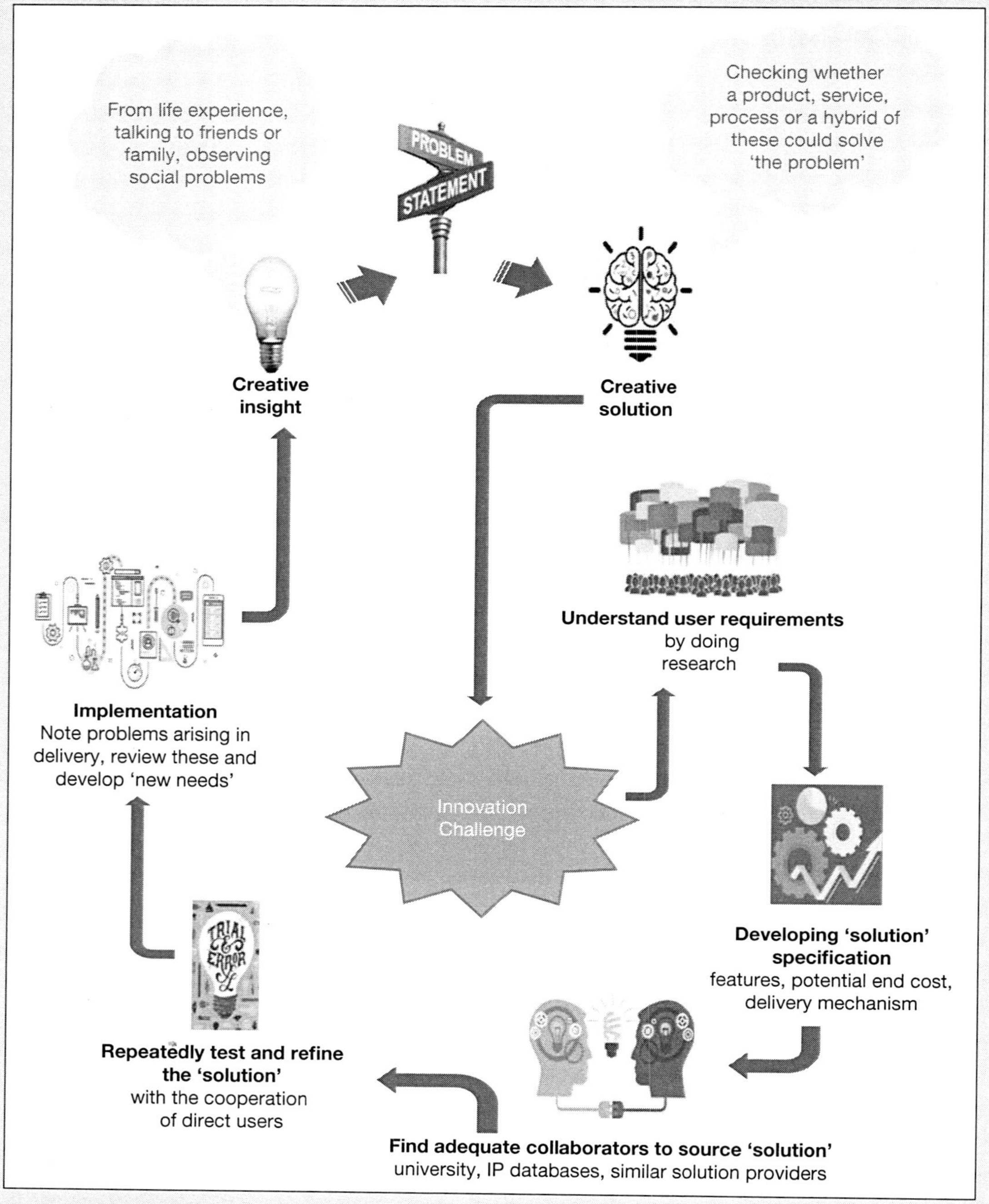

Source: The authors.

To solve a socio-economic 'problem' with innovation, the founders of Lijjat, M-KOPA Solar and Klong Dinsor created a business venture that did not rely on advanced science and technology but on innovative ways of doing business and delivering value to employees and end users. The extent of original science and technology-based research that entrepreneurs could license-out and commercialize in developing countries is somewhat limited. This is not to say that such research is not being conducted—it might very well be in most developing countries. However, it remains undiscovered due to lack of exposure and because of inadequate research commercialization mechanisms in place at universities and research institutes, we often do not see indigenous home-grown products launched in local markets based on outputs by local scientists and technologists.

Exercise 3.2. Form a group with your colleagues in class—your aim is two-fold; first, come up with an idea for a new product ideally (or service) that solves a known commercial (business) or consumer (general public) problem, for example, solar lights, portable water filters, alternate energy fans and so on. Use the creativity techniques described in the previous chapter to structure your thinking. You are encouraged to consider domains where your idea or 'solution' might produce a positive socio-economic benefit. Second, find a scientist(s) or engineer(s) at a university or research institute who are interested in your chosen idea's domain. You might have to make several attempts before you find the right individual—one who possesses an entrepreneurial mindset and has a commercial outlook. They might have published research, tested equipment or produced prototypes that could provide the technological basis for your 'solution'. Interview them face to face and understand how the technology works and as to when it would be ready for commercial/public use. Develop a plan to refine, package and promote the 'solution', develop a timeline and investment requirements to accompany your plan. Share this plan with your scientist/engineer partner and get their feedback.

4

Making Entrepreneurial Decisions with Effectual Thinking

LEARNING OUTCOMES

- Understand the difference between causal or managerial thinking versus effectual or entrepreneurial thinking
- Become familiar with the five core heuristics or mental shortcuts expert entrepreneurs use to take decisions
- Learn how expert entrepreneurs take steps to lower their exposure to risk

4.1. WHAT IS EFFECTUATION?

Spotlight on Kadir Koymen, Founder of Edelkrone: Photography and Cinema Products from Turkey

Kadir Koymen is a Turkish movie producer and director, and the founder CEO of Edelkrone, a company that produces and sells a wide variety of innovative equipment for the photography and cinema industries. In starting up Edelkrone, Kadir employed a process that minimized both risk and capital requirements. A number of years ago when he was considering making a feature-length movie and working on its script, he could not find a cost-effective 35 mm lens adaptor for his camera. He thought to himself 'why can I not develop my own lens adaptor'? and proceeded to put up a post on his personal website which claimed 'I will produce the world's cheapest 35 mm lens adaptor for cameras'.

He was setting himself up for a challenge making a public claim in this manner and without having a requisite background for designing and manufacturing such a specialized product. Thinking about the problem, he had an idea for his own adaptor, and posted a picture on his website of a camera and a lens which were strapped to each other with mere Sellotape. The public claim and the expectation he created within the film-maker community proved to be a great source of motivation for him, in a way forcing him to think unconventionally about how to develop such a product. With the help of comments and reactions online, he decided to put aside the writing of his script and the feature-length movie project and focused entirely on developing his lens adaptor.

He stated: 'If you want to quit smoking, first of all you should start with telling your friends'. The most significant challenge for Kadir was lack of investment capital which made it hard to employ the necessary support staff. He had to operate single-handedly out of his garage, near an industrial estate, for more than two years. Such a challenge was also an opportunity to keep overhead costs at a minimum, giving him the ability to correct mistakes, providing refunds and sending lots of free units. He taught himself the principles of quality control and over time, with the help of the professionals in the nearby industrial estate, he was able to perfect his innovative product. His camera lens adaptor was hailed as a miracle because it gave photographers and movie-makers the ability to record high-quality scenes with a great depth of field through the use of an average quality and affordable camera. In a way, his product paved the way for independent cinema, because film-makers could now meet the expectations of movie fans who believe unconsciously that a certain type of depth of field equals to high quality and high budget.

According to Koymen, his customers in Turkey did hold a negative bias towards local products and the idea that products developed by foreigners and imported from overseas are always good. He believes that there are a lot of opportunities and skill sets for improving existing imported products in Turkey. However, individuals usually abstain from undertaking any improvement work because of the above mindset. However, it is important to persevere against such a bias and to implement a new idea with your own approach and style. When a Turkish MSc student of Ali J. Ahmad interviewed Kadir Koymen in 2017 and asked him about his start-up journey, he stated:

> *Sometimes you have an idea, but you see that someone else has already done it, but when you work on this idea with your approach and your own style, it turns to another thing. Yes, what you produce might be similar to what already exists, but this does not mean that you can't do it better.*

The product sold very well initially until Canon and Nikon—two of the largest camera manufacturers in the world—released their DSLR cameras, which provided a better solution to photographers and movie-makers. According to Kadir, this is a very common and expected problem for any entrepreneur; and rather than giving up he saw the launch of the new DSLR cameras as a hidden opportunity. By taking advantage of his newly acquired knowledge in the industry and relationships in manufacturing, he set up Edelkrone to develop innovative accessories for DSLRs and video cameras, becoming over time, one the most eminent companies in the world for DSLR accessories. Their approach is to develop products which present all the existing features of competitors but offer one additional one at least.

Kadir's approach for both design and manufacturing was based on who he was, what he knew and who he knew: 'We were always using whatever we had in our hands, what took time was finding a product which we could make solely with what we had, and we got much better at this in time'.

Professor Saras Saraswathy, who is the Jamuna Raghavan Chair Professor in Entrepreneurship at the Indian Institute of Management Bangalore, in her very original work on effectual entrepreneurship, argues that there are important differences between a manager (like a sales or human resource director in a company) and an individual who starts a business (an entrepreneur). Usually both managers and entrepreneurs would possess a similar range of business skills like the ability to interpret cash flow statements, estimate sales or generate new business leads; however, they would greatly differ in their logics of viewing the world, making decisions and taking action (Figure 4.1).

Managers are allocated 'goals' (or targets) by their principals (company owners who hire them to work in their interest), and they develop strategies to achieve those goals. They rely on forecasting under the following two assumptions: (a) that the future is knowable, though somewhat uncertain and (b) that their operating environments are reasonably well-structured and predictable. Without these two assumptions, managerial action would not be possible. Imagine an exercise of budget creation: a sales manager attempting to develop a departmental budget would first need a set of

FIGURE 4.1 Causal versus Effectual Reasoning

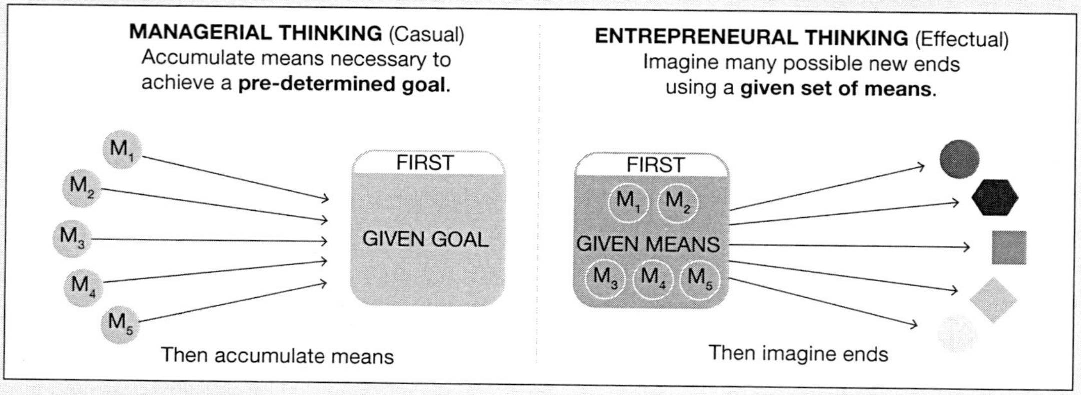

Source: Read et al. (2017).

clear goals (like reduce costs by 5%). Creating an acceptable budget would require looking at historical patterns and other parameters to estimate what the outgoings and incomings would be and that whatever problems might arise would be easily dealt with, with minimal impact on the budget. Her role is to ensure that she accomplishes the goals set by her principals in a fairly predictable and well-structured manner. Consider her difficulty if she had no basis for accurate forecasting because she has to assume that unexpected problems would keep on occurring unpredictably throughout the budget cycle.

Expert entrepreneurs, unlike managers, because they do not have principals, have no concrete goals. Instead, they might have a personal vision for where they might want to be in a period of time. They hold the firm belief that the future is entirely unpredictable and unknowable and the environment they operate in is unstructured. They understand the differences between known knowns (a predictable future under near perfect forecasting conditions—the sun will rise tomorrow), known unknowns (a somewhat uncertain future under imperfect forecasting conditions—weather predictions) and unknown unknowns (true uncertainty where accurate forecasting is impossible—a random draw from a perfectly set up lottery). Expert entrepreneurs, having internalized that the future in new venture creation is an unknown, understand that there is no basis for accurate prediction of what their actions might lead to. They do, however, have absolute certainty about their 'means'—known knowns; what they personally possess and control. They take action on the basis that the future does not as yet exist, but by using the means available to them and such means' various combinations, any new possible future may be created.

There is no value judgement on which logic or approach might be best, but to understand the difference between causal (managerial) and effectual (entrepreneurial) thinking more clearly, consider cooking. One of the two approaches might be used when preparing a meal; either a recipe is followed for a dish, for which all the necessary ingredients are made available, the required utensils are used and the described steps are performed to create the target dish. This would be the causal approach. On the other hand, an effectual approach would dictate that one would step into their kitchen and take note of what ingredients and other necessary implements are available at hand and by using those prepare a new dish. In both cases, for the dish to be appetizing and presentable, cookery experience and technique would certainly be needed; but practical considerations aside, it is instructive to realize that using causation leads to a known output dish (like a curry or a milkshake), whereas, by relying on effectuation one ends up with a completely new dish each time they cook. An effectual cook would take the ingredients for a curry and using those might end up making a savoury soufflé or any number of other possible dishes. He would understand that they might not all be perfect, but they would certainly be different—and one of such combinations might end up being the next culinary blockbuster.

4.2. HOW EXPERT ENTREPRENEURS TAKE DECISIONS

Expert entrepreneurs (as opposed to novice or first-time entrepreneurs), over many years of practice, have learned that the most interesting new ventures are built in circumstances where the future is not only unknown, but unknowable. They understand that they have the ability to shape this unpredictable future by using techniques that minimize the use of prediction. These techniques are best described as 'heuristics' or 'mental shortcuts' (discussed in Chapter 2). In this section, five such 'entrepreneur heuristics' are described along with example cases that highlight application.

4.2.1. THE BIRD-IN-HAND PRINCIPLE

Expert entrepreneurs start with their basic means or things that they have readily at hand. These can fall into three categories:

1. **Who I am:** Your beliefs, moral and ethical stances, your personal history and upbringing, traits, tastes, opinions about what constitutes 'success', social or political issues that infuriate you or make you happy, things you would never do under any circumstances. In other words, what makes you 'you'—an individual.
2. **What I know:** Your education, training and expertise. You could possess unique pieces of information, for example, my sister bakes the best cakes in our city or meaningful things you have learnt through your experience in the commercial world, for example, there is always a shortage of rubber tyres during a particular season.
3. **Who I know:** Your social and professional contacts. On average, each one of us have about 150 'good' contacts and by utilizing those contacts you could reach out to more individuals and develop relationships with them.

The above means are a dynamic complex, changing and being added to as progress is made in life and vocation. By using a combination of the above means, an entrepreneur begins to imagine new possibilities to take affirmative action. They usually start very frugally, how Kadir Koymen did in the case described earlier—operating from his own garage for two years, moving directly into implementation without any careful planning. Recall, within the effectual work view there is no merit in doing long-term planning because it is impossible to make accurate predictions about the future. As each step is taken, possible outcomes are reconfigured. In time, effects from actions begin to take shape into achievable goals, populating a blank map with way points to an end point imagined by the entrepreneur.

Dai Wei, CEO and Co-Founder of OFO: Chinese Bike Sharing Firm | Bird-in-Hand

Dai Wei, who at the time of writing this book was 26 years old, began his higher education studies at Peking University in 2009 and graduated with an undergraduate degree in Finance in 2013. The university had a very active cycling community which promoted the idea of combining sport with academics. During undergraduate studies, Dai became a member of this community, and this is where he met his future collaborators. He began to develop an understanding about the many problems that cycle commuters face and the gaps the cycling industry left in solving these.

Overwhelmingly, they believed that the industry at the time was totally unresponsive when it came to providing users with a convenient, efficient, green and healthy way of travelling around cities. They thought to themselves: why do not we offer a solution to existing and potential cyclists through a new method of 'bike sharing', thereby, taking away the burden of 'bike ownership' and the costs and risks that came with it (such as maintenance and theft). Various ideas for solutions coalesced and OFO was born—a firm combining smartphone applications with the idea of the 'sharing economy' to overcome the 'last kilometre of travel' problem faced by people living in large cities in China and beyond. They plunged into action to test the basic principles behind OFO—making use of the facilities and captive target audience (staff and students) in the large campus of Peking University. The founders' relationships and work experience in the students' union and their observations about the living conditions, life styles and commuting behaviours of teachers and students proved invaluable.

Like a vast majority of entrepreneurs, Dai proceeded without any business plan or a detailed analysis of possible strategic options and manoeuvers. He used 'bricolage', the idea that one works with what they have got, taking action to create OFO using the basic means he could readily control—'who he was', 'what he knew' and 'whom he knew'.

We can see from the case write-up that Dai was a curious student who wanted to make a difference—he was sociable, confident and demonstrated leadership quality. He knew economics and finance from his education, had some work experience in the students' union (and also a math teacher); he also knew about the gig economy and the rapid changes taking place in Chinese government policy to promote clean environment initiatives. Being a cyclist himself and through his observations of others, he also knew about the problems faced by cycle commuters and understood the reasons that hindered potential cyclists from adopting bikes for their commuting needs. OFO could not have been set up if Dai did not have his friends in the Peking University Student Union supporting him and along with other actors within the university's administration who came on board early with 'skin in the game' (that they had something to lose if the venture failed, which ensured their full attention and dedication). Finally, his parents' (though initially quite reluctant) support was also instrumental in the early stages of testing and trialling. Dai created OFO using these basic means.

4.2.2. THE AFFORDABLE LOSS PRINCIPLE

To launch a new product or explore any other business 'opportunity', managers conduct a market and industrial analysis and make strategic choices based on highest 'expected returns' (or profits). Entrepreneurs, on the other hand, when they wish to take action, think of outcomes in terms of 'affordable losses' rather than expected returns—what they might lose if they took action rather than what they might earn. Effectual entrepreneurs, therefore, do not create upfront budgets for launching their business and then expend energy in raising that money; because uncertain new venture opportunities are difficult to value upfront. Instead, they attempt to assess the downside (or things that could go wrong) and determine the worst-case scenario. Their decision for action is based on whether they would be able to recover from the 'worst-case scenario', if it ends up manifesting itself. If they believe that they could personally absorb the consequences and not be irrecoverably harmed if the worst case ends up happening, for example, their product failing mandatory government certification or the import duty on a key ingredient for their catering business skyrockets, they tend to plunge into action. The effectual entrepreneur, to reduce his/her exposure to the 'worst-case scenario', brings other stakeholders on board to spread the risk (and leverage expertise), to determine what all stakeholders could afford to lose together. What is important to understand about this principle is that an entrepreneur's assessment of his/her 'affordable loss level' depends primarily on his/her personal circumstances and would naturally vary from person to person, across his/her life stages and circumstances.

Kadir Koymen, relying on affordable loss, did not invest a lot of personal cash, but rather used his own garage and taught himself quality control and other technicalities related to developing a camera lens adapter. He understood that he was taking time off his usual line of work to pursue a new venture, which would mean a loss of income during this time he spent and the risk of potentially becoming redundant within the film-making industry if he wished to return should the venture fail. However, he also understood that the potential loss of income could be absorbed by reducing his personal living expenses and by relying primarily on 'sweat equity' to start his venture. Also, a return to film-making was always possible, because the industry works on meritocracy and output quality—if he could make good films before his venture, he could continue to make good films if the worst-case scenario ended up happening. His only loss would be time. Thus, the affordable loss principle allows cheap failure and learning that can be applied to the next iteration of the opportunity.

Samir Ibrahim and Charles Nichols, Founders of SunCulture: Kenyan Agri-Tech Firm | Affordable Loss

Agriculture in Kenya is the most common source of livelihood for a large proportion of the population. Due to a poor irrigation system, farmers have no choice but to rely on rain-fed agriculture. This leads to one of their biggest problems—unreliable rainfall patterns—which render much of the arable land unutilized during certain periods of the year, leaving them with little or no income.

Samir Ibrahim and his friend Charles Nichols based in New York and working full-time, in 2010, developed an idea together—using solar water pumps for introducing efficient irrigation systems in regions with unpredictable rain fall patterns. Charles had a background in engineering and had worked for a company developing solar energy projects, while Samir had a background in finance and was working at PricewaterhouseCoopers (PwC). To take their idea forward, they entered the New York University (NYU) Social Venture Competition but did not win—they achieved the second place. Reflecting on their loss, Samir stated in an interview, 'Don't take losing too seriously. Many people have great ideas but don't pursue them when they don't win the competition. Don't let that happen to you. We didn't win, but that didn't mean that we didn't have a viable business idea….' They built a pilot and asked themselves three questions: (a) Does the solution make economic sense for a for-profit business? (b) Does it make economic sense for farmers? (c) Does the technology work? When they got a 'Yes' to all the three questions, they knew they were ready.

They packed their bags and booked a one-way ticket to Nairobi, Kenya. According to Ibrahim, moving to Kenya and leaving behind his family, friends and a well-paying job in the USA was not easy but moving with Charles, who was a friend as well as a business partner made the move easier. The two developed a strong network of contacts before moving. Samir's family roots lay in East Africa and had some family living in the region, and Charles visited Kenya prior and networked with the start-up community in the country before the two made the big move. Speaking about their move, Samir said in an interview:

> *There was a really big problem that we say and that no one was addressing anywhere, and I have always been interested in East Africa, my family is from here, and the private sector's role in economic*

development, Charlie has spent some time in West Africa and were into conservation. We always had this drive to do something bigger—so this was attractive. We had time, we were young, we were stupid, we were like—why not try this. It was harder for my parents, because they were immigrants to the US…they were living the American dream…they put me through college and I was self-sufficient. So when I told them they were like—why are you going back? But they were very supportive and visited me often. Auerbach (2018)

After eight years of refining their AgroSolar Irrigation System, they have a thousand customers over East Africa. The system makes it cheaper and easier for farmers to grow higher quality crops and increase their yields by 300 per cent or more. Samir took action to jump-start SunCulture by only taking the amount of risk he could personally recover from should the worst-case scenario end up happening. Together with Charles, he acted based on the premise of 'why not try this—we have always wanted to do something bigger'. They were young and financially self-sufficient, had little direct family responsibilities, and had the time and the right mindset. They also had family roots and connections to help them manoeuver Kenya's business landscape. Coupled with this, they knew their product could make a real difference to the lives of impoverished farmers—which meant they could inspire others to join them on favourable terms, thereby, further reducing their exposure to risk. Samir and Charles did not start out by calculating how much money they could make by selling the SunCulture system; instead, they thought to themselves what is the worst thing that could happen if we ended up with a start-up in Nairobi—we might fail and go back to New York and resume our old lives and jobs. This would be 'affordable loss' thinking.

4.2.3. THE LEMONADE PRINCIPLE

Expert entrepreneurs, with years of practice, have developed the expertise to turn surprises or unexpected information, meetings or events, no matter whether these are positive or negative, into new opportunities. In contrast, managers tend to despise the unexpected; they do so because the unexpected occurring unexpectedly signals a degree of incompetence in contingency planning (preparation for worst-case scenarios). Expert entrepreneurs, on the other hand, work with surprises and take advantage of them because their ideas are not strongly tied to any preconceived target customer. Therefore, anything and everything unexpected occurring (like a chance meeting or a seemingly negative result from a trial) during the course of their venture's start-up phase is potentially a clue that could lead to a new opportunity.

New ventures are products of contingencies or surprises. Their structure, culture and core competence, if examined carefully, is determined by entrepreneurs fulfilling particular aspirations through interactions with other individuals, their geographic space, the circumstances in time they find themselves in and the technologies that are available. For example, Kadir Koymen, when he could not find an affordable adaptor for his camera, could have relented and bought what was available in the market and kept on working on his film project. This was his negative unexpected surprise event, which he viewed as an opportunity and decided to develop his own lens adaptor. He could have taken numerous routes to develop the adapter like taking out a bank loan to set up a company with hired engineers or partnered up with a university. Instead, he posted a blog on his personal website and claimed to take on the challenge for the adapter's development personally. This act, unexpectedly, created a lot of interest online and got him thinking about possible solutions.

When, after two years of effort, he finally did develop the product and it started to generate good sales, giant competitors launched DSLR cameras which eliminated the need for his adapter. This negative surprise could have resulted in him wrapping up operations and going back to his old line of work. However, he saw in the launch of the DSLRs a hidden opportunity; and diversified his venture to create unique accessories for these new cameras. Throughout Kadir's journey as an entrepreneur, and to this day, we can see him using the Lemonade Principle to work unexpected meetings, events and information to his advantage for creating new opportunities and strategic options.

Sachin and Binny Bansal, Founders of Flipkart.com: Indian E-commerce Giant | Lemonade Principle

A whole chain of serendipitous events brought India's e-commerce pioneers Sachin and Binny Bansal (not related) together. It was in the summer of 2005 when Sachin, 24, and Binny, 23, met as students at Indian Institute of Technology Delhi. They developed a close friendship while trying to improve their BTech's final project scores at the Institute's FPGA hardware lab. They might have never met had they got great scores in their first submissions and did not have to spend a whole summer attempting to meet course requirements. Though not related, they hailed from Chandigarh, were technically orientated, however, had different temperaments. Sachin is quick to take offence, whereas Binny is more laid back. Sachin has a dry sense of humour and is known to be intuitive, whereas Binny enjoys being behind a computer screen, working with data.

They found jobs together in Bangalore, though at different firms. Google rejected Binny twice, but Sachin joined Amazon. A little over a year later, in 2007, Binny too was recruited by Amazon and it was during this work experience that they developed an idea for a new start-up—a price comparison website. Market research, however, would force them to change their minds; direct e-commerce seemed much more viable. Thus, Flipkart.com was born in October 2007—the focus of the business was online book retail with delivery possible across all of India. A small investment of Indian rupees 400,000 (about US$5,500) equally split between Sachin and Binny provided the start-up capital. For the first 18 months of Flipkart's life, their parents supported them with an allowance and they worked from their two-bedroom flat, building the first version of the website and testing it live. When their first online order came through—a copy of John Wood's memoir *Leaving Microsoft to Change the World*—Flipkart was open for business. Sachin and Binny had to now procure that book from an offline retailer and ship it to their customer. However, as fate should have it, the book was not easily available in Bangalore. The order arrived a day late and the book was not in mint condition, but the customer was nevertheless happy with the founders who kept him informed about the delivery. After 20 successful shipments in 2007, they developed a degree of confidence.

In successive years, Flipkart focused on building its online book retail business with a number of innovations, such as, a 'cash-on-delivery' facility to win the confidence of Indian consumers when shopping online, book pre-ordering and a 30-day return policy. In 2011, they expanded their catalogue further and started offering personal care products, large appliances, laptops, cameras and stationery. Flipkart also expanded to 600 towns and cities across the country. In 2012, Flipkart forayed into the fashion and clothing segment and launched their mobile app as well.

Over the years, Sachin and Binny had successfully attracted investment from both local and international sources and their corporate structure had grown to keep pace with the growth in their business. Their 'negative unexpected event' occurred in 2012, when they came under Government of India scrutiny for alleged violation of Foreign Direct Investment rules. This created tremendous pressure on the founders; and to comply with government regulations and also to evolve their business for its next phase of expansion and growth, converted Flipkart—which was an online retailer at that time—into an Amazon.com-like online marketplace, where anyone wanting to sell any kind of product could use the Flipkart platform to host their e-shop. This led to massive expansion and their 'Big Billion Day' pre-Diwali sale in 2014, where they conducted US$1 billion worth of business in a single day. In 2018, Walmart, the world's largest retailer announced its plan to purchase a majority stake in Flipkart, around 77 per cent, valuing the Sachin and Binny's business close to US$20 billion.

Sachin and Binny took advantages of both positive and negative surprises to set up and grow Flipkart. They got unexpected information (e.g., customers' reluctance to pay in advance), met individuals in chance encounters who proved to be valuable (like themselves) and encountered unexpected events (e.g., their investigation by the Indian government). They started out with their basic means, and what these and other surprises did were add to their means; in other words, surprises revealed new clues and forced them to innovate and follow new strategic directions which they otherwise could not have planned for.

4.2.4. THE CRAZY QUILT PRINCIPLE

The growth of entrepreneurial zeal among the youth demographic in emerging and developing countries is evident from country-specific entrepreneurship surveys like the Global Entrepreneurship Monitor. Rates of 'perceived opportunities' and 'total entrepreneurial activity' across the developing world is surging. We find evidence of professionals leaving their jobs to set up new ventures as a part of an 'entrepreneurial team'. Common 'entrepreneurial teams' include student alumni, family members, former colleagues or husband–wife dyads. For instance, several technology-based ventures in recent years in India have been founded by a team of professionals who were alumni in higher education Institutes (e.g., Flipkart, featured earlier in this Chapter). However, one must ask: Why does this happen? The Crazy Quilt Principle provides a useful explanation.

Entrepreneurs tend to begin the new venture creation process under the assumption that they do not know the true characteristics of the market for their idea. Hence, they do not know who their competitors might be. The best, and least risky way forward is to build partnerships, ideally with potential new customers. These partnerships are formed on the basis of potential partners putting 'skin in the game', and ideally their first potential customers. These early partners commit to the venture with time, money and/or resources, self-selecting into the new-venture creation process. The entrepreneur remaining flexible, relies on these partners for directing changes to aspects of their idea so that it better suits market/customer requirements. The effectual entrepreneur is not wedded to any particular market for their idea, the network of early partnerships determines what market(s) their product (or even firm) might eventually end up entering or creating. In this manner, the 'Crazy Quilt' links well with 'Affordable Loss' to reduce uncertainty and bring the idea to market with little cash expenditure. This occurs because of early partners' (like potential suppliers, customers or technology providers) pre-commitments. For instance, Kadir Koymen, who was strapped for cash in the early days of his venture and was unable to hire R&D technicians, and would have found it nearly impossible to develop and perfect his first product—the camera lens adapter—had he not had assistance from technologists in the industrial estate near his garage operations. Further, the initial feedback he received from his early customers, to whom he would send the adapter for free, too proved be invaluable—not only did he get pertinent insight on how to tweak and improve the adapter but also built, in this manner, future customers who would be paying for his current and future products.

Gyanesh Pandey, CEO of Husk Power Systems: Indian Rural Electrification Pioneers | Crazy Quilt

Gyanesh wanted to make a difference by changing the lives of the most marginalized in society. He grew up in a small rural village within the West Champaran district of Bihar, India. After dusk, there was complete darkness because his village had not been linked up to India's main electricity grid. Rural households relied on burning expensive kerosene or candles for light. Gyanesh qualified as an electrical engineer from Banaras Hindu University and then moved to the USA for pursuing higher studies at the Rensselaer Polytechnic Institute in New York. Soon after, he started his career in the Los Angeles semiconductor industry. It was on a visit to his native village that he and a good friend, Ratnesh Yadav, started a conversation about the urgent need for rural electrification in India. This conversation and its potential implications proved to be a turning point for Gyanesh. He moved back to India, and together with Ratnesh set up a modest R&D operation in a village within their district—Tamkuha.

They explored various options for generating electricity in rural settings and began to rule out various means. Solar, for instance, was too expensive and Bihar did not experience high levels of wind flow or have enough water in reservoirs for wind or hydro power to be viable. They also ruled out biodiesel synthesis using the Jatropha crop due to concerns around yields and planting cycles. Soon after, Manoj Sinha—an electrical engineer and Intel employee in the USA and a native of the Bihar state who grew up in similar circumstances to Gyanesh and Ratnesh—joined the operations. Manoj too wanted to solve the problem of rural electrification and had been experimenting with farm waste as a source of fuel to generate electricity. He convinced a friend, who was studying for a master's degree at the Darden School of Business, University of West Virginia, Charles Ransler, to also join the operation.

Owing to a chance meeting with a gasifier salesman, Gyanesh learnt that rice millers in Tamkuha were utilizing a mixture of diesel and rice husk to power their mills. To him, this method seemed quite viable as rice husk was a plentiful resource in Bihar and had no alternative uses (like cattle fodder due to its high silica content)—the millers simply threw it away and left it to rot. He thought to himself: could only rice husk be used as a fuel source for electric generators? To explore its potential, the four partners set up an NGO —Samta Samriddhi Foundation—and started to seriously experiment and discover ways to eliminate the use of diesel alongside rice husk in the dual fuel method that existing millers were using. This method only allowed for 50–60 per cent of savings on diesel. Rice husk on its own, it appeared, could not be used as an independent source of power generation. Initially, results from their experiments were not encouraging—the husk produced a gas that was high in tar content, making it 'dirty', resulting in ceased generator engines. They believed that if the gas was adequately filtered before it reached the engine, the model could work. Using 'jugaad', trial and error and tinkering, they did succeed in creating a single fuel rice husk-based system. And in August 2007, after about five years of experimentation, the inhabitants of Tamkuha village enjoyed electric light after dark for the first time, 60 years after India's independence.

To commercialize their technology, they abandoned the NGO and set up a social enterprise instead—Husk Power Systems (HPS). Although their model was proven on a small scale, they had a grand vision for changing the lives of impoverished communities across India and beyond. The much-needed funding and exposure for HPS came through the efforts of Manoj and Charles, who took the model to various business plan competitions around the world. In 2009, HPS won the Cisco Global Business Plan Competition; in 2010, it was honoured by The Tech Museum of Innovation for applying technology to benefit humanity; and also in the same year, HPS ranked second in the BW Young Entrepreneurs Awards held in March 2010. With awards came direct investments. Shell Foundation, supported HPS with donor capital, coming on board early as a strategic partner, allowing the team to build a plant every month. In a year, HPS had scaled-up its capability to building a plant every two-and-a-half weeks. In mere three years, HPS succeeded in building 24 plants and electrified 80 villages through a franchising model. Village-scale entrepreneurs would invest in their plant technology, would set up their own electric grid using double-jacketed wire (to stop electricity theft and ensure safety) affixed atop bamboo poles. The franchisees earned an income by collecting a small usage fee from consumers upfront (therefore, no metering was necessary). The franchisees also monetized char (a black ash produced in the gasification process)—rural women were trained to make incense sticks, which were sold to big brands.

After many trials, by 2018, HPS had been able to set up over 75 plants in India and Tanzania serving 15,000 households and businesses. An announcement recently notified that a US$20 million equity investment had been secured via Shell Technology Ventures, Swedfund International and ENGIE Rassembleurs d'Energies. They are poised to grow rapidly over the next four years and envision adding over 300 mini-grids in India and Tanzania, deploying 15 MW of 100 per cent renewable power plant assets, serving over 100,000 customers. Commenting on their progress, Manoj recently stated: 'Together with our strategic partners, we are now confident of achieving our vision of becoming the world's largest rural utility company providing 24/7, 100 per cent renewable and affordable power to drive inclusive and sustainable development in growth markets'.

Gyanesh could not have achieved the above successes working on his own—his partnerships with Ratnesh, Manoj and Charles were crucial in bringing a new social innovation (rural electrification using rice husk) to market. To grow the enterprise, Gyanesh needed more partners—rural entrepreneurs who became their franchisees, the rice millers who sold husk to the franchisees, the big brands who bought incense sticks from the women workers, their various overseas donors, their strategic partners in Tanzania who took the technology to a new market and the agencies from within the Indian government who supported them and helped them refine their technology. HPS is a great example which shows how entrepreneurs, using the Crazy Quilt principle, de-risk and lower start-up costs and grow their business sustainably by working with partners who put real 'skin in the game'.

4.2.5. THE PILOT-IN-THE-PLANE PRINCIPLE

Expert entrepreneurs have well-developed personal effectiveness skills (recall from Chapter 1), which they can channel for exercising 'personal control'. Personal control is 'the desire for control over one's own life decisions'. Being the pilot-in-the-plane is an entrepreneur's 'mindset', and is linked to the notion of 'individualism', self-esteem, self-belief, autonomy and freedom. Entrepreneurs recognize the importance of personal control and choose entrepreneurship as a career because they want to be the 'pilot-in-the-plane'. The plane is a technological marvel that can perform a wide variety of functions, but it is the pilot that realizes this potential—the plane follows the pilot's directions. And it must, because without the pilot's direction, the plane would be mere 'undirected and utilized potential'. By exercising personal control, entrepreneurs can choose to work on things they believe are important, set their own schedules and work with whom they want. Such a feeling of personal control is never realized when undertaking traditional employment. The extent to which an individual might want to exercise personal control would be linked to one of their means: 'who you are', and may vary over the course of a lifetime, becoming stronger or weaker with feedback.

Kadir Koymen exemplifies the pilot-in-the-plane principle; he was an independent thinker and took upon himself a herculean challenge—developing a camera lens adapter, a product for which there was no precedent and he had no training or previous experience in optical engineering. What he had was self-belief and a desire for autonomy, controlling his actions and taking personal responsibility for their outcomes. He moderated his time, work schedule and priorities the way he saw fit—often working 18 hours a day, 7 days a week, because he could choose to and wanted to. By being in the pilot-in-the-plane mindset, he was able to use the other (previously discussed) four principles of effectuation to create a brand new product.

Daria Alekseeva, Founder of Charity Shop: Russian Social Enterprise | Pilot-in-the-Plane

Daria, at the age of 25, in 2014 decided it was time to venture out on her own after having worked at an NGO and other social enterprises like the American 'Goodwill' and having graduated from the Financial Academy of the Government of Russia. Although she had a limited amount of savings (₽700,000 or US$11,000) for the new venture, she knew her idea for a charity shop would work and deliver new value when compared to existing outfits. She also believed in her ability to negotiate and her instincts when it came to setting up the new venture. For example, before she started Charity Shop, she negotiated an agreement with the Moscow regional government for a reduced shop rental rate—a mere ₽3,500 per square metre per year when compared to the market price of about ₽12,000–13,000. However, the locations the government offered to her were in the Moscow suburbs where she knew people did not often shop—which would have meant very low footfall. This was an important decision, and she trusted her instinct and decided to rent within one of the main shopping districts close to the city centre and pay the full market rental (about ₽160,000 per month).

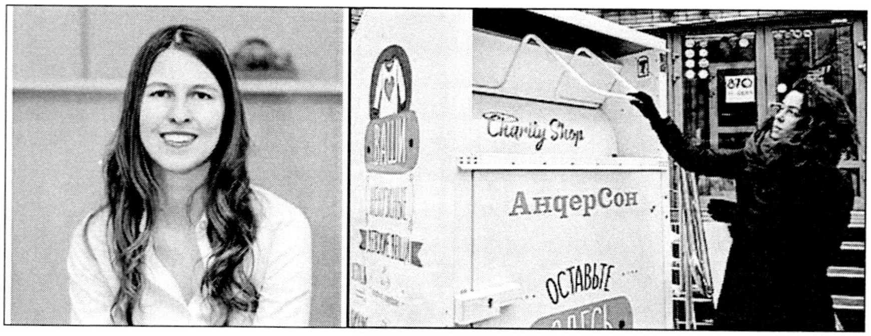

This turned out to be a good decision, because the location generated much more interest and footfall into the new shop was very encouraging. Daria knew that her concept would generate a lot of interest because of its link to charity and recycling. By advertising Charity Shop on Facebook, she was able to attract the interest of a variety of resourceful entities, for example, she negotiated with the architectural bureau 'Platforma' to develop the shop's interior design. A professional photographer then took high quality photos of the donated clothes in the shop. Even a well-known advertising company 'Russ Outdoor' allowed her to rent several billboards to advertise her venture around the district. All of these services were negotiated for either a discounted price or for free.

Daria understood what marketing in the social sector involved; she concentrated her attention on what she could do with what she had to do 'good things' for people. She allowed regional charity foundations and organizations to run social events in her shop for charity purposes. She thought about how to help people donate excess clothes in an easy way and set up containers located at 22 collecting points in shopping malls, company offices or other public places. Interest in the concept grew, and Daria had confidence in herself and in what she had created; thus, Charity Shop grew out of Moscow to other cities such as Adygea, Rostov-on-Don, Nizhny Novgorod, Kazan and Saint Petersburg. She started to cooperate with famous brands and big malls, placing special boxes for collecting unwanted clothing and collected a record 140 tons of clothes, shoes and jewellery in a single month. She had the confidence to work with big corporations; during one #UberSpringCleaning day, Uber drivers collected 3 tons of donated clothes from families who wanted to participate in this campaign. All the while, Daria has remained true to the original concept of charity and recycling. A large proportion of her profits go to a charitable foundation called 'Vtoroe dyhanie' (Second breath) which has special programmes that help people from vulnerable groups to find employment. A part of the profits are donated to the Equal Opportunities Development Center 'Вверх' (Up) that helps children from correctional orphanages to adapt to life outside.

Although she might not have studied effectuation, Daria thinks and behaves like an effectual entrepreneur. Her pilot-in-the-plane mindset empowered her with self-belief and confidence and accentuated her need for autonomy. She was in touch with her individuality and expressed it by taking effectual entrepreneurial action, forming relationships, keeping risks low, growing the venture organically and generating the right kind of public interest.

4.3. SUMMARY AND APPLICATION

Entrepreneurs have a different worldview and behaviour set when compared to business managers. As opposed to managers, they view the future as 'uncertain' and 'unpredictable', and the environment they operate in as 'unstructured'. To cope with the complexity and uncertainty inherent in the new venture creation process, entrepreneurs deploy a set of decision heuristics. In this chapter, five of these heuristics were discussed, and accompanying illustrative cases explained the manner in which developing country entrepreneurs deployed these with an effectual venture creation process. These heuristics help in the reduction of risk, the level of investment needed and for delivering new value. Figure 4.2 summarizes the effectuation process; the starting point is an assessment of one's means which leads to 'opportunity spaces'—goals and possible interactions. Using these, the entrepreneur can seek stakeholders who are willing to put 'skin in the game'; once they come on

FIGURE 4.2 **The Effectuation Process**

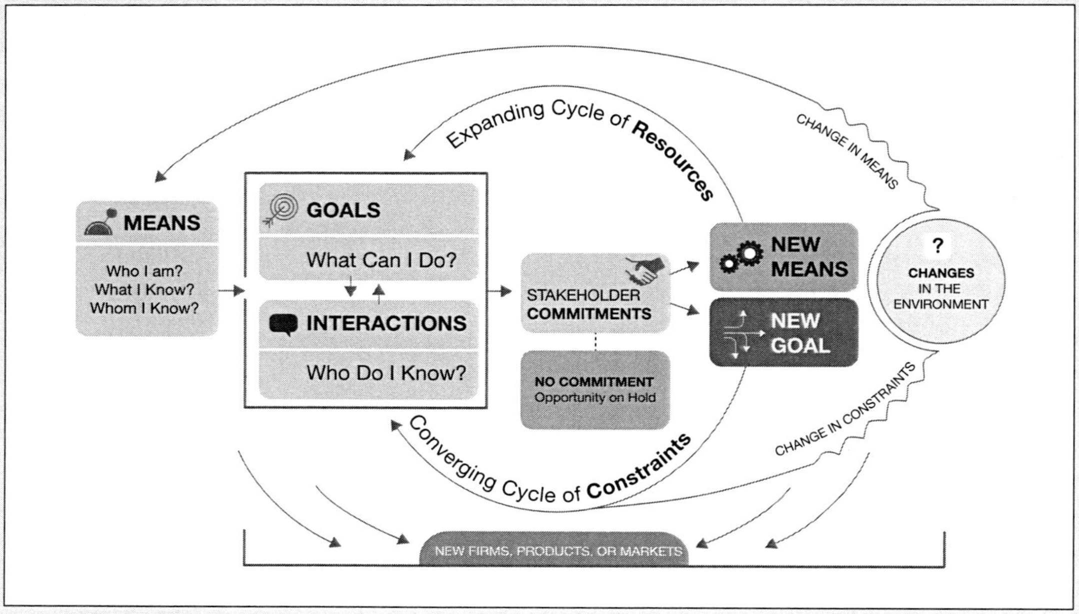

Source: Read et al. (2017).

board, they add more means and help the entrepreneur streamline his/her goals. Outside-of-control changes in the environment can also introduce new means and add constraints. Working with these 'means' and using 'constraints' as levers to trigger more interactions with potential stakeholders, the entrepreneur shields himself/herself from high risks and steers the new venture, product or market through stages of development.

Exercise 4.1. Opportunities for new venture creation or being enterprising in any other context are personal and linked to your means. This means that what might be an opportunity for you may not be one for someone else. To analyse where there might be opportunities for you, work through the following Bird-in-Hand template (Figure 4.3) to generate new, and personal, ideas. Take your time, even a few days, talk to your family members and friends. Share the completed template with your class; explain why you believe the developed ideas are *opportunities* for *you* specifically. Try and imagine how you'd go about acting on your ideas to implement them.

FIGURE 4.3 **Bird-in-Hand Exercise**

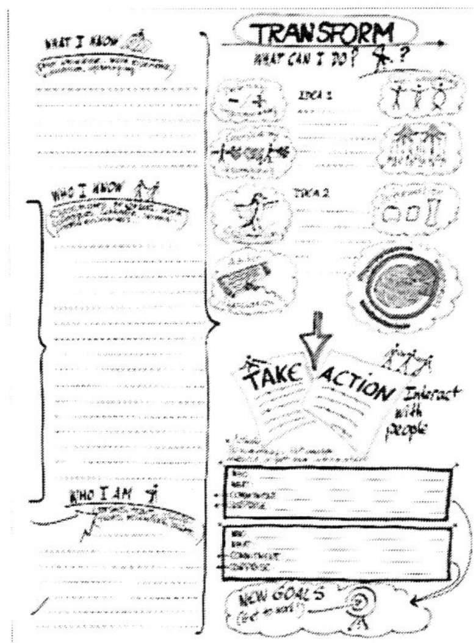

Source: https://www.effectuation.org/?page_id=666 (Accessed on 14 May 2019).

Exercise 4.2. The previous exercise would have helped you with the first stage of the effectuation cycle—the bottom 'Ask You' section in Figure 4.4. Asking questions is a good way to develop a working familiarity with the five principles of effectuation. Choose an idea you have generated from the previous exercise; using this idea as a focal point, visualize its implementation and move up from 'Ask You' to the other levels answering the prescribed questions. Do not be afraid of talking to strangers and considering unconventional answers. Take your time; once completed, prepare a one-page story with a plot and characters which captures the essence of the idea and its contribution/impact. Share this story with the class; try not to read from a written script, instead practise its delivery so you can speak free-flow, making eye contact with the audience. Solicit feedback and refine the idea.

FIGURE 4.4 Hierarchy of Effectual Asks

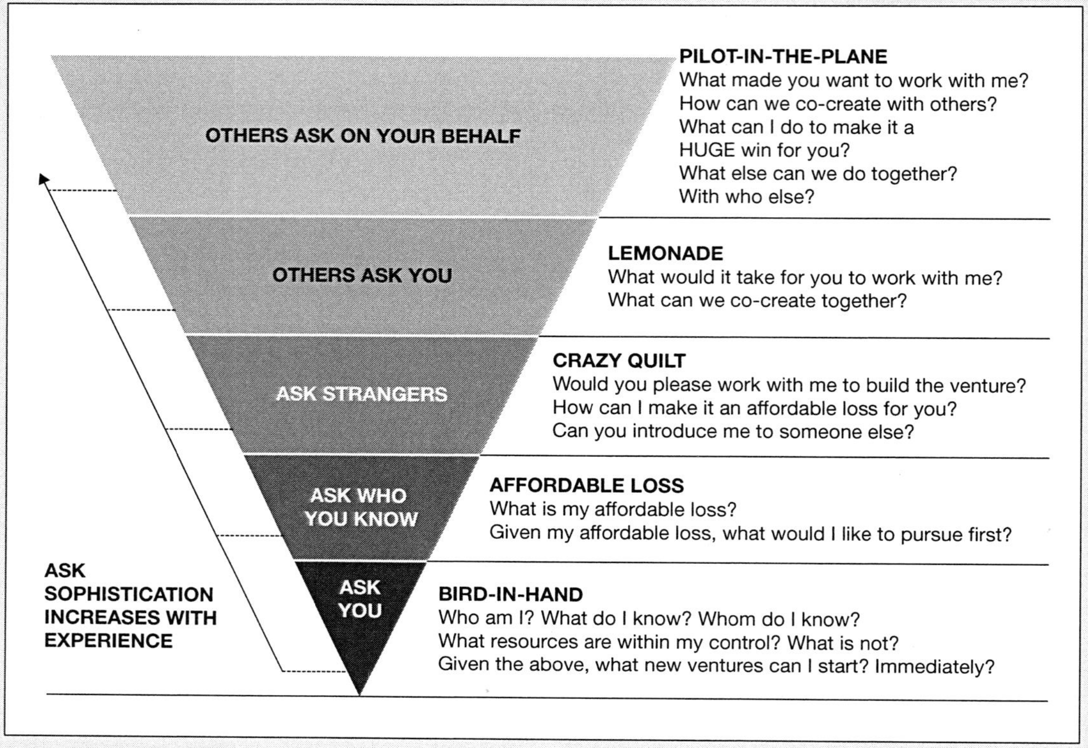

Source: Read et al. (2017).

SECTION B

ENTERPRISE DESIGN

5

Customer Research

LEARNING OUTCOMES

- Become familiar with the various types of customer research techniques
- Understand the requirements for undertaking indirect and direct forms of customer research
- Be able to create a data collection and analysis plan

5.1. WHAT IS CUSTOMER RESEARCH?

Spotlight on M-Pesa, 'a Money Transfer Service' from Kenya

At the time of M-Pesa's launch in 2007, mobile penetration in Kenya was at 39 per cent, with more than 15 million users. Simultaneously, about 35 per cent of people in Kenya either did not have access to financial services or did not use any financial provider. M-Pesa enabled millions of users with access to a mobile phone, but without or limited access to the banking system, to deposit, send and receive money. The platform allows users to pay bills as well as purchase calling credit. Registration to the service and deposits are free, while transfers, withdrawals and bill payments are priced along a tiered structure, enabling users with different income levels to use the M-Pesa platform.

Users are customers of the Safaricom mobile network in Kenya. These customers subscribe and register for the service at the nearest authorized agent (often a small retailer or mobile phone store). This allows them to deposit cash and receive electronic money in exchange as a confirmation of the deposit made. Accordingly, the customers can send this electronic money to their friends or family or pay bills. Once a client has signed up for the service, they are able to securely complete all the transactions they choose by entering a four-digit PIN; after which both parties, that is, the sender and the recipient receive a confirmation message in the form of an SMS, detailing the amount transferred.

Prior to the M-Pesa pilot project, Safaricom had not conducted adequate research to understand user requirements. They did remedy this, and during the pilot project, an extensive field study was carried out with trial participants to understand their needs, as well as their reactions towards the offering. The M-Pesa pilot implementation, which took place between October 2005 and May 2006, included eight agents and about 500 trial participants who transacted in three discrete geographical locations in Kenya. Many obstacles were encountered during the trial phase. Key hindrances were the levels of trust between users and agents. High levels of trust were needed which would encourage agents to process withdrawal transactions. Most of the agents were hesitant to give out cash from their till on the basis of an instruction received via SMS. To counter this problem, Vodafone offered the agents separate M-Pesa cash floats from which they could transact. In addition, the agents were encouraged to record the transactions processed on a separate paper log. This would help the agents keep track of their balances, separate from the M-Pesa system.

Another serious challenge encountered was the need for continuous agent training. It was apparent from the pilot project that agents needed to understand all the aspects of the system so as to help customers. To solve this problem, Safaricom offered additional resources in order to aid weekly agent visits, as well as continuous refresher training on the M-Pesa system. Lessons from the pilot phase and the key findings from the formal market study encouraged Safaricom to roll-out the service in full-scale.

Thus, the research from the pilot project enabled Safaricom to come up with various M-Pesa iterations. This happened via testing a variety of the system's features among its trial users until the core offering that aligned best with customer needs was identified. This offering became M-Pesa's 'core application'—national remittance.

To create robust value propositions (VP) and accompanying business models for their ideas, seasoned entrepreneurs rely on customer research. The purpose of doing customer research is to reduce the risk of failure (like potential losses or costs for reconfiguring the idea) due to misalignment of the business's/product's/service's core VP with customer needs, post implementation. Using customer research, the entrepreneur attempts to gauge the preferences, motivations and buying behaviours of the customers for the developed 'value proposition' or 'solution'. Since customer research can be time-consuming and requires atypical skills that need to be honed, some entrepreneurs make the mistake of avoiding it completely. This would be deemed too risky an approach to new venture creation. It cannot be stressed enough: customer research is absolutely necessary for validating the business idea's core VP, and without having conducted it, new entrepreneurs must be wary of taking any concrete steps to start up their ventures.

The depth and scale of Safaricom's research project would be difficult to match—a project on such a scale requires considerable resources. However, to validate a vast majority of new business ideas by individual entrepreneurs in a developing country setting, a stripped-down version of the exercise Safaricom conducted would suffice. Undertaking such an exercise would be inexpensive, and depending on the enthusiasm of the focal entrepreneur may be completed fairly quickly (in a matter of a few weeks), requiring only rudimentary literacy and numeracy skills.

Customer research may be conducted using either 'direct' (data collection by the entrepreneur) or 'indirect' methods (using already published material). It is a norm that in validating VPs, the 'indirect' method is used first. Material relevant to the VP, and linked to its potential customers, is drawn from internet searches, social media, magazines, books and other published sources and purposefully reviewed to identify trends and patterns. This helps the entrepreneur develop a 'feel' for the opportunity landscape and develop a semblance for which aspects of the VP might work, and importantly, which might not. Outcomes from indirect data collection allow the entrepreneur to set the general direction of the 'direct' data collection exercise, which relies on engagement with potential customers or other important stakeholders.

5.2. INDIRECT DATA COLLECTION METHODS

Indirect data collection requires the patient adherence to a systematic method for searching, reviewing and storing content published either online or in traditional offline sources. Start with this basic assumption: whatever you have conceived, in some shape or form, already exists. It would be quite rare for a new entrepreneur to conceive a solution/VP that is wholly original, never ever seen before. This assumption eliminates potential disappointment when similar solutions are found and helps the entrepreneur focus on finding ways of making refinements to their solution based on the problems with what already exists.

Free-to-search and view information available online is by far the most valuable means to start the VP validation exercise. In the following sections, three methods for indirect customer research will be explained: keywords, online trends analysis and social sentiment.

5.2.1. KEYWORD SEARCHES

Popular search engines can be used effectively to sift through vast amounts of content hosted online; it is important to note that when using such engines it is the quality of 'keywords' that generates the desired searches. Search engines, like Google, look for the 'keywords' in your query in the websites they search, bringing up web locations where those words appear. To use a search engine effectively, there is a need to be able to choose the best combination of keywords. Using several keywords is best after having thought about what needs to be searched for.

For instance, you believe to have found a new and much more efficient way of repairing bicycle tyre punctures. The first action to take is to check if your conceived method already exists, and if so, in what form and whether it is available where you are based or wish to start your business. Say you are based in Addis Ababa, Ethiopia, start by doing a basic search using the keyword string 'bicycle puncture repair Addis Ababa' (without the marks of quotation). Quite possibly hundreds or even thousands of results might be available to view, or very few, perhaps even none—you can never know in advance. Click through the results on the first and second pages of the search results and take mental notes. Next, become more specific; say your conceived method is meant for repairing tubeless tyres. Type in 'bicycle puncture repair for tubeless tyres'; the order of the words is not important and review the most relevant results carefully. If you are confident that your method has not yet been conceived or is in use by anyone else, especially in Addis Ababa, then conduct even more specific searches. For example, you believe what is unique about your method is that it does not rely on patches for the puncture repair, type in 'patchless repair of tubeless bicycle tyre'. Remember: you are not only searching to verify what already exists in terms of similar or competing 'solutions', but also, to learn if you could improve your own method by incorporating what already exists or find a potential partner (say an existing and popular puncture repair outfit). Do not give up if you find that someone else is already using your 'solution'; they might not be based in the same country or city and might lack the energy, drive and enthusiasm you might have, and there is also a possibility that you could work with them to refine their solution or acquire the rights to use their established name for your own venture.

Online video and image hosting sites are also important indirect customer research tools. Searching these sites equates to using the same keyword techniques described above for traditional search engines. Start with 'Google Images' and then the image search site 'Pinterest' using different permutations of words or phrases, such as 'cycle puncture repair tutorial', 'cycle puncture solution', 'how to repair a cycle puncture', 'cycle puncture Addis Ababa'. Clicking on any image of your choice will bring up further details, and you will be pointed to the original web source of the image—say an article or a corporate website. YouTube has an immense amount of user generated content which can be quite insightful. For example, a search with the keywords 'cycle puncture repair' produces hundreds of uploaded videos—clicking through these videos will allow you to view viewer comments, some of which can be quite insightful.

FIGURE 5.1 **Google Images Search Result (Accessed on 17 July 2018)**

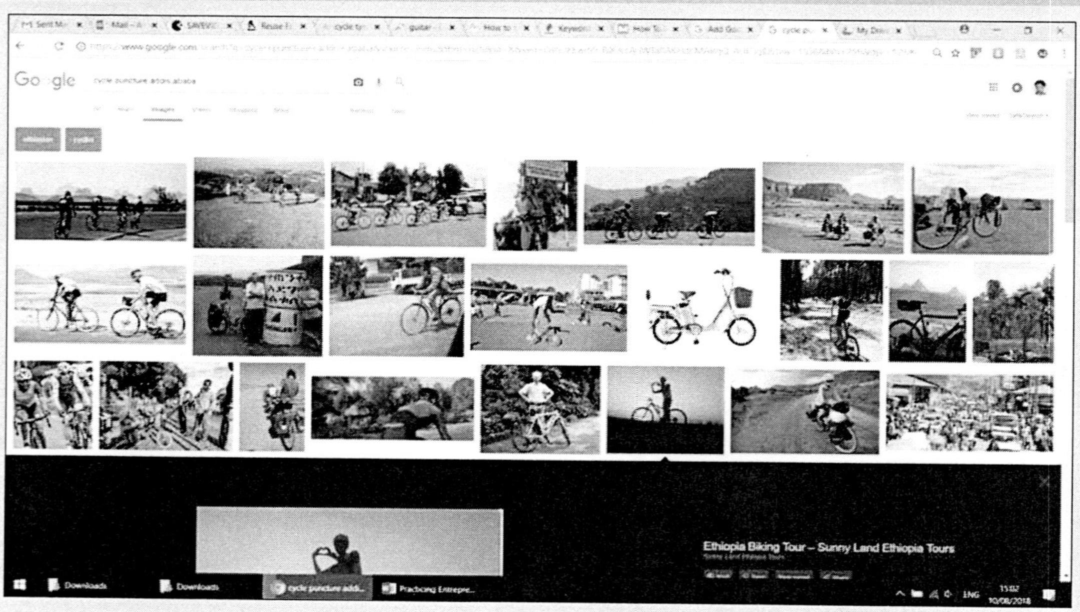

Depending on the nature of your VP, other more specific online platforms can be relevant. For example, if the 'solution' solves a problem within the hospitality or tourism sectors, then running searches on TripAdvisor would be pertinent. Alibaba should be used to search for products similar to your solution, where you should also be able to see their detailed specifications. Trustpilot and Amazon are useful for reading reviews of existing similar products. Country-specific e-commerce platforms like Jumia, if you are based in Nigeria, must also be searched. In countries where written and verbal communication is not in English, such as Turkey, Russia and China, local language search engines should be employed.

Reviewing the outcomes of keyword searches should create a mental impression about your solution's general viability, which would be difficult to articulate. This is common when dealing with qualitative data—written material, images and video. You should attempt to imagine modifications to your solution based on what you have reviewed online, such that it meets customer requirements better or is easier to manufacture or package. It would be important though to preserve the outcomes of your effort; for this, create a separate document for use as a 'data dump' in which you could copy-paste web content, insert screenshots, images and web links. Look through the data dump document, while thinking about your VP, run mental simulations to help it evolve and improve.

5.2.2. ONLINE TRENDS ANALYSIS

If your VP is targeted especially to consumers (rather than businesses), then online trends analysis would allow you to predict approaching shifts of direction in your industry and beyond. If you immerse yourself in the industry where your VP is going to sit (let us assume 'bicycle repair and maintenance'), by visiting events, talking to industry leaders and reading specialist publications/ newsletters, you are going to begin to notice new concepts and themes propping up with increasing regularity. But what about trends outside of your industry that could have a meaningful impact on your VP? Such as falling prices of motorcycles and availability of cheap vehicle finance, if your VP was based around bicycle repair and maintenance. Entrepreneurs, therefore, take an interest in wider trends outside their industry, and a good way to do this is via free online tools and locations such as Google Trends, Think with Google, BuzzFeed, Mashable, Reddit and AllTop.

By using Google Trends, you can see how often specific keywords, subjects and phrases have been searched for over a specific period. For example, by setting the utility to display data from 'Ethiopia', you can search for the term 'cycle' to check 'interest over time' and 'interest over region'. You can also see which keywords Ethiopians prefer to use when they are looking for cycles, by comparing the keyword 'cycle' with 'bicycle', 'bike' or 'pushbike'. While Google Trends is based around keyword popularity, Think with Google—a free subscription based service—will give you richer insights into emerging digital and offline marketing trends, techniques and actual practices. While the information gleaned may not be specific to cycles or repairing cycle punctures, it might spark thinking around how best to package the VP, brand and market it or sell it via a new sales channel (like mobile).

BuzzFeed, Mashable, Reddit and AllTop are news aggregator platforms that promote 'trending' (or popular) blogs, articles and news items linked to technology, business, science, popular culture, online behaviours and politics—any material trending in web searches and clicked through online. There is a considerable amount of material updated in real time on these platforms and it is useful

FIGURE 5.2 **Google Trends Comparison (Accessed on 21 January 2019)**

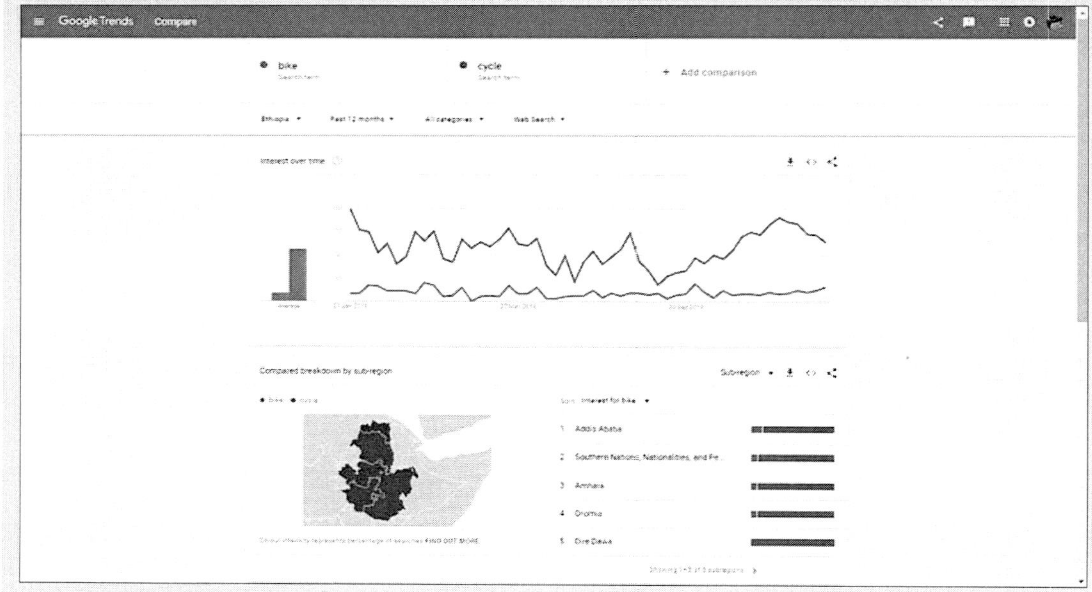

to choose a time window, say over a period of a week, to plough through the trending content of interest to you, even though you might find that it has little or no link at all with the VP you are validating. The value of this exercise is that it would allow you to maintain a cognitive state where unexpected creative connections could be made.

A final platform to search on is Kickstarter—for discovering whether solutions similar to yours (or whatever else in your industry) are underdevelopment via crowd funding—a mechanism for raising money from a large number of people who each contribute relatively small amounts. Review the outlines of projects that emerge from your searches, those which most interest you, and using the SCAMPER technique (discussed in Chapter 2) compare these with your solution—can you borrow, swap, adapt or adopt any features and/or specifications?

5.2.3. SOCIAL SENTIMENT

Discussions and posts on social media platforms such as Facebook, Instagram, Twitter, Pinterest and others can offer useful insights to the entrepreneur looking to identify and validate customer 'pain points' and 'value propositions'. Run keyword searches on all the popular social media platforms and check whether any dedicated groups or pages exist. Join those groups and read through threads of discussions posted to assess the general direction of the posters' sentiment—positive, negative or neutral? It is unlikely that no discussions online exist that might hold value—even if ancillary. If nothing or not much appears, test other keywords—persistence usually pays off.

In addition, free-to-use online social sentiment analysis tools help in the measurement of emotions behind social media 'mentions'. If for instance, you wish to see how your potential customers have reacted to solutions like yours or feel about causes of 'pain', like being faced by a punctured bicycle tyre, then online tools can help you gauge whether the sentiment behind the associated 'mentions' was (for instance) satisfied, happy, angry or annoyed. Hence, it is not enough to know that some topic of discussion is trending, adding context to that sentiment helps to contextualize—without which social media data can be misleading.

There is an online community for virtually every topic of interest one could think of, comprising users posting questions, giving opinions, reviewing gadgetry and engaging in all manner of discussion, mostly on topic. For example, Lugnet.com is a very large community of Lego fans and Aquariumforum.com has users discussing all manner of topics related to keeping marine pets. A Google query with the keywords '(your topic of interest—say cycle) online forum' will produce relevant results. Here it would be important to start with a broad topic of interest; in our case 'cycles', and then to search within the discovered forums for more specific content—say 'puncture repair'. Clicking through topics will bring up discussions on the topics posted after the 'original post (OP)'. Read through these posts to get a sense of sentiment on the topic, while thinking about, is the articulated pain point *really* a pain point, are users happy with existing solutions, are there any other things that are causes of pain, are users customizing existing solutions. The overall purpose being to get a semblance of user sentiment on the topic.

FIGURE 5.3 Online Forum Dedicated to Cycles and Cycling (Accessed on 21 January 2019)

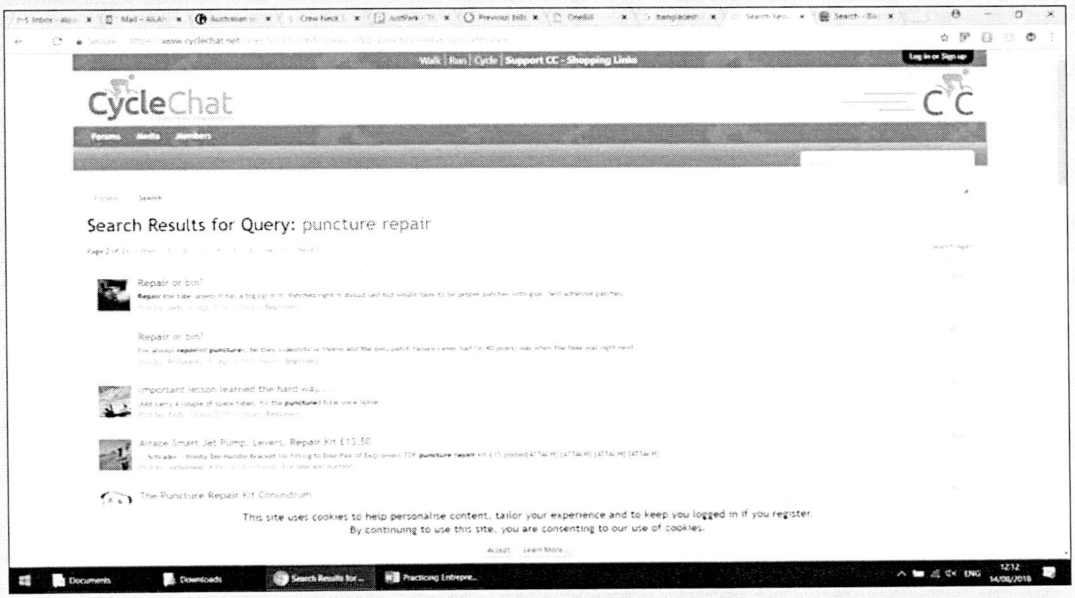

FIGURE 5.4 Social Mention Aggregator (Accessed on 21 January 2019)

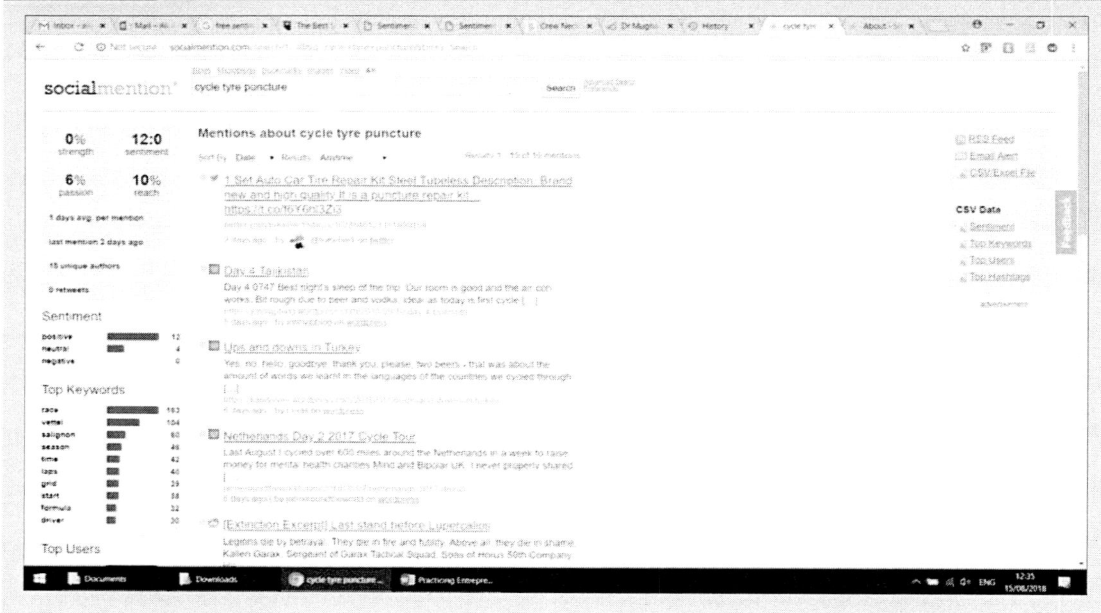

Although the following would be classed as a form of direct customer research but discussed here because of the method's link to online forums. A good way to solicit user feedback and to gauge sentiment is for you to create an OP, usually via registering on the forum first, to begin a discussion. For example, 'can we repair cycle punctures using shaving foam'. Post any pictures or your own thoughts, results from any experiments you have done and then wait for responses. In active forums, you could generate a tremendous amount of interest in a matter of hours. Take care when you craft your OP, moderate its tone and keep the content topical and interesting. You will have the ability to respond to users and generate further discussions.

Finally, several free-to-use online tools can also be used for social sentiment gauging. For example, Socialmention.com can be used to run searches for keywords related to your VP. Socialmention.com is a social media search and analysis platform that aggregates user-generated content from across various social media platforms. Running a search on the keywords 'cycle puncture repair' on this platform will allow you to gauge what the latest topics of discussion on these keywords are and numbers relating to related 'mentions' online.

5.3. DIRECT DATA COLLECTION METHODS

Direct data collection should be initiated after having undertaken an analysis of indirect data; developing a sense for the viability of the VP and consumer sentiment around the problem and associated pain points. To further develop and refine your understanding on the factors that might drive adoption of your solution by prospective customers, several key questions would first need to be formulated. These questions should be developed considering what you have found out via indirect data analysis and also, importantly, what aspects you need to know about a bit more, because data from indirect sources was perhaps unavailable or incomplete. For instance, consider the cycle puncture repair problem: indirect data might validate the need for a more convenient, portable, easy-to-use and inexpensive solution to the problem of random punctures, generally, and for a certain type of cycle user (let us assume the long-distance urban commuter). However, what about specifically in your locality/city and how much of a problem is it for what type of cycle user? You would need to use direct data collection to explore answers to the following questions: How do particular users in your city/locality presently solve the problem? How much on average do they spend on repairs? What annoys them about present solutions?

The three most popular direct data collection methods for initial VP validation are observation, interviews and focus groups. The choice of method would be dependent on the characteristics of the prospective customers and nature of the VP you wish to validate. Reasons for this will become clear as you read through the following three sections.

5.3.1. OBSERVATIONS

Observation, or simply looking at people engaged in an activity, can be a powerful way of assessing customers' responses to physical environments and when using products or any other form of interface (like a computer game or a website). The premise behind the method is that 'people often do not do what they say they do, so it is best to observe than to ask'. As the observer, you are attempting to gather data to understand 'why people do what they do'. A good understanding of the rationale behind people's actions—and there is always one to be discovered—can provide powerful insights for fine tuning VPs. Table 5.1 suggests a number of 'data categories' the observer can use for compiling his/her observational data set.

TABLE 5.1 A Basic Scheme for an Observation Study

Data Categories	Events to Look For	Observed?	Timings	Notes
1) Triggers for acquiring the product or service	• Why, when and how?			
2) Triggers for product usage	• Who, what, where, when, why, how?			
3) The environment	• Physical layout/objects • Actors • Activities/events • Time sequence			

(Continued)

TABLE 5.1 (Continued)

Data Categories	Events to Look For	Observed?	Timings	Notes
4) Interactions with user's environment	• Physical interactions • Social interactions			
5) Product usage	• Wasted time • Doing things right • Doing things wrong • Misuse • Confusion • Dangerous situations (for example physical or data)			
6) Intangible aspects and unarticulated needs.	• Emotions • Frustration and wasted time • Fears and anxiety • Linguistic signals • Extra-linguistic signals • Non-verbal signals (for example body language) • Spatial signals			
7) User customization	• User modifications of the product • User modifications of the (normal) process			

Source: Goffin and Mitchell (2017).

There are two ways of recording observations—as a 'participant' or a 'non-participant'. As a participant observer, to understand how your customers behave in a given setting and communicate with others, you would need to join in their activity such that, over time, you become an 'insider'—a trusted member of the group. As an insider, you will gain access to privileged information, such as observing players' behavioural norms (individually and in groups) and as to how they react to particular environmental or other forms of stimuli. You can wrap up participant observation when you reach a 'saturation point', that is, you stop taking note of anything novel, interesting or different.

Participant Observation Example

Consi...s a customer group for a new massively multiplayer online role-playing game (M... ch as World of War Craft and The Elder Scrolls Online. To understand aspects ...e features that create 'entertainment value' in existing platforms, which in turn ...nitted gamers, dedicating upwards of a 1,000 hours of playing per year, participant ... would be ideal. You would become a game player yourself and enter the virtual ...ne MMORPG with the objective of immersing yourself in the life-world of other gam-... the environment created by the platform.

Source: The authors.

You will develop friendships with other gamers and explore the world with them, and in the process over time develop a rich understanding of the existing MMORPGs' configuration that create entertainment value and a 'pull factor', which gets gamers hooked. It would be important to keep an objective distance when immersing yourself and to take notes after every play session, recording any significant detail that will help you create a rich picture—the ultimate objective being to capture data to validate the core VP behind your own MMORPG and to refine its configuration.

Non-participant observation requires the 'fly on the wall' approach—as the observer, your prese... goes unnoticed or is barely noticeable, and your objective is to carefully note aspects along s... 'data categories' (see Table 5.1), or whichever ones might be most relevant. It is important to ... your thinking prior, and to not approach the exercise with any pre-conceived biases, your role ... be to simply absorb and note what you see along the described data categories.

Non-participant Obse

Example

Say you are intending to validate a VP that would offer an arcade gaming-based solution. By using the outcomes from non-participant observation, you can take info sions about the configuration of the gaming arcade, its main platform (arcade machine vs. consoles) and even its pricing.

raditionally, gaming arcades are popular with young people and families with children; and they nploy coin-operated/token-based machines. Plan to visit a few such arcades in your city and ng the aforementioned data categories, while remaining inconspicuous, start to take notes of you see. Quite likely you will start to observe patterns around which game machines are more ar with which category of users, how long a typical game lasts, are the games played in single e player modes, which games generate the most interaction among players and between nd observers and so on. You can also start conversations with more engaged users and ask stions about their preferences, to double check the patterns emanating from your obser- hen you have repeated the process at a few arcades, you will begin to see strong and ns beginning to emerge. These patterns can help you configure your VP.

nce
even
clear
would

WS

gh degree of understanding on a specialized subject, holding conversations ly referred to as 'interviewing'—can be very beneficial. Entrepreneurs of 'incomplete information' because of 'asymmetric knowledge'. They ts would know more than them when it comes to various aspects of loping and then rolling out their VP. The method is interrogative in ing information. Consider the words 'inter' and 'view'— a 'view' is tween the interviewer and his/her subject.

consensus. This might lead to data bias problems—'you will hear what you want to hear rather than what needs to be heard'.

Take a number of precautions when recruiting your focus group participants—social media can be a useful means in this regard. You are looking for engaged users who are affected by the 'problem' and have experimented with available 'solutions'. Do not turn to individuals most conveniently available, like friends, classmates or family members. Getting unbiased data would require that you look for participants from outside of your immediate circle of contacts. Take your time and choose carefully by setting up selection criteria. Such criteria maybe based around an age range, income level, number of years of work experience and so on. This does not mean though that you would end up recruiting the same types of participants, which in turn might lead to predictable outcomes. Rest assured, everyone will bring different experiences and views.

Book a location that can comfortably host between six and eight participants (maximum), you, the facilitator, and a note-taker. Ideally, the following too should also be available: a whiteboard and markers and a means to display (like a plain wall) any drawings or written work produced by the participants. The rule of formulating questions in focus groups are the same when compared to interviews, but with the additional requirement where you as the moderator will move from participant to participant to elicit responses, picking up cues and asking for elaborations and seeking other participants' inputs to either validate or present arguments to disagree. At the end of the allocated time, thank the participants and present concluding remarks to summarize the major outcomes from the focus group. It is tradition and a sign of courtesy to offer refreshments after.

Carefully read through the note-taker's material and using a highlighter pen mark out key points that relate to the product's/solution's VP—what statements made highlight potential problems in use, any frustrations it might cause, unanticipated side effects, what might cause your potential customers to start using it, and more importantly, the absence of what features or key fundamentals might cause them to ignore it. Do not simply accept the outcomes: you might get a good sense of direction on the manner in which your VP needs to be modified but assume that *you may be wrong and that you need to double-check what you know*. Hence, prepare to conduct another focus group. Sometimes, due to a wide array of minor and unavoidable mistakes, focus groups can yield bogus outcomes—but you would never know unless you cross-checked findings.

5.4. SUMMARY AND APPLICATION

The first premise behind the value of customer research is: 'customers do not know what they want until the time you give them something they did not imagine they needed—then they start wanting it'. Consider the cycle tyre puncture solution example used to frame thinking in this chapter; existing users of bicycles understand that if they have been unfortunate enough to have encountered a punctured tyre, there are one of two ways to undertake a repair, by DIY (do-it-yourself) or by using a qualified repairer, with costs and benefits associated with both ways. If they opt to DIY, then there are known ways (like rubber patches). However, asking them to imagine using an unknown one (like shaving foam) without them having witnessed or used it directly, is unfair and an exercise in futility. Therefore, asking customers what they need is not very useful, because they do not know what they need because they do not know what is possible. Hence, customer research needs to be conducted in a manner that takes into account this premise.

The direct and indirect customer research methods described in this chapter are relatively simple and cost-effective ways to compile the necessary evidence to bestow confidence on the entrepreneur. Without a high degree of confidence in the validity of their VP, for an entrepreneur, acting towards implementation would be akin to fighting against oneself—they simply would not, the risk of failure would be too high. Using 'indirect data collection methods', start exploring 'what we already know'. Safaricom undertook such research prior to launching M-Pesa via commissioning a feasibility study and accompanying business plan. For these pieces of research, data was drawn from sources already published and in the public domain or accessible in some other way. This allowed them to create an outline VP which explained the core features of M-Pesa, which in turn led to the system's specifications and the development of an initial prototype. They understood that they might be wrong, the system's features may still be misaligned with customer needs—there is no guaranteed way to know in advance. Therefore, they initiated a pilot study which utilized 'direct data collection methods', observations and interviews primarily, and many aspects of the VP were indeed misaligned. Only after making due adjustments that Safaricom felt confident enough for a market launch.

Recall Figure 3.1 from Chapter 3, 'Innovation Process in Developing Countries'—to develop the solution specification, the entrepreneur would traditionally deploy the following data collection methods in stages (Figure 5.5).

FIGURE 5.5 Stages of Data Collection Leading to Solution Specification

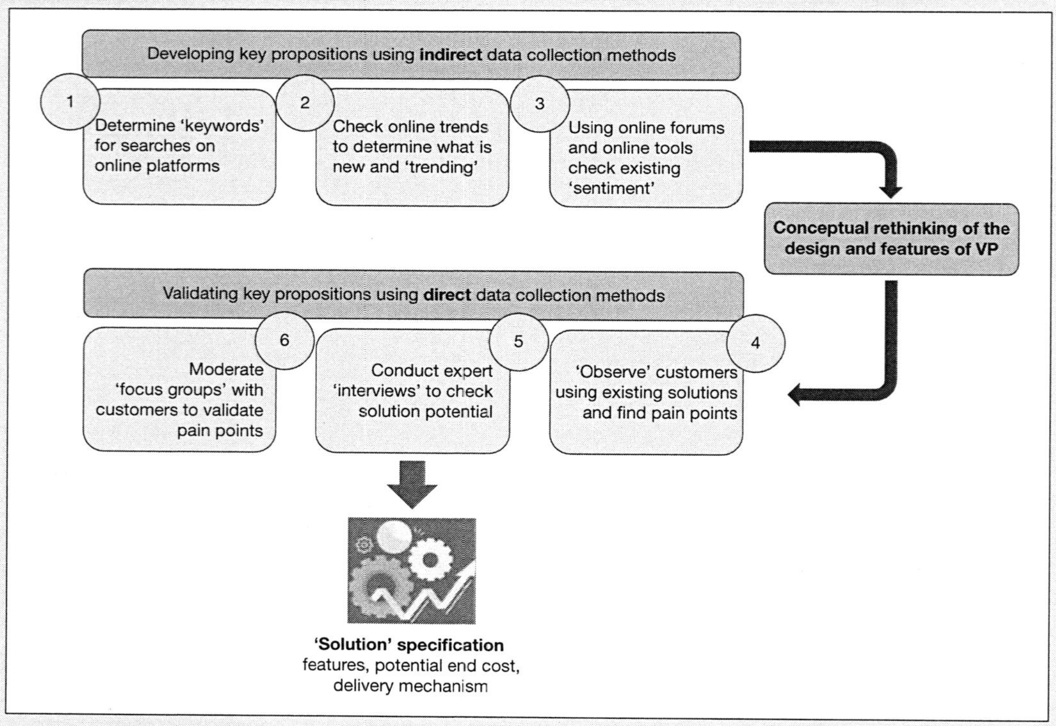

Source: The authors.

Exercise 5.1. Consider the outcomes of the exercises you undertook in the previous three chapters of this section. Now that you have, conceptually, unpacked and reformulated your idea and a VP has emerged, undertake indirect data collection to develop to check whether, conceptually, your VP shows general alignment with customer needs. Use Figure 5.5 to guide your plan—start by testing keywords and running searches on the described and relevant online platforms (be wide and varied in your choices). Check the content aggregator websites to find out what related aspects of your VP are presently trending. Finally, crawl through social media and use sentimental analysis tools to determine the direction of customer sentiment. Capture your findings in a 3–5 minute presentation.

6

Applying Jobs-to-be-done for Framing Problems

LEARNING OUTCOMES

- Understand how jobs-to-be-done (J2BD) can be used to define a market from a customer's view of the world
- Become familiar with the J2BD market definition and sizing process
- Learn how to use J2BD as part of new enterprise design

6.1. WHAT IS JOBS-TO-BE-DONE OR J2BD?

Spotlight on Fax Machines

Fax or 'facsimile' is a technology not many of us use these days. With an illustrious history of invention going back into the 1800s, it was Xerox Corporation in the 1960s that is credited with the launch of the world's first commercially available fax machine.

The Xerox LDX (1964) consisting of two units—a scanner and a printer

Imagine a Xerox salesman trying to sell the LDX model to a potential customer—say a clearing and forwarding agent. The agent uses the postal service or the more expensive courier to send and receive important documents to and from domestic and overseas clients. One of their *jobs* is, therefore, 'to send and receive documents quickly and securely to and from clients'. A fax machine would certainly make the agent's *job* of sending and receiving documentation from clients 'simpler', 'less expensive', 'quicker' and 'more convenient'. The post is not 100 per cent reliable—documents sometimes get lost in the system, not instantaneous, takes several days to deliver and requires the agent to commute back and forth from the post office. The Xerox salesman probably thinks that the agent would buy his new fax machine right away—it would be an easy sell, because the benefits of the fax over post and courier are so obvious. But they would be wrong. Why would that be the case? The agent would object to the Xerox salesman, 'nice idea, but why should I buy your fax machine, no one else has one, so who would I send my fax to?' Until and unless enough clients of theirs have fax machines, the agent would not be able to make use of the benefits the new machine offers. There were other problems with the fax machine as well—it was costly, complicated to use and quite bulky.

By the 1970s, however, many companies around the world, especially from Japan, started to manufacture and market their own fax machine models. These machines competed well with Xerox's models because they were more compact, easy to use, faster and more efficient. Sharp from Japan was one of the big winners when in 1984 they introduced the first low-priced fax machine and sold about 80,000 units within the USA alone. For the next three years, businesses steadily bought more and more fax machines, until in 1987, enough people had faxes that it made sense for everyone to get a fax. In 1987, a million were sold and by 1989—two million. By 1990, it became almost impossible to do business without using the fax technology—companies had to have them.

Only a few years later, a new technology emerged. In 1995, emailing became possible due to the lifting of restrictions placed on commercial data traffic on government-owned networks. Think about the clearing and forwarding agent now. Their *job* is still the same as it was when they bought the fax machine—'to send and receive documents quickly and securely to and from clients'. They adopted the fax machine because it made their *job* 'simpler', 'less expensive', 'quicker' and 'more convenient'. But now, with email available as an alternative to fax, they would be thinking to themselves: 'Our fax machine is costly to maintain, runs out of paper and ink, they are not secure because anyone standing beside it can peek at confidential documents coming through, it is also labour intensive and for faxing long distances we need to bear international calling rates'. Would not email make their *job* 'simpler', 'less expensive', 'quicker' and 'more convenient'? It certainly would, not immediately but certainly by the 2000s, it became impossible to do business without an email address. And this spelled the demise of the fax machine.

What is the lesson from this case? *People do not care about technology*, they care about getting their *jobs* done. 'Jobs' do not usually change, they remain stable. Better technology makes doing *jobs* 'simpler', 'less expensive', 'quicker', 'more convenient', 'accessible'—just *better*. If a technology does not make doing *jobs* 'better', people simply do not use it. We need to think about the *jobs* people want to get done and not *technology* when we design new 'solutions'.

There are different ways of segmenting (or dividing) markets. Think about fax machine manufacturers in the above case; corporations like Sharp used to design, price and sell different models of fax machines to suit the requirements and budgets for different types of customers, such as small business owners, commercial operators and home office users. These three types of customers were essentially three different 'market segments' and their expectations from a fax machine, what it could do for them and how much they would be willing to pay for one would be different to one another. But there was a problem in this way of market segmentation that is relying on customers' expectations and willingness to pay (WTP) for a 'product'. This is a part of the reason why corporations like Sharp are no longer market leaders for fax machines; in fact, they do not sell fax machines anymore—that entire line of business has vanished.

It is important to understand that people do not buy 'products', they buy 'solutions' that help them do *jobs*. To segment different types of customers based on what *jobs* they want done is a much more viable and stable way when developing 'solutions'. For example, think about photography; why do you take photos? Most people take photos because they want 'to capture, store and share *memories*'. Your grandparents wanted the same job done, the 'solution' that was available in their times was a photo film camera. Your parents too, wanted the same job done, but they probably used a different 'solution'—a digital camera. In your parents' and grandparents' era, the 'solutions' were suboptimal—there was a cost per photo taken, there was a finite number of photos that could be taken and sharing photos was not as easy—they had to rely on physical photos in an album that could be passed around when they would have guests at home. Think about the 'solution' available to you; remember: the *job* is still the same, 'to capture, store and share *memories*'. You probably own a smartphone with a camera that is connected to mobile broadband, and you most likely have a Facebook account, are on Instagram/WeChat/WhatsApp/Snapchat/other social media. Has the original *job* not become much easier to do?

'Solutions' Change, Jobs Do not

Kodak Retina Xenar Its postwar film camera	Kodak Compact Digital Easyshare	No Kodak Smartphone? Why? Product focused not *job* focused

J2BD is *a way of thinking* that helps entrepreneurs focus on 'what precise *jobs* do customers want done'. By thinking about customer jobs, entrepreneurs can more accurately define markets and align their product's innovative features to a group of customers. Such thinking originates from one of the most famous quotes in marketing by Harvard Business School professor, Theodore Levitt: 'People don't want to buy a quarter-inch drill machine. They want a quarter-inch hole!' J2BD has evolved over the last 25 years but it is still an emerging practice in business and marketing. Professor Clayton Christensen introduced the J2BD perspective in his seminal book on disruptive innovation '*The Innovators Dilemma*'. Anthony Ulwick has developed and published two books over the past decade on his version of J2BD methodology called '*Outcome Driven Innovation*' and Bob Moesta and Chris Spiek have also been at the forefront of developing J2BD thinking and tools, including the 'Progress Making Forces' diagram introduced in the following chapter.

6.2. WHAT ARE THE DIFFERENT JOB TYPES?

J2BD thinking helps entrepreneurs to systematically frame the market which they wish to enter and uncover opportunities by understanding the customer's decision-making process and how different customer groups measure success around a specific job.

The following case study will help you see how J2BD thinking can be retrospectively applied to understand why a new 'solution' to an existing and stable job is better than previous solutions. We will do this by first identifying the 'core jobs' the 'solution' is helping customers do *better*, and then what aspects of its 'context' of use and customers' 'success metrics' make the 'solution' *better* than competing alternatives. Remember: customers are 'solution neutral', they will use whatever solution is *best* at getting their *job* done.

DiDi Taxi App Part 1: A Customer 'Jobs' View of the Market Definition

DiDi Chuxing is a Chinese ride-hailing company founded by Cheng Wei in 2012. He worked for Alibaba for 10 years before founding DiDi as 'he missed several flights because he could not hail a cab in time'. DiDi is among one of the several global players currently in the process of fundamentally changing the traditional taxi industry. Although the taxi industry worldwide might have differences from country to country, but the industry as a whole is fundamentally based on a model where small taxi companies compete with each other in a city or region and are regulated by local authorities. The global taxi industry is very large and employs millions of persons, for example, in large cities like Beijing there are around 68,000 cabs in operation.

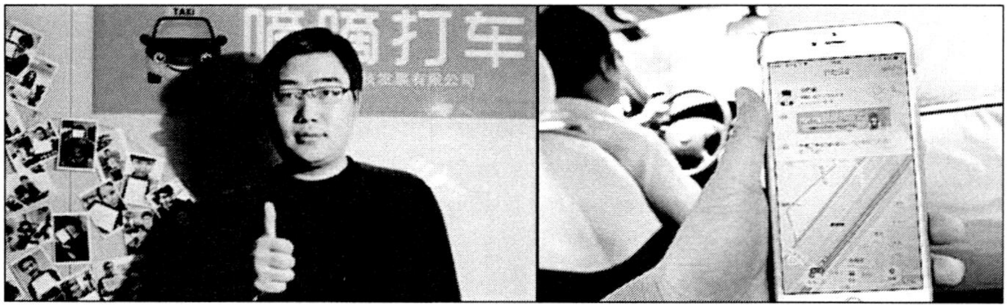

From left to right: Cheng; Wei: CEO, DiDi Chuxing; the DiDi App which tamed Uber in China

Traditional taxi businesses work on the basis of a number of long-standing assumptions, for example, 'local knowledge of taxi drivers to navigate' and 'local taxi routing businesses'. DiDi has completely turned these assumptions around; and not just in China but also in the broader Asian taxi industries. Its ride-hailing business has broken many of the traditional industry rules.
A *jobs* perspective on the taxi industry is that passengers really do not care about where the taxi comes from and who is driving the taxi—they are just trying 'to get from point A to point B'. DiDi's ride-hailing customers are trying to 'get to the airport on time', 'get to work on time', 'get back home on time' and so on. These would be the 'core jobs' that taxi passengers are really trying to achieve. Linked to these 'core jobs' are passengers' 'success metrics'. DiDi's goal is to help passengers get these important 'core jobs' done quicker, more reliably or cheaper. DiDi, therefore, is not just competing with other taxi companies to help passengers get these 'core jobs' done but with other industries as well, such as trains, buses and personal cars.

There are three key job types we need to understand which are as follows:

1. Core functional jobs
2. System dependent jobs
3. Emotional jobs

6.2.1. CORE JOBS

Core jobs are equivalent to Levitt's 'hole' analogy. Consider the following job statement, 'create a hole in a brick wall'. This job statement describes the *end* the customer wants to achieve. We can also ask a higher-level question, '*Why* a customer needs the hole in the brick wall in the first place?' The answer to this question would be a higher level 'core job' like 'hang a picture' or 'store a coat ready for use'.

Core jobs represent the hundreds of practical things people are trying to get done every day. Consider which of the following core job statements are relevant to you: 'eat breakfast', 'remove plaque and food particles from my teeth', 'prepare a hot beverage', 'get to work on time ', 'wake me up on the bus before my stop', 'create an assignment', 'store important documents', 'eat lunch while working', 'arrange an informal business meeting', 'prepare accounts for a tax return', 'listen to music', 'create a mood with music' and so on. Core jobs are often stable over time and can be around for decades, centuries and even millennia, unlike products which often change frequently.

Unfortunately, for entrepreneurs looking to design new products or 'solutions', people—their customers—do not naturally describe what core job they are trying to get done. People often codify the world through product names, for example, consider the statement your friends might often make: 'I need coffee'. This statement does not tell you *why* your friend is needing coffee. 'Product centric' thinking offers a very narrow view which is not that useful for developing new 'solutions'. It is fraught with bias around a customers' emotional attachment to products, giving a limited and skewed view of what customers *really* value.

When thinking about 'core jobs', you will need to first define 'success metrics' or the indicators through which you will test how successful your 'solution' really is—otherwise how would you know whether your solution is *actually* helping customers do a particular core functional job? For example, the core job 'create a hole in a brick wall' has some key broad success metrics that can be defined as follows:

1. The *time* it takes to create a hole in a brick of the desired shape, diameter and depth.
2. The *accuracy* of creating the holes of the desired shape, diameter and depth.
3. How *reliably* a hole can be created in the brick to achieve the accuracy requirements.
4. Total *cost* of creating a hole in the brick wall.

The above four indicators are just the broad metrics. To really understand these metrics further you would need to interview the customer group carrying out the job. For example, for metric A, time, we would ask about the amount of time taken. What might slow down 'creating a hole in a brick wall'? When does it go off track? What situation are you in when it is most difficult? Answers to these questions will help you think about the ways through which you can refine your 'solution'.

6.2.2. SYSTEM JOBS

System jobs are the jobs that need to be done when using a *specific* product or 'solution'. The drill's 'system jobs' can be stated as follows: 'mark the location where the hole is needed', 'set up the drill to create a hole', 'pack away the drill in its storage box', 'store the drill when not in use' and so on. How well the designed 'solution' is performing on each of these jobs can be tested with 'success metrics'. For example, 'set up the drill to create a hole' will have the following 'success metrics':

1. The total *time* taken to set up the drill for a specific hole width and depth (e.g., connect drill to power outlet, adjust drill settings, change drill bit and so on).
2. The *cost* of the setting up a drill for drilling to a specific depth (e.g., purchase of specific masonry drill bits, adapters required, and so on).

Unlike core jobs, 'system jobs' can be eradicated altogether. This is because a customer *does not* want to do these jobs, rather they must do them to get value out of the 'solution' (the drill). The customer wants a hole as *quickly*, *accurately*, *reliably* and *cheaply* as possible. All the jobs they have to do to create that hole (such as marking the location and setting up the drill—the 'system jobs') are hindrances, obstacles in the way that they would rather not do. Opportunity will come from finding creative ways to improve on the most painful ones of these system jobs or entirely eradicate unnecessary ones in your new 'solution'. Remember: *customers would rather not do 'system dependent jobs'.*

6.2.3. EMOTIONAL JOBS

Emotional jobs have two dimensions—personal and social. An emotional job statement expresses how people want to 'feel' themselves (personal) or be 'perceived by others' (social). For example, when trying to do the core job 'create a hole in a brick wall' a carpenter or mason may want 'to be perceived as an efficient professional'. Emotional jobs can relate to many related 'core jobs' and 'system jobs' and are often broad in nature. For example, the emotional job 'to be perceived as an efficient professional' will be relevant to many carpenters' or masons' core functional jobs like 'to cut wood' or 'to give a quotation to a client'.

Each emotional job, like the other two categories of jobs, has its own set of metrics. It is important to remember that emotional job metrics help entrepreneurs and businesses to understand how people want to 'feel' when getting the 'core functional job' done. They are particularly useful for marketing and appealing to a customer's ideal emotional states or feelings or the broader emotional frustrations they are trying to avoid that might relate to a core functional job. Remember: while doing core functional jobs, *customers want to feel good* or *avoid frustration and pain.*

6.3. USING THE SOLUTION DECISIONS MAP TO UNDERSTAND CONTEXT AND METRICS

When customer groups are trying to get their jobs done, they find themselves in a particular context or situation. For example, a tradesman might find jobs that require him 'to create a hole in a brick wall' at 'the bottom of a garden' or 'up a 15 ft ladder'. These contexts can significantly increase the difficulty of getting the core job done which changes the 'success metrics' (see previous section) a tradesman will have for the job 'to create a hole in a brick wall'. The key question for an entrepreneur is which context is relevant enough or in which context does the above tradesman frequently find themselves in to be worthy of investment in a specific 'solution'. Another important question to think about is: How does a context impact on the tradesman's 'willingness to pay'?

Consider the DiDi taxi case discussed above: taxi businesses get passengers based on the *decisions* such passengers make around the 'success metrics' associated with the 'core job'. We can analyse this customer *decision-making* process using a 'solution decision map'. Figure 6.1 describes a solution decision map for the core job 'get to the airport on time'. We know through secondary research that getting to the airport on time for a flight departure is a frequent 'core job'. In 2017, there were more than four billion passengers scheduled onto flights globally.

The taxi 'solution decision map' above defines the customer group as 'flight passengers' with a core job context of 'five family members with four large suitcases'. Consider Stage 1—solution decision-making in Figure 6.1; flight passengers have to decide which 'solution' out of the several available gets the job done *best.* Defined further are five key broad success metrics[1] of how flight passengers might evaluate the job 'get to the airport on time'.

1. Reliability of arriving at the airport check-in counter by the deadline.
2. The total journey time from home to the airport check-in area.

[1] These are just the broad metrics, in reality the metrics will be far more granular.

FIGURE 6.1 Taxi Solution Decision Map

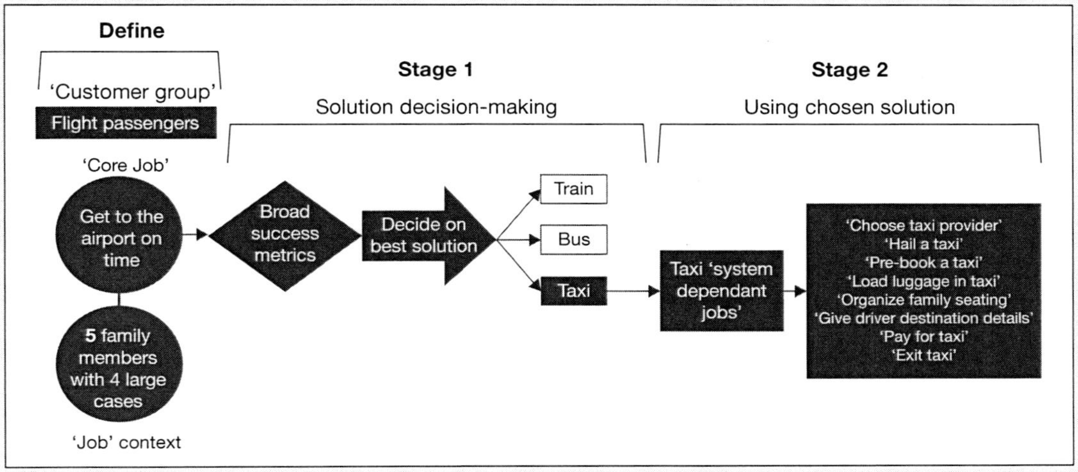

Source: The authors.

3. The time and effort required to move required luggage.
4. The time required to plan and organize the other co-travellers.
5. Total cost of getting to the airport on time.

These core job metrics help flight passengers decide which type of solution fits best. A particular flight passenger with four heavy suitcases will weight those 'solutions' highly or better that can move such suitcases with minimal effort. The taxi solutions here are the likely winner, unless the cost becomes a critical deciding factor.

At Stage 2—using chosen solution, the flight passenger is now mentally focused on seeking out the *right* taxi solution and using the taxi service. From a *jobs* perspective, the flight passenger now has a set of 'system jobs' that come about from using a taxi service. These jobs all have the word taxi at the heart of the job statement, for example, 'hail a taxi', 'pre-book a taxi', 'request taxi driver to go to a destination', 'pay the taxi driver' and so on. Each of these jobs will have a new narrower, more specific set of metrics.

When we start to analyse the market for DiDi, what becomes apparent is that when it comes to helping passengers do the 'core job' of 'getting to the airport on time', its ride hailing service is largely equivalent to all other taxi companies. However, there is one metric, metric 5 in our list, 'the total cost of getting to the airport' on which it far excels. As DiDi's ride-hailing service is positioned as a lower cost solution, this metric will score DiDi higher on the flight passenger's success metrics, particularly price sensitive flight passengers.

Optimizing on taxi 'system jobs' presents the biggest opportunity for DiDi. From the taxi system job statements presented in Figure 6.1, six out of the eight jobs (see under Stage 2), require significant improvement. In one instance, a 'system job'—'pay taxi driver' has now been made entirely redundant by taxi apps like DiDi. Passengers now do not have to worry about carrying cash to pay the taxi driver or asking for a receipt. They also do not have to worry about fair pricing or haggling with the taxi driver. By eliminating one 'system job', DiDi has succeeded in improving on the passengers' 'success metrics' linked to a number of core, system and emotional jobs.

6.4. DOING J2BD—STEP 1: DEFINING THE MARKET

When using J2BD thinking, your first task is to 'define the market' from your customer's perspective. Like in our case, DiDi's ride-hailing service, entrepreneurs need to understand which types of customer jobs and success metrics are most important to focus on to create new customer value. The following five steps will help you to begin to put J2BD thinking into practice.

1. By observing and questioning a specific product's consumption, define as many 'core jobs' and 'customer group' as you can. Ask yourself what goals does this product help the customer group to achieve?
2. Do these customer groups have particular 'contexts' that are noteworthy? Defining these contexts is not always required, but the context affects how each customer group will define the success metrics.
3. Select three to five of these 'core jobs' that you see as most attractive to your business idea. If you have lots of 'core jobs', it is likely you will need to select the few that are most relevant to your business idea. However, if there are lots of potential core jobs, then a jobs survey may be required to establish the most promising ones. Do the same for 'customer groups', that is, which groups of customers need the chosen 'core jobs' done most.
4. Now you are ready to think through how 'core jobs' success metrics relate to the 'solution' you are designing. Create a solution decision map (like the one in Figure 6.1) around each 'core job', its broad-based metrics, a list of likely solutions and the 'system jobs' for each solution.
5. Evaluate each solution decision map using the evaluation questions outlined as follows (also see Figure 6.2).

6.4.1. SOLUTION DECISION MAP EVALUATION QUESTIONS

These questions are to be used as an initial starting point for J2BD thinking. Further questions will develop when considered against important business objectives.

1. Which core job metrics are most problematic to the customer group in this specific context?
2. When the customer group is deciding on the solution to be consumed, are there any significant factors not defined by the core job success metrics which might bias the customer group towards a particular solution? For example, a particular solution is already owned.
3. Which solution is most likely the 'natural' choice for this customer group and their core job and job context?

FIGURE 6.2 Example Solution Decision Map for a Tradesman

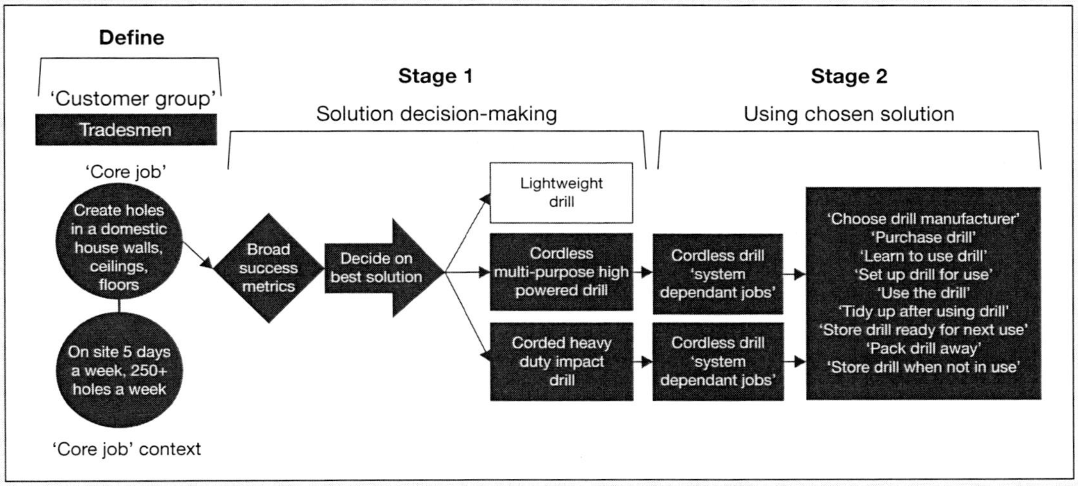

Source: The authors.

4. Which 'system jobs' does the customer group struggle to achieve?
5. How does the solution decision map change when other contexts are considered? What is the significance of these contexts?

6.5. DOING J2BD—STEP 2: SIZING A MARKET

Sizing a market is an important part of your business case, which will describe your 'solution's' market entry and product strategies. The 'market entry' strategy needs to be first clear before an optimal 'product' strategy can be formed. A good market strategy needs to answer two big questions:

1. From where can I acquire my initial customers?
2. What is my venture's realistic growth potential once an initial tranche of customers has been captured?

To answer the above questions, market data would be needed. You could use market data on 'current solutions' to assess their past performance and future growth potential (competitors) or use market data based on the 'core job' that your potential customers are trying to get done. Market data on 'core jobs', it is advocated, will be a much more valid and reliable means through which to build your business case. To understand the value of jobs-based market data as a means for sizing markets, let us turn to part 2 of the DiDi Taxi App case study as follows.

DiDi Taxi App Part 2: Market Size Hypotheses from a Customer Jobs Perspective

For entrepreneurs seeking investment, it becomes critical to build a clear picture of the market. Investors need to see evidence that the current product strategy is being successful based on the current rate of customer acquisition and that future customer acquisition is possible based on market size.

In June 2012, DiDi was just an early stage start-up looking to attract investment. By late 2012, they had raised $3 million 'Series A investment' by GSR Ventures, followed by a further $15 million 'Series B investment' from Tencent in July 2013. These investments were based on the early traction DiDi achieved with Chinese customers. The figures were impressive: by end of 2013, 300,000 daily bookings were being made through the app. How did Cheng Wei convince the above investors to part with such volumes of cash? From a customer *jobs* perspective, there were two ways for Cheng to build a future market investment case. Market data on the 'current taxis systems' and market data based on the 'core job'.

Market Sizing Based on 'Taxi System'

It is estimated by Goldman Sachs that the global taxi market in 2018 was worth $108 billion. They also provide an estimate that the current ride-hailing taxi market is worth $36 billion, around one third of the current taxi market. It is also estimated that 15 million ride-hailing trips are made each day which equates to about 5.5 billion trips per annum.

Goldman Sachs predicts that by 2030 ride-hailing will experience over a six-fold increase and rise to 97 million trips a day, about 35 billion trips a year.

This data is based on taxi usage rather than the 'core jobs' passengers are trying to get done.

Market Sizing Based on 'Core Job'

A market size can also be hypothesised for the core job 'get to the airport on time'. This market size provides a much broader perspective and is one of the few real markets which taxis are competing for. It must be emphasized that this is just *one* core job that DiDi satisfies. Table 6.1 provides a global estimate of $146.2 billion for this one job. This estimate compares relatively to the global expected revenues for the airline industry in 2018 at $834 billion. Based on this hypothesis, the cost of getting to and from the airport is around 17.5 per cent of the total cost of a flight, so each trip is 8.75 per cent (half of 17.5%) of the cost of the flight.

Consider Table 6.1; in the fourth row we observe that of the 4.36 billion airline passengers taking flights and commuting to and from airports on an annual basis (column 2), 35 per cent (column 3), which is approximately 654 million passengers per annum (column 4), would be willing to spend $12.80 for 'getting to the airport on time'. This assessment suggests that the size of the market for just this segment (those passengers willing to pay $12.80) is an astonishing $16.7 billion.

TABLE 6.1 Market Size Hypotheses 'Get to the Airport on Time'

WTP Segment $ (Hypotheses of Willingness to Pay per Trip, per Passenger)	Global Passengers per Annum	Segment Size % (Hypotheses)	Segment Size (Total Number of Passengers)	Number of Airport Trips Required per Passenger	Estimated Spend in $ per WTP Segment
$1.20	4,358,000,000	5	217,900,000	2	$522,960,000 00
$3.80	4,358,000,000	10	435,800,000	2	$3,312,080,000 00
$8.90	4,358,000,000	15	653,700,000	2	$11,635,860,000 00
$12.80	4,358,000,000	35	653,700,000	2	$16,734,720,000 00
$25.60	4,358,000,000	18	784,440,000	2	$40,163,328,000 00
$38.40	4,358,000,000	10	435,800,000	2	$33,469,440,000 00
$57.60	4,358,000,000	5	217,900,000	2	$25,102,080,000 00
$76.80	4,358,000,000	1.5	65,370,000	2	$10,040,832,000 00
$120.00	4,358,000,000	0.5	21,790,000	2	$5,229,600,000 00
				Global market size	**$146,210,900,000**

Source: The authors.

Notes:

WTP Segment $: These values represent the range of costs per passenger. Road tolls, parking, hotel stayovers are included.

Global Passengers: In 2018, 4.358 billion passengers flew around the globe. This is calculated as each individual flight rather than a return.

Segment Size %: This is the percentage of customers estimated to be at each of our WTP thresholds.

Segment Size (total number of passengers): This is how each WTP segment translates into numbers of passengers.

Number of Airport Trips Required per Passenger: As each flight has two airports, there are two trips required per flight.

Total Spend in $ per Segment: This is calculated by multiplying WTP Segment $ by the total number of passengers in that segment.

The growth potential for any 'solution' you develop is determined by defining and validating the size of the market opportunity—the bigger the market, the more enticing your case for attracting investors. Sizing a market through the J2BD lens helps entrepreneurs to keep horizons broad but also focused on the customer. It enables a structured view across multiple industries that customers can use to get the job done. It can also be used to assess what share that industry has of the 'core job' and the untapped growth potential. Using J2BD thinking, an entrepreneur will be equipped to foresee the potential of growth outside of their industry as well. As is the case with DiDi, their success is linked to the size the market they serve from both a 'core job' and 'system job' perspective. It is the combination of these job perspectives that entrepreneurs can use to make a business case. A J2BD reliant business case can help identify the precise customer segments entrepreneurs would be able to get early traction from and also from which segments subsequent market growth could come from.

6.6. DOING J2BD—STEP 3: HYPOTHESES DEVELOPMENT

The process for market sizing discussed in Stage 2 leads to hypothesis development. Hypotheses about the 'core' and 'system' jobs are typically formed using published secondary data (industry reports, newspaper articles, blogs, review aggregator websites like www.channelsignal.com and so on) combined with your instincts, assumptions and experience. From the market sizing exercise undertaken in Stage 2, which would be based on valid and reliable, good quality information—what do you hypothesize are the unserved 'core' and 'system' jobs that your potential customers are trying to get done, but the solutions they use right now are suboptimal? These initial hypotheses may be labelled as 'arm chair' research or mere guesses but you should not get discouraged. Many very successful businesses began as mere guesses about core jobs—Airbnb is a great example of this (research how it was set up). Returning back to the DiDi taxi app case study, observe how they kept their hypotheses about core and system jobs very broad initially, then using secondary and primary data, they made them more specific.

DiDi Taxi App Part 3: Broadening the Market Definition

From DiDi's business perspective, the job of 'get to the airport on time' is very attractive, but it is only one of many 'core jobs' a taxi service can satisfy. Other example jobs could include 'get me to work on time', 'get the kids to school on time' and so on. There are many jobs that have the similar objective 'get somewhere on time'. It makes sense, in this instance, to broaden these markets into one succinct definition 'get to a local destination on time'. This broad definition would allow you to take the common attributes among a set of specific job statements into one overall statement. See Figure 6.3: for DiDi, it was important to find the highest level of abstraction for a group of similar jobs that still makes sense to a customer. Therefore, their broad market definition or hypothesis would be that a certain segment of customers want to 'get to a local destination on time'. This 'get to a local destination on time' hypothesis defines a huge market of all local journeys where arriving on time is a key driver of success for customers/travellers/passengers.

FIGURE 6.3 Higher-level Hypothesis

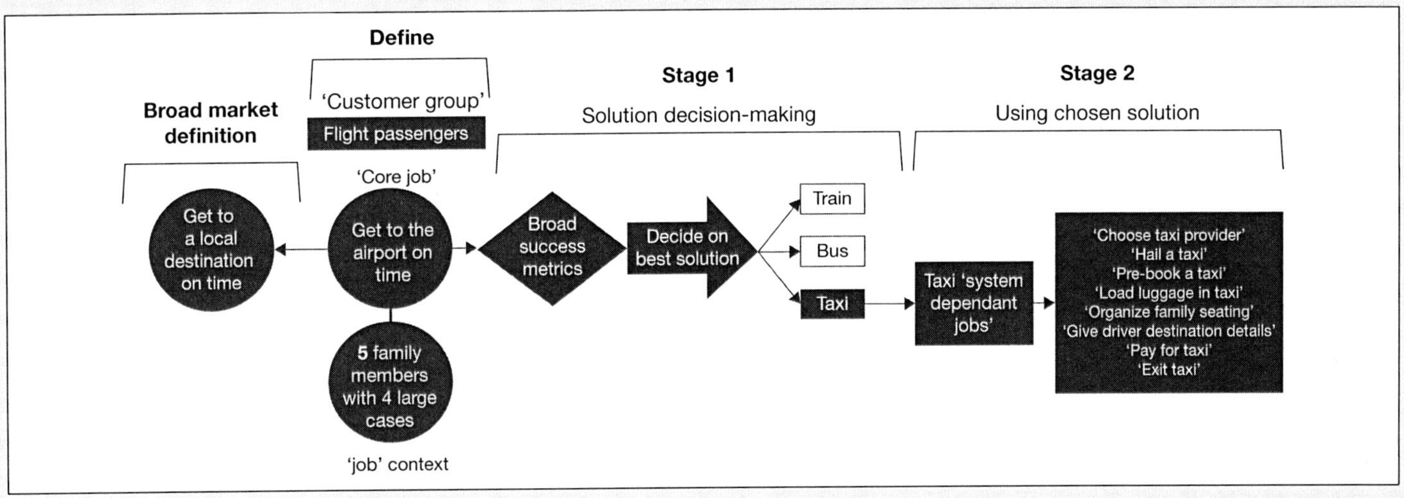

Source: The authors.

A realistic hypothesis about the 'revenue' that DiDi could generate by helping customers do the more defined 'core job'—'get to the airport on time'—also needs to be developed. For this exercise, it may be that data is very hard to find or does not exist in the right form. Research reports similar to the one by Taverner (shown below) for Sydney Australia (from December 2014) might exist which provide a useful indicator of the broad purposes of taxis trips. Specific jobs-based data, however, are not usually available and needs to be extrapolated and extracted from more general broad datasets. Hence, it is likely that primary research would be necessary to establish specific jobs and revenues attributed to such jobs within the taxi industry.

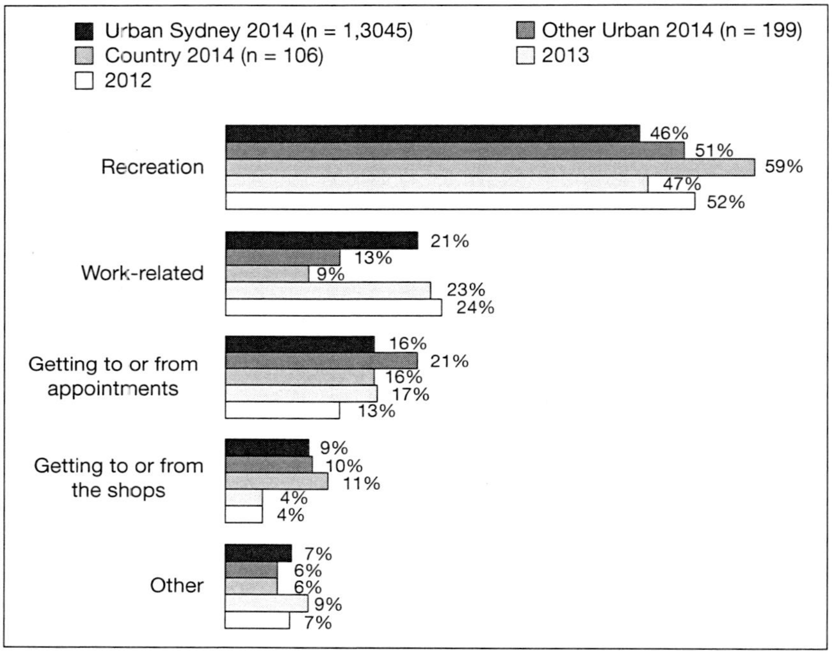

Source: https://www.ipart.nsw.gov.au/files/sharedassets/website/shared-files/investigation-administrative-taxi-passenger-survey/consultant-report-survey-of-point-to-point-transport-use-february-2017.pdf (Accessed on 21 January 2019).

To be taken seriously by potential investors and for you to have the confidence to move forward and put your idea into implementation, primary data collection would be necessary to validate your hypotheses—to see which ones are more important, which jobs do customers care more about and for which jobs are customers willing to pay more to get done to a certain expected standard. The primary data collection phase requires a structured approach; where the initial starting point is to define good research objectives (see previous chapter). Once you have defined your research objectives, you can move ahead and conduct interviews, undertake observations and deploy surveys to collect primary data. The research objectives would normally include a collection of the target customer group's success metrics to establish dissatisfaction with current solutions used to help customers do their jobs.

A market size hypothesis is very much dependent on how the core job has been defined, so first make sure you have good quality primary data to scope and probe a clear job definition using the solution decision map. Once this map is completed, you will need to size the core job using the 'four steps to market size hypotheses development' approach. The approach's four steps are as follows:

1. Number of customers trying to get the job done
2. Job frequency
3. WTP to get the job done
4. Context frequency

6.6.1. STEPS 1 AND 2

When trying to complete the first two steps you are identifying data to uncover the total number of jobs being done per year. In DiDi's case, for the core job 'get to the airport on time', we do not actually know how many customers are going on 4.3 billion flights. But 4.3 billion flights give us the total number of jobs data which we are looking for. This would be enough to give us an accurate size of the market, which is 8.6 billion taxi trips as passengers have to get to and from the airport.

6.6.2. STEP 3

There are two ways to calculate WTP. First, a calculation of what different 'priced-based customer groups' will pay today. Second, what different 'price-based customer groups' will pay today if they could to get the job done *perfectly*. We are mainly focused on the first as the second requires highly specific and very complete data sets. 'Priced-based customer groups' need to be approximated based on the entrepreneur's experience or industry, professional and market knowledge. Typically, between 5 and 15 'price-based customer groups' are defined for market size hypotheses development.

6.6.3. STEP 4

The specific contexts that are defined in the solution decision map will significantly narrow the market size. Again, careful consideration would need to be given to what data exists to validate the chosen contexts; or what data could be used to inform a reasonable set of hypotheses. Market sizing is fraught with data collection challenges and the entrepreneur needs to work hard to obtain data from good secondary and primary sources. It is often the case that it seems too hard to get good data and market sizing is done hastily. Job-based market sizing requires both hypotheses development and primary data collection in order to be reliable and truly insightful.

6.7. SUMMARY AND APPLICATION

An entrepreneur must understand that the customer, and how they measure value, their success metrics, is one of most important aspects of building an enterprise with solid foundations. J2BD provides a structured and systematic approach to breaking down the market into a customer-centric view of the world. J2BD helps entrepreneurs define customer success metrics using 'core jobs'. In this chapter, the J2BD process has been explained; it can support entrepreneurs in undertaking two critical activities when building the foundation of an enterprise. It helps in (a) 'framing the market using the customer' and (b) sizing-specific, job-based, markets. Completing these two activities will build the basis for an entrepreneur's customer knowledge development and deeper awareness of what customers really want in new 'solutions'.

Mastering J2BD thinking is like any critical thinking skill, it will take time and practice. The best way to learn is by starting to apply it. Over time, it can be applied systematically to your own venture's development, including: market definition, market sizing, market segmentation; customer profiling; competitor analysis; product strategy; market differentiation; market positioning and market messaging.

Exercise 6.1. Understanding the customer is the foundation of your business and it is going to be important to get thinking about the many 'core jobs' a customer group is trying to get done. Using the five steps of the solution decision map template (explained in 'Doing J2BD—Step 1: Defining the Market'), carry out the initial steps of building a deeper understanding of how your potential customers are getting their jobs done and are measuring success. A simple way to start is to informally talk to friends or family about why they bought a product X or Y and start to dig deeper as to what competitive set of solutions were being measured against this purchase.

Exercise 6.2. In the previous exercise, you should have developed several solution decision maps. Identify a 'core job' and 'customer group' that you think are of most interest for your business idea. Now, ignoring any specific context, calculate a market size hypothesis based on the defined 'customer group' and 'core functional job'. Follow the first three steps as outlined in 'Doing J2BD—Step 3: Hypotheses Development'. You will need to think about ways to improve the accuracy of your hypothesis from both secondary data and discussions with easily accessible people with knowledge of the customer group and/or 'core job'. It is important that you do not spend too long on this hypotheses stage as it will never be fully accurate. The purpose would be to identify avenues for further data collection.

7

Designing New Value Propositions

LEARNING OUTCOMES

- Understand how a compelling value proposition (VP) message drives user adoption and product purchase
- Become familiar with the new VP design process
- Learn how to design new VPs as a part of new enterprise design

7.1. WHAT IS A NEW VALUE PROPOSITION?

Spotlight on the 'Generator Economy' in War-torn Syria

As a consequence of the ongoing conflict, vast populations in Syria have suffered from extreme power shortages. Many solutions have been proposed to provide stable electric supply, including solar power and biomethane from organic manure and green waste. However, set-up costs for these systems are too high, and the results are not instant, sustainable or reliable—especially in cities burdened with war and fleeing populations. Since 2011, people have relied on car batteries for powering lighting, TVs, charging phones, laptops and network routers. The local manufacturing of car batteries, chargers and inverters has, therefore, flourished. However, car battery-based systems themselves need to be charged and they have limitations when it comes to powering domestic appliances for extended durations. Providing electricity through privately owned backup generators is the best alternative to mains electricity and represents the pinnacle of social innovation in Syria. The strong need for stable electricity has led to the creation of a new 'generator economy' in the country.

understood by knowledgeable salespeople who attempt to elevate and strengthen the two forces that promote a customer to make a change and 'take action'. If these two forces are greater than the opposing two forces, the customer will take the desired action. It is important to understand that just building a product that fills an important 'value gap' is not enough. Communicating and positioning a compelling, succinct message is equally critical. Poorly communicated VPs are just as likely to halt a customer's action as the viability of the overall product.

7.2. VP DESIGN PROCESS

A design process is required to support an entrepreneur's VP's development. This process comprises eight steps for building a compelling new VP that can drive frictionless customer acquisition. These eight steps are as follows[1]:

1. Use the 'solution decision map' (explained in the previous chapter) to get clarity on the core job the target customer group is struggling to get done.
2. Define the customer group's 'value gaps' and the most important 'value gap' that is to be addressed.
3. Explore possible 'value creation promises' that can fill the most important 'value gap'.
4. Compose a concise definition of the new VP for internal use.
5. Compose a VP message for the customer group: a succinct, memorable articulation of the 'value gap' and the 'value creation promise' that strongly resonates with the customer group.
6. Define the key action required by the customer group to get commitment.
7. Define the two forces blocking change and evaluate why change might not take place.
8. Develop a pricing model that can promote adoption of the VP by aligning pricing with customer segments' WTP.

Let us consider a well-known case, the Apple iPod, and go through each step of the aforementioned VP design process in more detail. In October 2001, the now infamous, memorable new VP message 'iPod. 1,000 songs in your pocket' was launched by the Apple CEO, Steve Jobs. It was a new music player called the iPod.

Apple's slogan for the iPod '1,000 songs in your pocket' was a customer facing message defined in step five of the aforementioned new VP design process. Apple wanted music lovers to remember the value their iPod would create for them. They needed a succinct and memorable message. They needed it to be easy for customers to remember and would help facilitate WOM between early adopters.

The message 'iPod. 1,000 songs in your pocket' is actually a compelling summary of the most important 'value gap' that music lovers needed filling at that point in time—'access my personal music collection, when on the go'. Knowing this 'value gap' provided Apple with a solid foundation for its message as it connected music lovers to what they really needed. Knowing the 'value gap' is the most neglected part of designing a new VP, and that is why propositions fail to resonate. Many entrepreneurs make the mistake of not clearly understanding their product's or service's 'value gap'

[1] If your business has multiple customer groups then repeat the steps for each group.

and make big decisions based on *assumptions* about what they *think* are their customer group's 'value gap'. Some entrepreneurs neglect the 'value gap' outright.

7.3. VALUE GAPS

From the previous chapter, a concept was introduced that customers do not care about your product or service, they care about getting their jobs done. As a customer group tries to get a job done, they have a set of success metrics based on the *core job*. They then have a set of system jobs based on the solution they choose. Using the J2BD approach we can frame the market from the customers' understanding of value and how they prioritize and make decisions when it comes to choosing a product or service. Defining these success metrics and system jobs and measuring how well satisfied they are is the key to understanding the most important 'value gap' that exists for a particular customer group. The groundwork for understanding the basis of 'value gaps' should be derived from the solution decision map explained in the previous chapter. In the case of the iPod, Apple wanted to successfully enter an existing market of music players, and to be successful, they needed to get the job done better or cheaper than the competition. The initial questions Apple needed to answer were as follows:

1. How do we define and frame the market for music players?
2. What value must a new music player create to win customers in the market?
3. What customer group will likely be the early adopters of an Apple music player?
4. What core job and context are most unsatisfied when using existing music players?

A solution decision map is the best place to start to answer these questions and would provide a great frame of reference for Apple's new VP design (Figure 7.2).

FIGURE 7.2 Solution Decision Map: Listen to Music, while on the Go

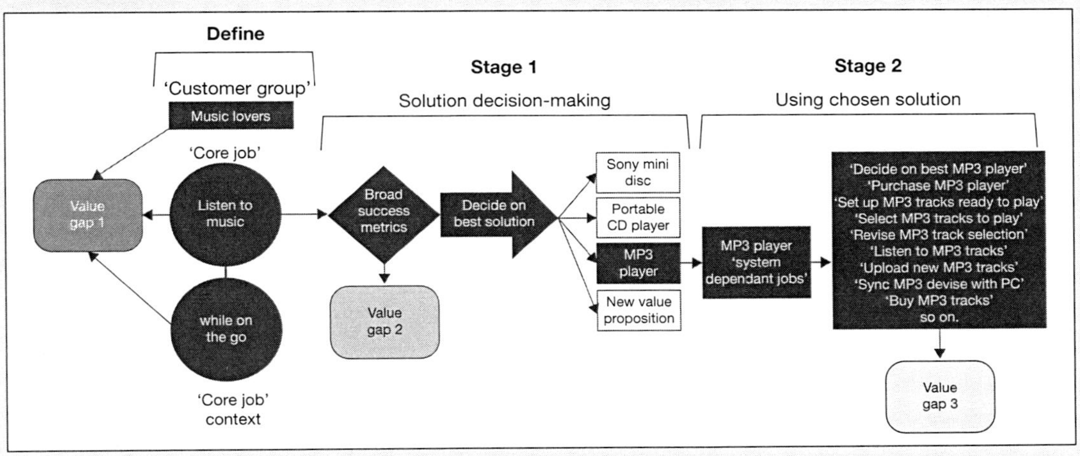

Source: The authors.

The market for the iPod—based on its J2BD analysis—can be defined as 'music lovers listening to music, while on the go.' There are three 'value gap' areas to be considered for the iPod. These are explained as follows.

7.3.1. VALUE GAP 1

'Value Gap 1' considers the *define* stage of the solution decision map. The define stage combines the three key aspects of the market: 'customer group', 'core job' and 'core job context'. The first, 'customer group' can be redefined as either a broader group or a narrower group. In the case of Apple iPod, 'music lovers' is a broad definition. A narrower definition of early adopters would make more sense to Apple: 'music lovers using Apple Mac PC'. Narrowing helps us focus on a more specific and more relevant group of early adopters that are of interest to Apple. The potential value Apple can create for this narrower group would be greater as they would have already invested in other Apple products, like their laptop or PC. Any digital music file formats that the iPod would use should then be compatible with Apple's Mac PC, allowing the narrowed down group to avail of maximum value that the new iPod would create.

While the second aspect of the market—'core job'—is 'listen to music', other related jobs are also of interest to Apple. For example, 'build my music collection', 'buy music albums', 'buy a song' and so on. The key question is which of these related jobs are satisfied and which are unsatisfied? Apple understood that these three other jobs were unsatisfied. A year and half after the iPod launched, Apple launched iTunes targeting these other jobs. Emotional jobs are also related to the core job. A core functional job can be delivered well by other brands too, but Apple excels on how it can make customers 'feel good about themselves' and how they can be 'perceived as *cool* by others'. The 'think different' marketing campaign Apple ran in 1997 was about building an underlying emotional connection with customers and that Apple is the company that can 'empower people to change the world'. Aspirational marketing and emotional design execution all focus on delivering these important emotional jobs.

The third aspect of the market—'core job context'—can be used to create either a narrower or broader market definition. The context, 'on the go', could become narrower by focusing on a specific situation of being 'on the go'. For example, 'while driving a car', 'while on the train' or 'while running'. These contexts subtly change the success metrics of getting the job done. A specific 'value gap' becomes greater or smaller depending on context, or the frequency a context has for a specific customer. Knowing if there are contexts that create bigger 'value gaps' becomes an important insight for the entrepreneur. A specific context can help create greater focus and bigger 'value gaps' for the business. Alternatively, it also important to know if there are common success metrics unsatisfied across a range of contexts and hence a larger market.

7.3.2. VALUE GAP 2

The broad success metrics for the 'customer group', 'core job' and 'core job context' help us to understand, in general terms, the areas where customer dissatisfaction lies. Given further are some broad success metrics which could be defined for the further narrowed down group 'music lovers using Apple Mac PC, trying to listen to music on the go':

1. Know what songs are best suited to my current 'on the go' situation (e.g., when running around a park, when driving a car, when commuting on a train).
2. Time it takes to gather and store the required songs when playing in that situation.
3. Time it takes to select, gather and order stored music songs in that situation.
4. Reliability—that music songs play as intended in that situation (e.g., without skipping like how a CD would).
5. Time taken to revise song selections, order, or deselection in that situation.
6. Total cost of listening to music across various 'on the go' situations.

In October 2001, the metrics above were unsatisfied in many ways. MiniDisc players, portable CDs and emerging MP3 players had varying levels of strengths and weaknesses for getting the core job done. For example, users of Sony MiniDisc players would have been satisfied that when playing music while running, the music did not ever skip or jump tracks unintentionally. The Sony MiniDisc could withstand skipping for most jolts apart from extreme shocks, like when dropped on a hard surface. A CD player would jump or skip if you started to move more vigorously. Therefore, broadly speaking, satisfaction of metric '4' above is dependent on two variables which are as follows:

1. **The context the customer is in:** For example, for running while listening to music, avoiding track skipping is important. However, listening to music sitting on a train, track skipping is unlikely to pose a problem.
2. **The solution being used:** Portable CD player is likely to skip or jump. A Sony MiniDisc is unlikely.

Apple needed to know what metrics were most unsatisfied. Frequency of the context has a bearing on how often a customer might be struggling. If they only struggle once a year, this may be bearable, while customers struggling twice a week will need help more often.

The reality is, when the stakes and investment are high in product development, it is important to get more detailed and granular customer success metrics through qualitative and quantitative research. To get absolute validation on the 'value gaps', Apple would have conducted customer research which would have resulted in addressing more specific actionable metrics, some of these are defined as follows:

1. **Relates to metric '2':** Increase the likelihood that a personal music collection is available when 'on the go'.
2. **Relates to metric '3':** Increase the likelihood that music album information is available when finding or playing songs (e.g., album artwork, artist info, track details).
3. **Relates to metric '2':** Reduce the time spent searching for a desired music track or album.

7.3.3. VALUE GAP 3

The DiDi taxi case study, discussed in the previous chapter, highlights how *system jobs* offer the right lens to find important value gaps for customers. In DiDi's case, several system jobs of traditional taxis were unsatisfied or not required at all. The system jobs for the iPod market were linked to the problems of existing music platforms such as portable CD players, MiniDisc players, flash players and hard drive players.

Only a very small percentage of Apple's target customers were users of existing MP3-based solutions. Most of their target customers were using already established solutions such as portable CD players and the emerging Sony MiniDisc players. Portable CD players were still the dominant platform, and most people were heavily invested and owners of vast CD collections.

The following unsatisfied 'system jobs' would have been defined for portable CD players:

1. Select the CDs to be played when on the go.
2. Store the CDs ready for use when on the go.
3. Change the CD when a new music album is required.

If a historical format like the CD is approaching the end of its life, a new platform concept like digital music is likely to displace many of these portable CD player system jobs.

Job 1 above can be improved on by the new digital platform. The job would still exist and would become 'selecting digital tracks to be played on the move'. The quantity of songs that can now be selected and put onto a portable music player would be very high.

Jobs 2 and 3 above can be entirely eradicated as there would be no requirement anymore to store or change the physical CD. A new digital platform would eradicate the need to store a CD or change a CD when on the go.

To better understand how value gaps are identified for creating new VPs, the following OFO dockless bikes case study is instructive—the approach is applied step by step to identify the three value gaps.

OFO Dockless Bikes from China Part 1: Value Gaps Identification

We became familiar with OFO's background in Chapter 4 and understood the processes that led to its start up. OFO is the original dockless bike service provider and is now one of more than 50 companies competing globally. Dockless bikes are unique in that once rented, the user does not need to return the bikes to a designated 'dock'. They can be left anywhere (within reason) and are tracked, traced, collected and transported back to an appropriate 'hire' location.

Within less than two years, OFO's dockless bike sharing system expanded from one campus at Peking University to over 200 university campuses across China. To achieve this level of success, a compelling 'value proposition' needed to be succinctly communicated to the adopting university's students and staff. Staff and students would adopt and use 'dockless bikes' if they believed that OFO's 'solution' would create more *value* and help them get a *job* done better and/or cheaper than their existing solutions. What is the most important 'value gap' that OFO needs to address to drive adoption?

The solution decision map, introduced in the previous chapter, can be used to highlight potential 'value gaps' that created the foundation for OFO's VP. The map below is for the customer group 'Peking University students and staff' who are trying to 'move between university campus sites and buildings'.

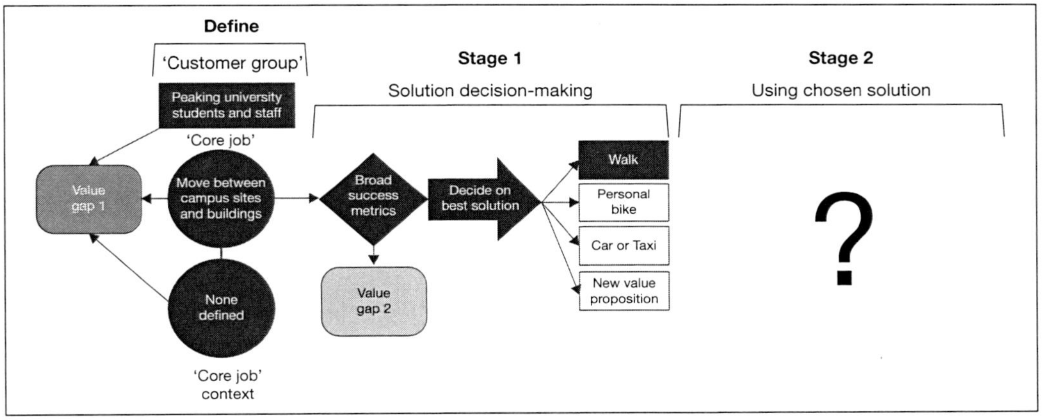

Source: The authors.

Let us consider 'Value Gaps' 1 and 2 that appear on the above solution decision map.

Value Gap 1

To identify Value Gap 1, we need to consider other customer groups, core jobs and core job contexts that are relevant to 'moving between campus sites and buildings'. Understanding specific value gaps here will require qualitative and quantitative research. However, it is important to understand where to first look; often, other solution decision maps maybe required for further investigation.

Other core jobs: Other related core jobs could be, 'get to Peking University campus from home' and 'get back home from Peking University campus. 'Complete errands or chores during downtime at Peking University campus' could be another related core job. Jobs such as these would depend on the distance to be travelled. Qualitative research would uncover other related jobs and quantitative research can validate other jobs that are unsatisfied.

Customer groups: Broader or narrower customer groups that OFO could target can also be defined. A broader customer group could be 'Beijing commuters and tourists'. A narrower customer group could be 'Peking University bike owners'. This narrower group would be of interest to OFO in understanding the deeper issues of bike owners when moving across campus and other bike ownership system jobs.

Core job context: Developing more specific job contexts would help us understand where getting the jobs done is harder. Qualitative research would reveal other more specific contexts that would be important to OFO.

Value Gap 2

Value gap 2 is about understanding the unsatisfied success metrics that 'Peking University staff and students' have when trying to 'move between campus sites and buildings'. The broad success metrics can be defined as follows:

1. Know the most efficient route to get to the target campus destination.
2. The total journey time from current location to campus destination.
3. The personal effort or energy consumed to get from current location to campus destination.
4. Effort required to move any personal belonging to campus destination (e.g., bags, books, materials and so on).
5. Total cost of getting from current location to campus destination.

The 'value gaps' here are predominantly linked to metric 2, which relates to journey time, and metric 5, which relates to the cost of the journey. Both these gaps are dependent on the distance to be travelled. There is a *time vs. cost* trade-off when campus buildings are dispersed over two miles or more. However, for very short trips of less than half a mile the cost factor would be negligent—simply walking would be more convenient over taking a cycle or any other form of transport.

Trips of two miles would typically mean a 40-minute walk vs. a 10-minute taxi ride. A two-mile trip would be virtually free to walk or cost around \$6–\$8 in a taxi. However, if the solution was a personal bike, interestingly the trip time would also be 10 minutes, comparable or even quicker than a taxi. The cost, on the other hand, would be approximately 25 times less than a taxi. This saving is calculated as the proportional cost of bike ownership and maintenance, and can be estimated to be between 1 p and 25 p per trip—depending on bike and equipment purchase cost, maintenance, frequency of use and so on. On this basis, the cost of a bike trip maybe even 625 times cheaper than a taxi. Therefore, for a two-mile trip, assuming access was not a problem, a personal bike would present a very good choice for many people.

Now let us consider a half a mile trip. A taxi is unlikely to be considered for a very short distance. Walking would take 10 minutes, whereas a personal bike would take 3 minutes. Walking is virtually free, whereas a bike ride is estimated at between 1 p and 25 p per trip. If the trip time is an important factor, then the personal bike is a very good choice, should one be available. If trip time is not a factor, then walking is a very good choice.

Metrics 2 and 3 have key value gaps when travelling longer distances of around two miles. However, metric 2 is the key value gap for shorter distances of around 0.5 miles.

Value Gap 3

Value Gap 3 considers the system jobs when a solution is chosen or is strongly desired to be chosen but cannot be due to one or several constraints. In this case, consider the same solution decision map as earlier in this case above, but with the choice of personal bike in Stage 1 'solution decision-making'.

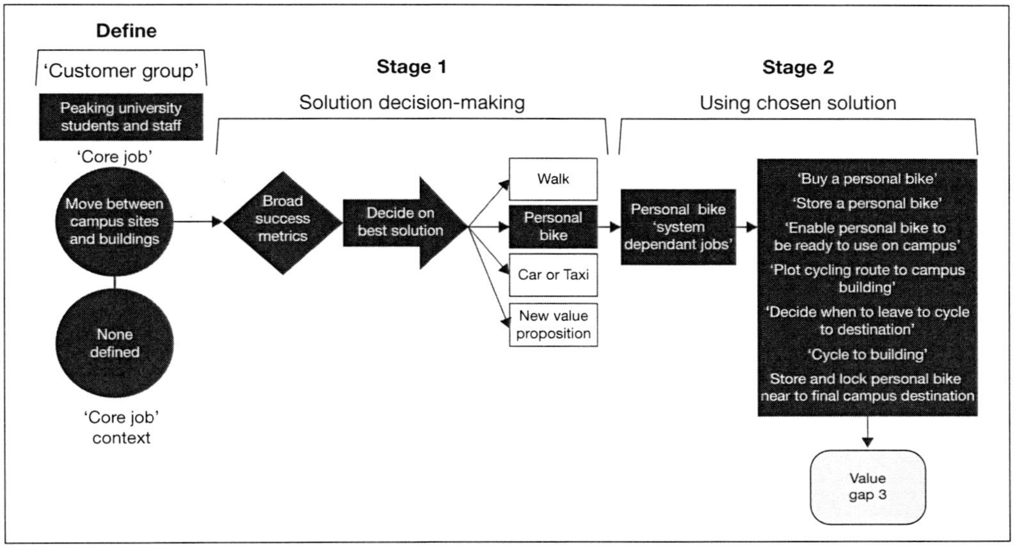

Source: The authors.

The personal bike has many system jobs that need to be achieved for this solution to be viable. Seven of the most common personal bike jobs are listed, however, there may be many more which would need to be uncovered using qualitative interviews. From the seven jobs listed, analysis would reveal that the following four jobs represent significant value gaps for Peking University students and staff.

'Buy a personal bike': If you strongly desire to use a bike and do not own a bike, then you have to buy one. Bikes can be expensive and come with ownership commitments of constant storage and maintenance.

'Store a personal bike at home': If you own a personal bike, then you have to store it when at home. This can be in porches, corridors, front gardens and so on. Students do not often have the right space or enough space to store a bike. Limited home storage adds an extra barrier to bike ownership.

'Enable a personal bike to be ready for use on campuses': If you own a bike that would be useful to use on campus, then getting it to campus can present a problem if you do not live nearby or the road routes are not suitable for bikes. Additionally, weather can also prevent you from getting your bike to campus. Once on campus, it needs to be safely and securely stored as bikes are also at risk of theft. Limited locations and solutions for locking up bikes securely create problems for bike owners.

'Securely store a personal bike near to final destination': This too can be problematic when there are limited locations for storing bikes securely. Which might mean an additional walk from the storage point.

In summary, the 'value gap' analysis above helps us frame OFO's target market for its Peking University dockless bike sharing service's launch. Value Gap 1 helps OFO to identify and understand other related 'value gaps' for which solutions may be required to support future growth into similar and related markets. The analysis of Value Gaps 2 and 3 lays the foundation of OFO's early adopters' VP.

7.4. THE VALUE CREATION PROMISE

A value creation promise has two components. The first is a 'viable method' of filling the 'value gap' and getting the job done better or cheaper. The second is a 'promise' to the customer that the defined solution is proven to 'reliably' get the job done better or cheaper. If execution risks are too high, then the entrepreneur will not be able to make such promises to the customer. A value creation promise requires that the specified solution will reliably deliver *value* to the customer. The promise ensures the technical and delivery risk to the customer is minimal and forgivable. If the customers are exposed to too much risk from the adopted solution, they will no longer be customers. If you overpromise and do not manage expectations, your customers will find a better, more reliable 'solution'. A failed promise will go seriously against you.

A potential customer will be constantly evaluating the risks posed by a new VP. Typically, they will look at the new VP from a 'perceived risk' and an 'experienced risk' basis. An entrepreneur will have to overcome both these risks to successfully acquire and retain customers. If the *perceived risks* are too high, a customer would not believe that the VP can be 'promised' and therefore will not take any action to adopt. There could be many reasons why a high risk is perceived. For example, the customer had a bad experience with a product feature. The best way to find out about perceived risks is to interview customers and find out why they are concerned or worried. Are they concerned that the technology the VP uses might not be reliable? When it comes to *experienced risk*, it *feels* more real to customers; for example, a customer's friend has told them they used the VP and it failed to create the *promised* value.

To create the value desired by a customer group, an exploratory approach to the ideas gathering process is needed. The entrepreneur needs to uncover many ideas, without judgement, that have the potential to fill 'value gaps'. Once ideas have been generated, they will need to be filtered based on the 'value gap' and the ability to execute the idea with low risk to the customer. The following three questions should guide an entrepreneur's idea prioritization process.

1. Does the idea *actually* fill the 'value gap' identified?
2. Is the idea executable with available resources?
3. Does the executable idea present low risk for the customer group?

A functioning business is the culmination of many good ideas that align with customer expectations and can be executed efficiently. Filtering out the ideas that are not aligned to the customer's core job is a really important way to use available resources efficiently. Putting poorly aligned ideas into action is wasteful. Many ideas are not technically achievable or require sophisticated capabilities outside of an entrepreneur's capabilities and resources to execute to the standard required to create *value* for a customer group.

7.5. VP CANVAS

The VP canvas is a conceptual tool created by Alexander Osterwalder to support entrepreneurs and businesses when designing new VPs. The VP canvas enables an entrepreneur to create a coherent well-flowing narrative behind the rationale and design of their new products and services. There are two sides to the canvas (see Apple iPod's canvas at Figure 7.3). The right side frames the customer *J2BD* and builds a picture of the customer group's associated *pains* and *gains*. The left side of the canvas frames the *solution space* for entrepreneurs to explore and includes the methods and technologies that can kill the pains called *pain relievers* and create gains called *gain creators*. These *pain relievers* and *gain creators* lead to the final step of defining a clear product or service. The canvas's key strengths lie in its simplicity in creating a 'unifying story' of how customers get the job done better and/or cheaper.

To better understand how the canvas can be used, let us go back to the Apple iPod example. Apple needed a coherent proposition that addressed the most important 'value gaps' it had identified in the music consumption space. The canvas in Figure 7.3 represents the adoption logic of the iPod's early adopter group, 'music lovers using Apple PCs' and the core job and its context 'listen to music on the go'. These aspects occupy the right side of the canvas where the customer group's most important 'value gaps' can be mapped onto the *pains* and *gains* sections.

7.5.1. APPLE iPOD VP CANVAS: INTRODUCTION

In Figure 7.3, the most important 'value gaps' from the previously discussed Apple iPod solution decision map have been mapped into the *Pains* and *Gains* sections of the canvas. These most important gaps come from all three value gaps. A refined definition of the 'customer group' is selected: 'music lovers', with Apple being only interested in early adopters within them, that is, those 'using Apple PCs'. The early adopter is specified on the premise that Apple's file format will only work with the Apple PC. Most early adopters will own an Apple PC to get the full value from the iPod.

The core job and context remain the same as defined in the earlier solution decision map. To explore other opportunities around the job would require a broader VP or the development of another VP. The core job 'context' could be narrowed to be more specific, like 'while running'.

Keeping Figure 7.3 in view, let us now go through, in greater detail, the two main sections (and associated sub-sections) of the VP canvas as applied to the Apple iPod.

7.5.2. APPLE iPOD VP CANVAS: VALUE GAP SECTION

This section of the VP canvas requires the entrepreneur to define only the most important and common *gains* and *pains* across the entire customer group. It is common to try to list all the *gains* and *pains* that might exist in all different types of 'on the go' contexts. However, this would be a mistake and would signal that the entrepreneur does not know which *gains* or *pains* are most important. It is pertinent for the entrepreneur to gather both qualitative and quantitative data to validate which of these are the most important to the defined 'customer group'.

The *gains* identified include the following:

1. Music collection to be accessible when I am 'on the go'.
2. Quickly find any music tracks from my music collection.

FIGURE 7.3 VP Canvas Adapted for the Apple iPod

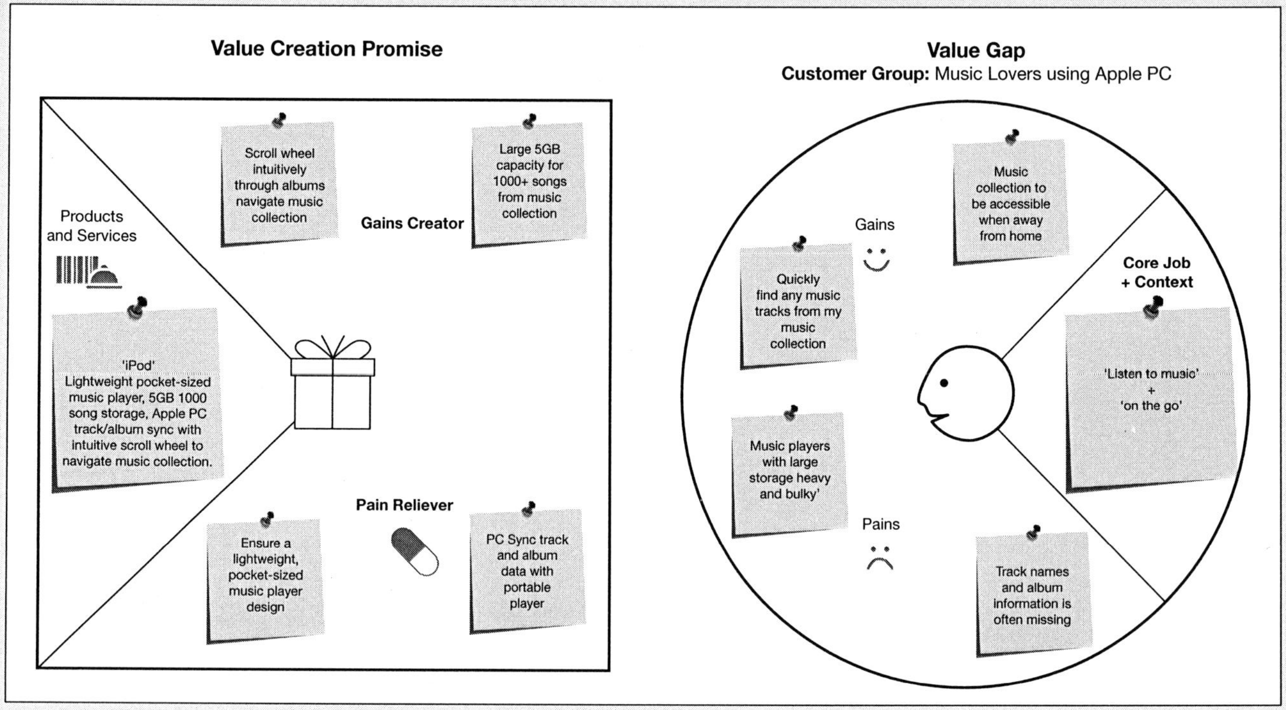

Source: The authors.

Gains are typically metrics that current solutions are not addressing or trying to promise. These are the metrics that everyone else misses as they are not discovered through analysing a product but built through understanding the goals of the job.

The *pains* identified include:

1. Music players with large storage are heavy and bulky.
2. Track names and album information not available.

Pains help us understand the 'success metrics' the customer group already expects as part of the existing solutions they have adopted. They experience non-performance on these metrics as pain as they can tell you 'the music player is too heavy'. Again, the entrepreneur should focus on validating the most common pains across the market. Many other pains might exist—and, as with gains, it is pertinent to gather data to support validation.

7.5.3. APPLE iPOD VP CANVAS: VALUE CREATION PROMISE

In this section, gain creators, pain relievers, and products and services are plotted. Two gain creators for the Apple iPod were identified which are as follows:

1. Large 5 GB capacity for 1000+ songs from music collection.
2. Intuitive scroll wheel: Navigates music collection through albums.

Gain creators focus on enabling the *gain* to happen as easily as possible for the customer group. Apple needs to enable as many albums in a customer collection to become readily discoverable and playable while 'on the go'. One key limiting factor is affordability of the storage size. A customer group's WTP to get the job done will influence this specific limiting factor. However, an increase in storage also increases weight and overall player dimensions—which is not desirable when 'on the go'.

Being able to access 1000+ songs from your music collection anywhere also creates a new success metric, 'being able to navigate a music collection quickly'. A simple scroll wheel or dial is one such method of intuitive navigation. This solution can also create a tangible and visual distinction from existing music players in the market.

Two pain relievers for the Apple iPod were identified which are as follows:

1. Ensure a lightweight, pocket-sized music player design.
2. PC sync track and album data with portable player.

Pain relievers focus on solving the two most important *pains* for customers when using existing solutions. The weight vs. size trade-off has already been discussed earlier, but the important factor here is to deliver this large storage capacity of songs but also a small, compact lightweight device. Apple had already been investigating compact and lightweight hard drive-based innovation in partnership with Toshiba. The ability to promise to relive customers' pains while introducing gains is paramount to an entrepreneur's success with acquiring and satisfying customers.

Finally, a product name, iPod, and a definition is provided as a summary of the gain creators and pain relievers that were selected on the ability to promise to deliver value to 'music lovers using the Apple PC trying to listen to music on the go'. In the products and services subsection, a brief description of the 'solution' to help customers do the above job is offered. For Apple, it was the 'iPod'—a lightweight, compact music player, with a 5 GB hard drive capable of storing 1000+ songs using Apple PC album information sync, with an intuitive scroll wheel to navigate large music collections.

7.6. BUILDING A VP STATEMENT

The VP canvas has helped to develop an outline of the new VP from Apple—the iPod; however, the VP statement we proposed in the previous section is 'internally facing'—a guide for Apple's designers and not be used for selling the product. Now, a concise and compelling consumer facing message can be created using the following formula:

A (*label*) called (*product name*), which allows (*customer group + core job + context*) to (*fill value gap*) using (*value creation promise*)
Label: A portable digital music player
Product name: Called iPod, which allows
Customer group + core job + context: 'music lovers' 'listening to music' 'on the go' to
Fill value gap: Instantly access anywhere 1000+ songs from their personal music collection, using
Value creation promise: A lightweight, 5 GB, pocket-sized MP3 player with simple, intuitive album and track navigation.

This statement reads as follows: 'A portable digital music player called "iPod", which allows music lovers listening to music on the go, to instantly access anywhere 1000+ songs from their personal music collection, using a lightweight, 5 GB pocket-sized MP3 player with simple, intuitive album and track navigation'.

This structure will bring consistency to all VP statements an entrepreneur may need to develop, but only for internal teams and other stakeholders—not customers. It allows for easier constructive criticism to take place. Remember, different markets will require different VP statements targeted at specific customer groups, like business customers or athletes. Consistency is going to be important if multiple VP statements are to be developed efficiently; and such consistency is possible using the above formula.

However, the structured version of the VP statement presented above is too long for any consumer to remember. A shorter version is required that will create engagement through a simple message. This simple message needs to be compelling, succinct and memorable.

1. **Compelling:** This means surprising the customer that new value can be achieved. Quantifying how many songs could be transported around makes a case, acts as evidence, increasing the value of the compelling narrative.

FIGURE 7.4 **iPod's VP Message**

Source: Apple Inc.

2. **Succinct:** The message needs to be short, to the point. It should capture the essence of the value, not the detail. Use as few words as possible.
3. **Memorable:** A message is helped if more meaning can be captured through analogies (one word if possible) that are easy to remember. For iPod, 'pocket' means: portable, compact and conveniently stored on a person. That is five key points made with one simple word, 'pocket'. Also, it is important to reference the core job. 'Songs' becomes the key reference to the core job and the specific customer success metric, the iPod, will improve on.

Finally, the phrase 'a picture is worth 1000 words' becomes true when helping potential customers *believe* what you are promising. The promise is evidenced in its full glory that the value creation promise is tangible and is within touching distance.

To cement learning and clarify further, the OFO dockless bikes case study part 2 below takes us through the process of using the VP framework to create compelling new offerings to help customers perform their jobs.

OFO Dockless Bikes from China Part 2: The VP Development

OFO's launch at Peking University was phenomenally successful. Its VP sits at the heart of that success. OFO needed a VP that would quickly resonate with staff and students trying to 'move between campus sites and buildings'. The foundation of this VP is in understanding the most important 'value gaps' that were examined in the first part of this case study. The identified 'value gaps' provide the raw material to develop a VP canvas and VP statement.

OFO's VP canvas has been mapped out below and brings forward the five most important 'value gaps' from the solution decision map (from part 1), which are mapped onto the right side of the canvas.

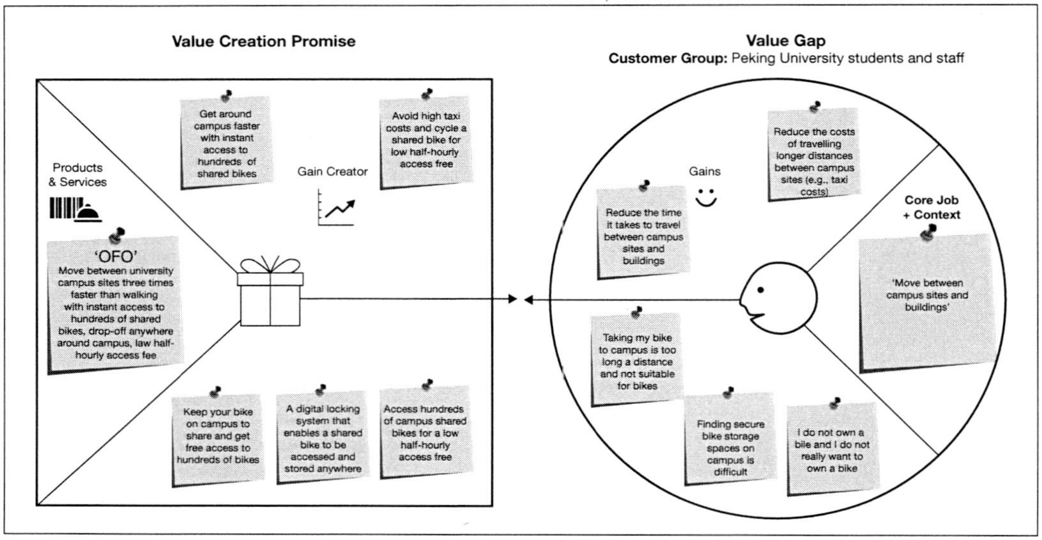

Source: The authors.

The right side of the above canvas defines OFO's market and its most important 'value gaps'. The customer group and core job and context can be defined as 'Peking University students and staff' trying to 'move between campus sites and buildings'.

Two *gains* and three *pains* are defined as follows: *Gains*—'reduce the time it takes to travel between campus sites and buildings'; and 'reduce the costs of travelling longer distances between campus sites (e.g., taxi costs)'. *Pains*: 'Taking my bike to campus is too long a distance and not suitable for bikes'; 'Finding secure bike storage spaces on campus is difficult'; and 'I do not own a bike and I do not really want to own a bike'.

The left side of the canvas is about exploring the solution and finding the coherent story that addresses the identified 'value gaps'. If we consider the two *gain creators* and two *pain relievers*, then there are three basic solution concepts that emerge.

1. Instantly access hundreds of shared bikes for a low, half-hourly, access fee.
2. Share your bike to access hundreds of shared bikes for free.
3. Hassel free locking systems to access and store bikes anywhere.

The simplicity of the solution definition above is enticing for customers. Delivering this VP does have some significant challenges, but at this stage it is about it being *believable*.

A more formal VP statement can now be defined that builds out in more detail its accompanying 'solution'. Using a simple five-point structure below, OFO's formal VP statement can be defined as:

Label: A shared bike mobile app,
Product name: Called OFO, which allows

Customer group + core job + context: Peking University students and staff moving between campus sites and buildings to
Fill value gap: Travel faster than walking and cheaper than taxi rides around campus by
Value creation promise: Open access to hundreds of shared campus bikes with instant GPS bike locating, digital locking and anywhere drop-off features.

Once a campus bike sharing model proved successful, OFO quickly spread to other universities across China. The next frontier was cities. The following VP canvas maps an evolution of the OFO VP to target the significantly bigger market of cities.

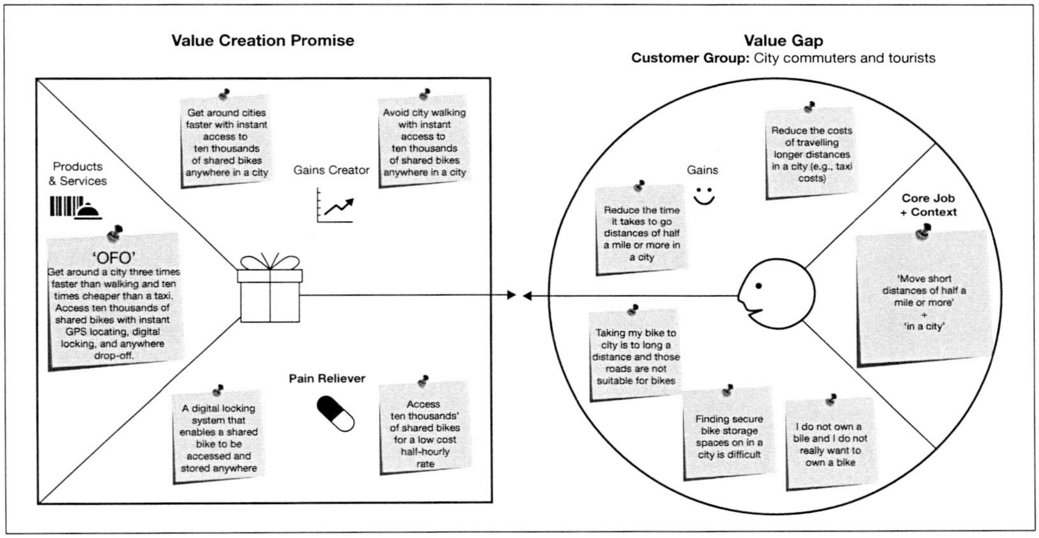

Source: The authors.

The updated VP canvas above is very similar to the previous university campus canvas, which is not surprising as the jobs are very similar. However, the product positioning has shifted from bike sharing to dockless bikes. And the product execution challenges are greatly increased due to less predictable supply and demand and the total number of bikes required to deliver that demand. The structured VP statement reflects aspects of these changes as follows:

Label: A dockless bike mobile app,
Product name: Called OFO, which allows
Customer group + core job + context: City tourists and commuters to move short distances around the city to
Fill value gap: Travel short distances faster than walking and cheaper than taxi rides by
Value creation promise: Open access to ten thousands of shared bikes with instant GPS bike locating, digital locking and anywhere drop-off features.

The attractiveness of OFO's VP to customers stems from the simplicity of the overall story and its ability to remove bike ownership risks. The technology behind OFO becomes almost invisible to the customer. OFO achieves this by leveraging GPS technology for tracking and locating bikes and established technology like QR codes as a locking system. This allows OFO's bikes to be located, picked up and dropped off easily.

7.7. ACQUIRING CUSTOMERS BASED ON THE NEW VP

The iPod's new VP needed to acquire a sufficient number of early adopters to be a viable line of business for Apple. Efficient acquisition of early adopters is required which essentially means achieving a low cost per customer acquisition. In other words, to keep the cost of getting one customer as low as possible. Steps 6, 7 and 8 in the new VP design process discussed earlier in this chapter are all closely interlinked to customer acquisition and aim to collectively reduce purchase 'friction'.

In marketing, many tactics have been developed to help achieve commitment from customers with lower risk to the marketer/promoting company. This is often achieved by asking for a smaller commitment than is required if the lead proposition was purchased. For example, a product or service that costs $10 is very different to those that cost $10,000. If the developed VP is expensive, then it would be sensible to build an entry level proposition that allows the customer to take a small first step. The ultimate goal though is still to sell the lead, more expensive, VP; however, this is not always possible. Any first step should always ask for a significant commitment from the customer in either money, time or reputation. If a customer's initial actions do not add up to an adequate commitment, then the entrepreneur risks that customer becoming a drain on the marketing and sales resources of the business.

At launch, Apple was seeking to achieve one key action: purchase the iPod device for $399.

As discussed earlier, most customers experience dilemmas when considering new purchases. The four forces model helps to explain why some customers purchase and others do not. However, not all customers experience the same strength of forces at each point. A customer might initially be enticed to commit to purchase the iPod but, as they start to realize, they do not own an Apple PC, and are not financially prepared to invest in an Apple PC—they might resist purchasing the iPod. This customer has an additional job to 'get access to an Apple PC'.

Figure 7.5 depicts a scenario of a sceptical, but also a very interested early adopter of the iPod. The interest stems from the iPod's VP which builds excitement in the mind of the customer. However, a bad experience with buying other 'portable music players' created disappointment and

FIGURE 7.5 **Progress-making Forces, Apple iPod**

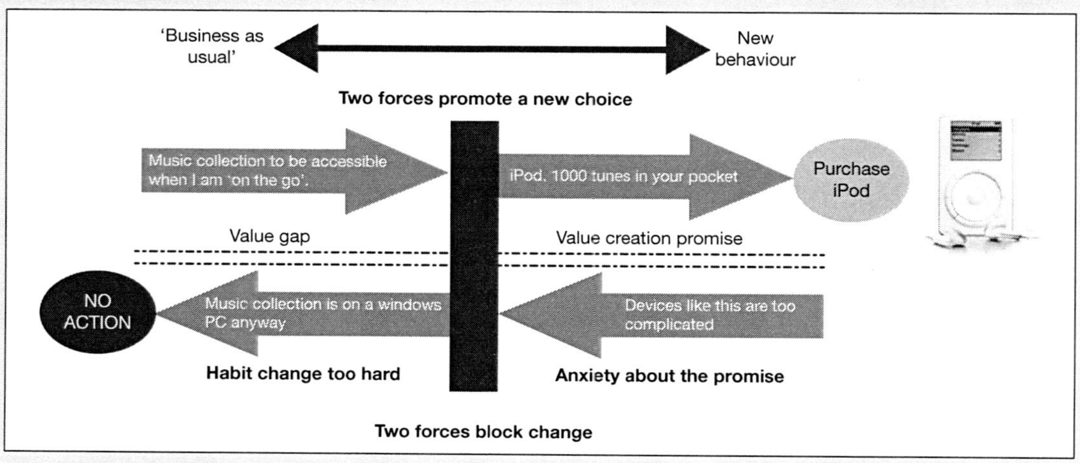

Source: The authors.

purpose as a temporary organization designed to 'search' rather than 'execute'. 'A start-up is an organization formed to *search for a repeatable and scalable business model*'. *Repeatability* and *scalability* are two key factors of how investable a start-up is. Consider the following definitions for repeatability and scalability:

A repeatable business model is when 'it is able to generate recurring sales effortlessly'.

A scalable business model is when 'it can increase sales and profits without incurring a proportionate increase in costs'.

Validated learning is an approach to systematically test and optimize the entire business model to be *repeatable* and *scalable* by starting with its riskiest parts.

8.1.4. INNOVATION ACCOUNTING

Measuring a start-up's progress is notoriously difficult, because there is no single set of metrics that can be applied universally. Each start-up has to determine what its key measures of success are. 'Innovation accounting' is a term introduced by Eric Reis as an antidote to the *vanity* metrics start-ups often report to give off a sense of success. For example, a start-up might suggest the number of user signups, which is useful to know. However, in and of itself, it is just a *vanity* metric, as it fails to indicate if those signups are engaged and receiving value. This is the trap of *egotistical big numbers* over the reality of *customer value*. The lean start-up movement seeks to 'improve entrepreneurial outcomes, and to hold entrepreneurs accountable, we need to focus on the boring stuff: how to measure progress, how to set up milestones, how to prioritize work'.

8.1.5. BUILD–MEASURE–LEARN

Build–measure–learn is feedback loop as a part of a scientific, design and testing methodology. The goal is to move through this feedback loop with speed and efficiency, with minimal waste and maximum learning. Figure 8.1 highlights three key goals—code or build product faster, measure faster and learn faster. It also highlights the many different techniques for achieving these. However, every start-up is at a different stage; when building a unique business they are required to learn different things at different times, so each technique's relevance really does depend on the *stage* and *requirement* of the start-up.

Lean start-up is deceptively simple to grasp but difficult to put into practice. One of Reis's most popular concepts is the minimum viable product (MVP), which truly personifies this theory into *practice* challenge. An MVP is the smallest feature set a product/service needs to have to create real and sustained value for a customer group. Its goal is to help entrepreneurs avoid creating products with too many features that create very little value for customers. However, in practice, this definition is a stretch in different directions. On the one hand, an initial marketing or VP test is often referred to as being an MVP. However, an MVP is *not* a product, nor can it achieve the desired *minimum* level of viable customer value. Second, an MVP is still an incredibly difficult product to

FIGURE 8.1 The Build–Measure–Learn Feedback Loop

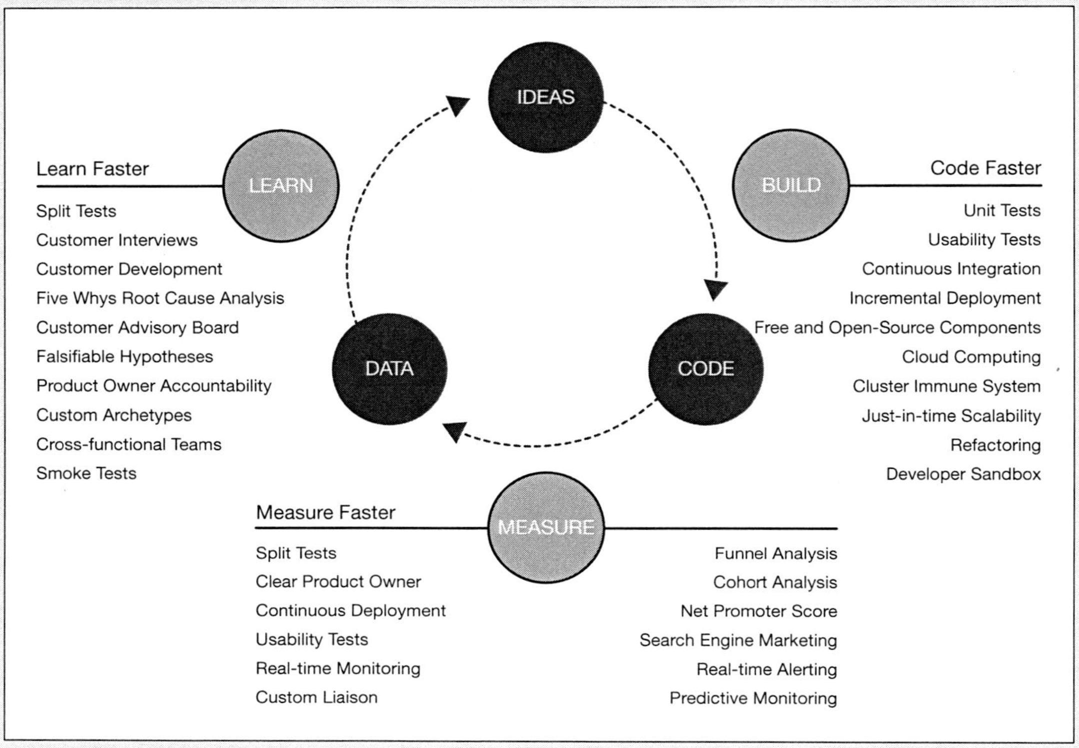

Source: Eric Reis (Theleanstartup, http://theleanstartup.com/).

specify as some MVPs could just have one feature, while others may need 50. There really is no predetermined formula for an MVP other than 'how the customer understands value'.

The practice of lean start-up is, therefore, exemplified as following the five principles combined with the mastery of specific methods and techniques that will yield maximum insight (validated leaning) and efficient progress (build faster, measure faster and learn faster.)

8.2. WHY TEST A NEW VP?

In the previous chapter, an eight-step process for designing a new VP was described. This chapter proposes some steps entrepreneurs can take to apply the lean start-up principle of validated learning to optimize the *proposition message* and overall offering. Testing a new VP is not about testing the product experience or its functions—that comes later—it is about answering the question: 'Is this product concept going to be accepted and deliver the value the customer needs?' It formalizes and tests the customer's willingness to take action based on the simplest possible presentation of a VP message and accompanying proposal.

There are two high-level objectives of testing VPs:

1. To validate any outstanding hypothesis from the market analysis and value creation promise conducted in Chapters 6 and 7; and
2. To move as fast as possible towards the goal of frictionless customer acquisition.

The first objective is about *validation* and *filling gaps* in knowledge about the target customer group, its target J2BD, the most important 'value gap' and the acceptance of the 'value creation promise'. This objective is achieved through qualitative testing of the VP using interviews with prospective customers/users. These interviews combine gathering background information on the customers J2BD with VP tests using marketing materials.

The second objective is about gathering qualitative insights and quantitative measures about 'why a customer does or does not take action'. The quantitative measures also determine the effectiveness of the channel (like an app, website or a retail unit) used to reach the customer. To summarize, qualitative interviews and quantitative tests together provide the necessary insights into:

1. **VP objections and acceptance:** Obvious or subtle ways that customers accept or object to the VP. Understanding the details of VP *objection* and *acceptance* helps the entrepreneur to align product concepts, optimize messaging, improve market positioning and modifying the product's market entry tactics.
2. **Early adopters:** Which customers from the target customer group are most likely to act and adopt, and are there other customers (with VP modification) that might also take such action?
3. **Channels:** What channels increase the number of customers that will receive and accept the VP for the least amount of cost per customer (this is commonly referred to as CAC—customer acquisition cost)?

An MVP has a key benefit that entrepreneurs often fail to recognize—it is a highly versatile *proposal*, not a *product*. It is far easier, faster and cheaper to revise a *proposal* than it is to revise a *product*. In some instances, the product will be useless to a customer and needs to be discarded. The fact is: most products require significant investment in time, money and energy to build the functions that actually get the job done better or cheaper. It is entirely possible to test the key aspects of an MVP without having to offer a fully functioning product.

Testing in this way is sometimes referred to as a *smoke test* or *sell-it-before-you-build-it*. The goal here is to validate that the MVP drives the desired action. Can the MVP lead to a sale, the acquisition of a paying customer? S*ell-it-before-you-build-it* is actually about getting presales based on marketing, product design and business proposals.

An early stage MVP test needs to be centred on the effectiveness of the VP (value gap + value creation promise + WTP). This requires devising marketing materials to package up the compelling message, position and covey the key VP benefits and illustrate the product to be offered. They

FIGURE 8.2 **MVP Testing Types**

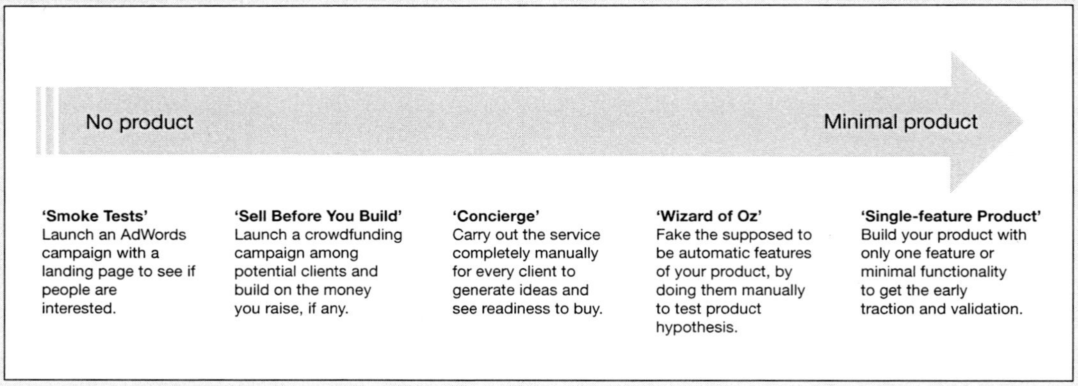

Source: Katerina Reshetilo, https://greenice.net/type-mvp-right-startup/ (accessed on 14 June 2019).

should attempt to present the VP in such a way that it drives the customer towards the desired action and simulate, in the customer's mind, the value the eventual product will provide. Customers taking the test should not know that the product does exist.

Testing the VP through an MVP helps entrepreneurs reduce product execution risk. This risk has two dimensions:

1. Building the *wrong* product; and
2. Building the product or feature set *wrong*.

It is important to note: the first of the above dimensions, building the *wrong* product, presents the biggest drain on a start-up's resources. If an entrepreneur is building the *wrong* product, they are on the wrong strategy. This is a bad situation that is often not recognized by the entrepreneur. A typical cause of building the *wrong* product is a cognitive phenomenon called 'confirmation bias' (more details in Chapter 3). Confirmation bias comes into play at some point in most start-ups and entrepreneurial decision-making. However, its impact is greater when an early stage start-up becomes heavily invested in building the functions and features of a product and then looks for *narrow* examples of customers, sometimes friends and family, and obtains product-centric feedback to validate and justify what is being built. The risk is, the feedback from this narrow sample *confirms to the entrepreneur* that the product he/she is building will create value, and this justifies to the entrepreneur further product development—because that is what the sample thought was what the entrepreneur *wanted to hear*. 'Confirmation bias' becomes stronger the more invested in the product an entrepreneur becomes. This approach unfortunately leads the entrepreneur to put the product before the customers J2BD. So rather than the J2BD being the unit of analysis, the entrepreneur's product takes centre stage.

Unwittingly, the desire to seek feedback friendly customers increases the confirmation bias from the customer side too. People do not like to be critical of other people's hard work for fear of upsetting them or demotivating them, so they will often give undue positive feedback, further reinforcing to the entrepreneur that they are on the right path. This is a self-reinforcing loop, and the more invested the entrepreneur becomes into the product, the harder it is to undo their work. This is why many invention-led entrepreneurs struggle with commercialization. They invest so much time, money and energy acquiring patents and building expensive prototypes that they have time to only superficially engage with the market. Eventually, when the product is finished, they expect the market to beat a path to their door. However, it is only when the market does not do this that they realize that the product they have built is not a good fit for the target customers. Testing the VP (using an MVP) rather than the product helps to overcome this problem.

8.3. PRODUCT–MARKET FIT OR MARKET–PRODUCT FIT

It is very important to realize that the core product concept of a start-up fixes in place many aspects of its strategy. If there are 100 viable product concepts, then an entrepreneur arguably has 100 strategies to choose from. Which one of these 100 concepts is going to align precisely to the customer group's J2BD and most important 'value gap'?

The problem is that many entrepreneurs already have a product concept formed when they create their vision. This is absolutely natural and fine until the entrepreneur starts investing in building this product concept in the form of an MVP. This product-led approach is commonly known as '*product–market fit*'. When a product concept is committed to and is being built, then only tactical variations linked to its strategy become possible. It becomes increasingly difficult to align the product to any emerging early stage insights. It is quite easy for an entrepreneur to fall into a product-led mindset, confounded by the first question most potential stakeholders or investors ask: Can I see your product yet? Stakeholders naturally want to see the entrepreneur's product and to see if they can actually build a good product. But as we have explored in Chapters 6 and 7, what an entrepreneur really needs to understand, and ultimately any stakeholders, is where is the most attractive market opportunity (the most important 'value gap') that aligns with the entrepreneur's vision, passion and motivation?

'*Market–product fit*' is when an entrepreneur seeks to uncover an attractive market opportunity that aligns to his or her vision, passion and motivation. A product concept should emerge from the market opportunity rather than the vision. Chapters 6 and 7 advocate this 'market–product fit' enterprise design approach. The customer group, the J2BD and the most important 'value gap' are put first and the product definition is a secondary, next step. 'Market–product fit' reduces the likelihood that an entrepreneur becomes too invested in one product concept. It actively drives the entrepreneur to become heavily invested in the market, seek out the right customer J2BD and align the resulting marketing, product development and sales strategies to right customer group and the most important 'value gap'. Using a market-led approach, the entrepreneur's confirmation bias will be minimized and is far less likely to build the wrong product. We saw Frank Wang take this very approach with DJI: he began not with a drone concept, but a VP that would help photographers and videographers shoot aerially.

Building the product or feature set *wrong* is a slightly different problem. The product concept might be well aligned to the J2BD and 'value gaps' but the execution of the concept is poorly thought through. Maybe it has become too complicated and for most customers is oversimplified and missing critical functionality. Specifying the *right* product features is required, and early stage VP testing can help get to the right 'feature set' faster than by iterating the product *as it is being built.* Minimizing rework and discarding features that were built but then later discarded is a key tenet of building a lean start-up.

8.4. QUALITATIVE VERSUS QUANTITATIVE VP TESTING

Testing a VP is best done when using a combination of both qualitative and quantitative testing. Let us remind ourselves what testing aims to achieve.

Increase the likelihood that a specific early adopter group is known (an early adopter profile), and through a defined channel (or set of channels) the early adopter will take a desired VP action with minimal friction at the most profitable price point.

Qualitative testing's purpose is to get to the 'why' of a specific customer action or non-action, and the objections or acceptance they have towards the VP. It also helps to determine *why* a customer group might be an early adopter (or not).

The following seven questions guide the purpose of the qualitative VP testing phase:

1. What is the frequency, context and relevancy of the customers' J2BD to the VP?
2. How quickly and accurately did the customer understand the core VP?
3. How memorable was the customer facing message of the core VP?
4. Why did the customer take or not take the desired action?
5. How well does the VP pricing model fit the customer's WTP?
6. What would be an optimal MVP feature set for this specific customer?
7. Which channels the customer uses and through which of these would expect to discover the VP?

A quantitative VP test, on the other hand, should seek to quantify the critical insights established at the qualitative testing phase. Such testing will focus on specific identifiable metrics and use different variants of the VP message, core benefits, technology positioning, pricing model and so on. Using quantitative testing methods allows for larger sample of the target customer group to participate, but only a limited number of metrics can be tested. Understanding what the testing objectives are is critical to a successful test and understand how to improve the VP's performance.

The following questions provide a good initial guide directing the *quantitative* VP testing phase.

1. Which customers completed the desired VP action and which ones did not?
2. Which channel yielded the highest levels of interest?

3. Which channels yielded the highest number of converted actions?
4. Which VP variants of the message, core benefits, technology positioning, pricing model and so on performed best?

The Meituan Takeaway Mobile Application, China

Meituan takeaway is an online ordering platform in China. It is built on the Meituan network, a group purchase website of the Beijing Sankuai Online Technology Co. The platform was officially launched in November 2013, based on the online to offline (O2O) business model. Customers can download the Meituan app to their mobile phone and choose their favourite restaurant or café and place an order for delivery. In the past, customers ordering takeaway, could only place their orders via phone and pay cash on delivery. Meituan takeaway solves two problems with ordering takeaway: first, it provides a platform that can integrate a large number of takeaway restaurants' details and provide multiple choices to customers. Second, it allows online payments.

There were four iterations of the Meituan takeaway app as a result of customer testing (both takeaway restaurants and ordinary customers ordering food were its customers). Initially, developers produced a very simple website and an Android app for customers, without any facilities to register restaurants. Once a customer would place an order via the website or the app, the developers would call the restaurant on behalf of the ordering customer to place the order. This process required the restaurant staff to manually record the order's details. The developers were met with two problems during this trial testing phase; first, it became costly to manage the ordering process when a large proportion of Meituan's staff were busy calling restaurants to place orders. The second problem was that there were too many gaps between what the customer wanted to order and what the restaurant had available.

In order to solve these problems, Meituan developers developed an app for restaurants as well, using which they could capture more order details more precisely and quickly, direct from the ordering customer. To bypass the need for manual processing, the developers linked a printer to the app, which meant that once a customer would place an order on their Meituan app, a printer connected with the Meituan restaurant app would produce a strip of paper that included accurate information for the chefs.

With further testing, Meituan found out that the system was still not convenient enough for its restaurant customers. The developers started experimenting with cloud printing to replicate the functionality of a point-of-sale debit/credit card machine. Using this approach, a cloud printer, which would be much smaller than a traditional printer, would automatically print out an order's full details. This approach finally aligned well with Meituan's restaurant customers. At the end of their order-placing customers, during testing, Meituan discovered that they really valued quick delivery and to be able to track their order's progress. In order to introduce functionality to meet these customer jobs, Meituan decided to set up their own delivery teams. In this manner, they could provide real-time location-based tracking for customers.

The various iterations of the Meituan takeaway app highlights the value of direct customer testing, which allowed the developers to fine tune and routinely configure the VP (not the product), and in the process discover new unmet jobs (delivery tracking)—making the VP better with time.

8.5. A VP 'SMOKE TEST'

A VP 'smoke test' is a method of engaging a customer through believable marketing materials leading them to take a specific desired action, which even though the product is not built, and they were not aware of this fact when they took the action. It is a way to achieve early stage 'validated learning' and gather insights about what might stop a VP being accepted. It is also a great way to iterate, test and optimize your VP.

The most common type of VP smoke test is the 'landing page' smoke test. Let us consider Buffer—a social media management and post scheduling company. The success of Buffer all started with validated learning from a simple smoke test. Founder, Joel Gascoigne, explains that he actually started off the Buffer project by making the mistake of coding a product, before quickly realizing he needed customer validation on the VP first. Joel stated:

> *With my first start-up, I learned a huge amount about the principles (of Lean Startup) and I tried to implement them as much as I could. I found that practice is much harder than theory. I even started coding Buffer before I'd tested the viability of the business. As soon as I realised that, I stopped, took a deep breath and told myself: do it the right way this time. It was time to test whether people wanted this product. (Gascoigne 2019)*

Joel stopped building and started to put his plan together and test whether people actually wanted Buffer's VP. He built out a three-page landing website (see Figure 8.3). A landing page or site is a URL which serves as the entry point for a soon-to-be launched website. The first two were designed to test how motivated target customers were and if they would pay for the offer. Finally, the test ends on the 'smoke screen' which states: 'Hello! You caught us before we're ready'. It finishes with the final qualifying action 'remind me'. If a customer left their email address, they give permission for Buffer to reach out to them at a later date.

The result of Joel's Buffer VP test was that lots of people were providing him with their email address and a small number of these people were also clicking on paid plans. While this test could be improved, Joel had got valuable data on what percentage of vesting customers would use the service and what percentage would pay for automating twitter posts. His pricing hypothesis was that Buffer should be a freemium business model, a free plan with payment required for increased features or user activity and so on. Seven years later, Joel's test is still intact (Figure 8.4). A freemium model still exists although other segments can now be served with high demanding business now being catered for.

A quantitative VP smoke test like Buffer's can be conducted with minimal resources but it is important to stress that the communication needs to be refined and simple. To get to refined communication, most entrepreneurs will need to use a qualitative phase to improve and refine the message, pricing and the overall proposal.

FIGURE 8.3 Buffer VP Testing Landing Pages

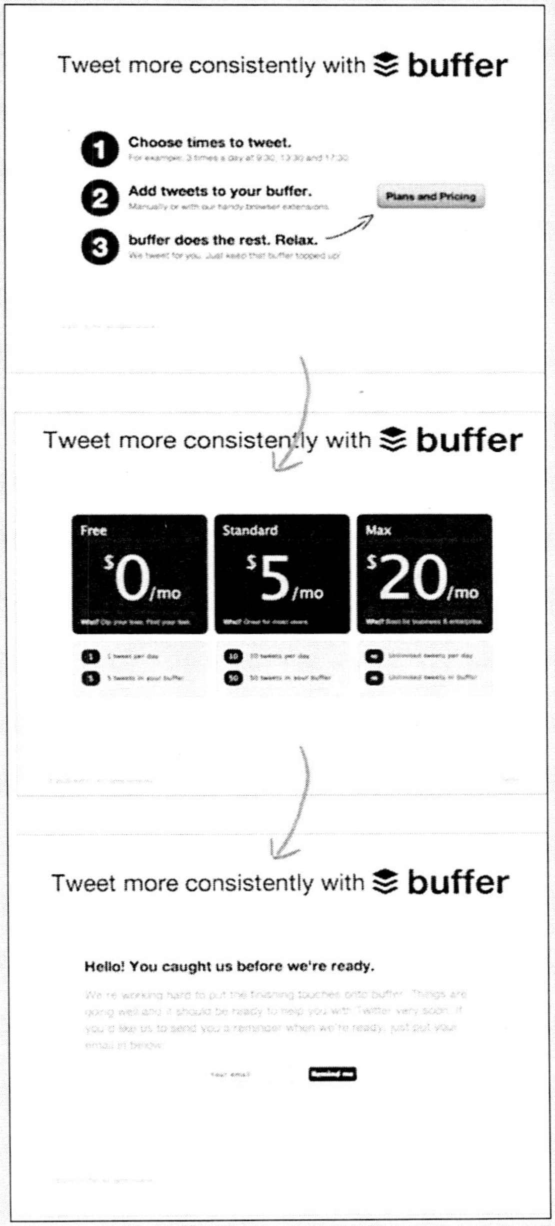

Source: Buffer.com (https://buffer.com/resources/idea-to-paying-customers-in-7-weeks-how-we-did-it; accessed on 14 June 2019).

FIGURE 8.4 **Buffer's Still Intact Freemium Model**

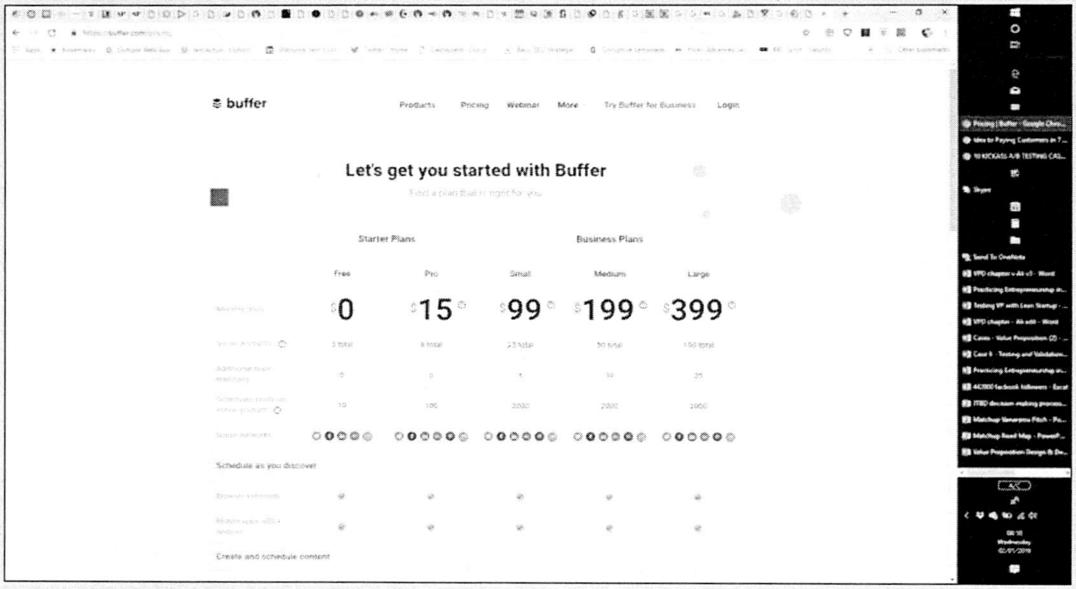

Source: Buffer.com (https://buffer.com/pricing accessed on 14 June 2019).

8.6. CONDUCTING A VP SMOKE TEST

For an entrepreneur to conduct an effective qualitative and quantitative VP smoke test, a structure for conducting and analysing test interviews would be required. The test will evolve from the interview phase towards more refinement in the second quantitative phase.

Designing a *qualitative* VP smoke test is always going to be an iterative task. It would be important to get your qualitative testing objectives clear by making sure you are addressing the key unanswered questions following your VP design process from Chapter 7. Start with a quick sketch, include your compelling, top three benefits and lead the participant into the first call to action. How many actions do you want the participant to take? How important is an image of the product to create trust? For software products, a quick mock-up image of the software illustrated on a desktop, tablet or smartphone may be enough. How else can you create trust in the proposition? Every proposition is different, some propositions will be very short and others will need to be longer to convey all the benefits. Sometimes a one-minute explainer video will do the job.

Once a plan and ideas for marketing material have emerged, some entrepreneurs may benefit from getting some professional input with their production. Consult with a professional designer or copywriter, get their input and suggestions for improving your content. Like with Buffer's case above, the opening landing page of the proposition needs to be understood quickly in as few words as possible. Look for examples of simple landing pages that have worked and seek inspiration from them.

Once the test is ready, it would be time to finalize the interview structure. The following provides a template for any qualitative VP testing.

1. **Recruit participants:** Identify six to eight members of customer group
2. **Schedule interview time:** 45 min to 1 hr (remember to record)
3. **Interview stage 1:** *Job discovery*
   - Validate the customer J2BD and gather info about the job frequency
   - Plot a solution decision map with the participant about when they struggled with the J2BD recently
4. **Interview stage 2:** *Conduct the test*
   - Present the test: Online through a website or mobile device
5. **Interview stage 3:** *Understand customer 'actions'*
   - Review the action taken
   - Reprocess the logic of the decision: Plot a progress making forces diagram
6. **Interview analysis**
   - Transcribe and code responses
   - Identify any correlation between J2BD attributes and action taken
   - Create a 'value gap' graphic
   - Create a product objections graphic
   - Create a product acceptance graphic

The interview process is often an exciting and engaging activity for both entrepreneur and participant. However, remember what the objectives are and stay focused on completing the analysis. This analysis is going to inform your objectives for a *quantitative* VP smoke test.

The quantitative phase is about measuring and quantifying the market. Review the data you want to collect from your participants. The following questions will help to guide your testing metrics:

1. Which customers completed the desired VP action and which ones did not?
2. Which channel yielded the highest levels of interest?
3. Which channels yielded the highest number of converted actions?
4. Which VP variants of the message, core benefits, technology positioning, pricing model and so on performed best?

In the Buffer example, it would have been good to know how many tweets are posted a day by all site visitors. Hence, focus on key data sets most likely to offer some correlation between the objections and acceptance graphics plotted after the smoke test interviews. Once the final quantitative test is set up, two more steps are required.

1. Identify a landing page testing tool integrated with an analytics tool that will collect and collate data.
2. Identify the channel or channels to present the landing page to the market.

There are many sophisticated but intuitive landing page testing tools like *Instapage* or *Unbounce*. From your original landing page, develop a test to meet your testing objective(s). Finally, the channel insights need to be harnessed from the interviews and some background research would be needed to understand how best to present your test to the target audience.

The quantitative results should, in most cases, become self-explanatory. However, it is important to have some guiding hypotheses around the business's viability in correlation with customers' WTP. Does the business viability hypotheses still stand up when the results of the test are considered? The result of the qualitative and quantitative tests are going to give you a barometer of how likely your VP would acquire early customers.

8.7. A 'SELL-BEFORE-YOU-BUILD' CAMPAIGN

Selling a product before it is built is generally a good idea. However, it is not risk free and requires substantial investment in marketing and presentation of a product that needs to have been carefully designed. This is the catch, while the product is not built yet, it requires significant investment in terms of feature scope, design and professional product visualization. Therefore, it is recommended that validation and VP optimization is firstly conducted through smoke testing, before committing to a selling-based campaign that requires investment in design and visualization of the product. A selling-based campaign emphasizes that the entrepreneur is focused on transacting with a customer rather than learning about and optimization of the VP. In the sell-before-you-build scheme, the scope for learning and re-scoping the VP becomes narrower and much more limited.

A 'sell-before-you-build' strategy de-risks a start-up that has validated its VP. Here is a comparison between a traditional seven steps to profit versus a pre-selling approach.

Traditional Approach:	1. Product idea 2. Prototype 3. Test 4. Build MVP 5. Launch 6. Ship 7. *Profit*
Sell-Before-You-Build:	1. Market gap 2. Test VP 3. Launch, 4. *Profit* 5. Build MVP 6. Ship

A pre-selling campaign is particularly important to start-ups that require significant capital investment to build a functional product (e.g., the Keexs spotlight case in Chapter 9). It may be too risky for investors to back as there is no proof of customer demand. Pre-selling addresses both these concerns, raises investment and provides proof of customer demand.

SECTION C

START-UP ENTERPRISE MANAGEMENT

9

Pitching to Potential Investors

LEARNING OUTCOMES

- Become familiar with main types of pitches and their structures
- Understand the requirements for preparing for a pitch
- Be able to deliver a convincing pitch to potential investors or stakeholders

9.1. WHAT ARE PITCHES?

Spotlight on Jide Ipaye, Nigerian Entrepreneur and Founder of an 'Innovative Social Footwear Brand'

Jide Ipaye is highly qualified with a PhD in microbiology and worked as a successful IT professional in Nigeria. However, he had the urge to do something totally different—he wanted to create stylish footwear for the youth. He was a shoe enthusiast himself, though, the options available to him were limited because of his shoe size—a size 48 (European). This meant, finding shoes that are the right size and fit was always difficult. He thought to himself, why not make bespoke shoes for not only myself, but for other youth who would value 'cool' and high-quality footwear in Nigeria. That is how Keexs, a unique Africa-inspired footwear brand was born. The brand name Keexs is a portmanteau between 'KICKS'—urban slang for sneakers or casual shoes with rubber soles and 'KEEK' which means to peep or glance. He began his journey by first investing in himself: he travelled to the Netherlands to attend a programme at SLEM, an international institute for footwear design where he learned how to make sneakers from scratch.

When the time came to launch his brand, he needed capital, which unfortunately he did not have of his own. To attract capital, in 2015, Jide teamed up with a friend, Moyosore Olowo, to create a story and pitch for the global crowd sourcing platform Kickstarter. Keexs's pitch on Kickstarter comprised of a video of Jide explaining his background and grand vision. This 3:45 clip conveys a number of powerful subliminal messages that resonated with African youth —his potential backers—such as creativity, dedication, self-sufficiency and initiative. He comes across as seasoned and confident, someone with integrity who could be relied upon to deliver on his commitments. His backers can ascertain these qualities when he makes statements like:

'We the citizens need to take more individual and collective initiatives towards correcting some of our social issues (economy and society) rather than sitting around complaining and waiting for our leaders to solve everything' (Jide lpaye).

The remainder of Keexs's pitch page has details on Jide's plans to create jobs and to give back to the community. His pitch was very successful, and £17,871 were raised from the backing of 72 individuals. This capital injection allowed him to produce the first batch of 1,200 sneakers that effectively launched the brand.

All entrepreneurs, without exception, will at some point in their new venture creation journey pitch their idea or solution to potential investors or other parties in a position to offer assistance. A pitch is an opportunity that allows an entrepreneur to sell (a) themselves (their candidature, skill set and experience) and (b) their 'idea' or 'solution' to individuals who are able to help in creating new value for what has been 'pitched'. The entrepreneur understands that coming up with an 'idea' or 'solution' is the first and somewhat easier stage in new venture creation; implementation is the much harder stage where without multidimensional help, chances of unanticipated problems becoming overwhelming are significantly higher. Consider alpinists (mountain climbers)—it is well known that a lot of preparation is made for climbing; however, most accidents, injuries and mortalities occur during descents. Climbing a mountain (or coming up with the idea/solution) is the easier stage, coming down alive and well from the summit to tell the story (implementation) is the much more difficult stage.

Pitching allows entrepreneurs to attract the help they need for taking their idea/solution forward to implementation. Help needed might include monetary input, advice, a need for mentoring, connections to other resourceful parties, perhaps access to facilities (such as inexpensive or free office space, use of a commercial kitchen or a booth in an existing shop) or a combination of these. Seasoned entrepreneurs understand that to win over the help they need, it is important to put themselves in the shoes of their potential investors. A key assumption they hold is that such individuals are 'gate keepers' and are 'self-interested'. Investors invest, monetarily and also with their time, expertise, experience and connections, because they are looking to multiply by many folds their original investment. They think about their 'exit' from the 'deal' they make with an investee right from the very onset. They do not wish to tie their original investment for an indefinite amount of time. The term of the investment is usually two–three years after which they expect to not only get their original sums back but also exit with a considerable mark-up. In addition to being self-interested, they are also 'loss averse'—the idea of losing their original sums invested is a lot more worrying than the *potential* utility or satisfaction from future gains. Hence, for investors, making the investment decision is quite difficult because it is fraught with uncertainty (whether gains in the future will be made or not) and risk of losing the original investment (and potentially other adverse impacts, like a loss of reputation).

Therefore, an entrepreneur vying to attract investment, in preparing for their pitch, should consider the following questions: How does the investor benefit in the short, medium or long term by investing in me? Why would it be worthwhile for them to take any risk to support me? And what gains can they make as a result of investing in me and my idea/solution? Investors ultimately want to make a 'deal'; however, it is the pitching entrepreneur's responsibility to allow deal-making to occur by presenting well-reasoned and believable answers to the aforementioned questions. Serious effort ought to be made to think about answers to these questions and to prepare for their delivery in a variety of scenarios.

Pitches can be impromptu or formally organized; in some instances, the entrepreneur might serendipitously find themselves seated next to a potential investor on an airplane or be introduced to one at a function. The window of opportunity might be wide open or very narrow; being opportunity obsessed, the consummate entrepreneur will always have their idea's pitch ready-to-deliver, practised and even memorized for an impactful, emotive and theatrical delivery that builds rapport draws in the interest of potential investors for a more formal pitching opportunity in the future.

9.2. THE ELEVATOR PITCH

Pitching is an important event in any new venture creation journey and its good execution could result in the opening of previously locked doors for the entrepreneur. Therefore, it must be taken very seriously, which means preparedness is vital. Some pitching opportunities are via invitation, for example, being shortlisted at a business plan competition or contact initiated by investors themselves. Mostly though, serious pitching opportunities need to be created by the entrepreneur by reaching out to potential investors and/or other parties (even the public at large, e.g., crowdsourced finance). To create the formal pitching opportunity, ironically, entrepreneurs need to first pitch—this initial pitch is called the 'elevator pitch'. This pitch could be via email, a message on a social media platform or a planned/chance face-to-face conversation.

For example, imagine the scenario: You are Jide Ipaye (whom we met in our spot light case) desperately seeking an investor's input without which Keexs may never come into existence; by chance whilst queuing for coffee at the airport you notice that the person in front of you in the queue is Jason Njoku (a prominent Nigerian technology entrepreneur and investor)—there are only three other people in front of him, you have perhaps 30 seconds to say something to him to grasp his attention, after which he would be at the top of the queue, purchase his coffee and walk away. What you say to him in this short span of time to get him interested in you and your idea/solution is deemed your 'elevator pitch' (the amount of time an elevator takes to move from floor to floor) and it is fundamental that would-be entrepreneurs always have one ready and prepared with them.

Preparing an elevator pitch requires the iterative refinement of thinking until the time one can say something intelligent and interesting in a short sentence. Rather than Jide saying 'I am a shoe designer who wants to launch a new African-inspired shoe brand', to which an investor might turn around and say 'so what?'; Jide could instead say 'I have created shoes that make older people feel youthful and the youthful feel more fashionable'. Consider a few other examples: rather than saying 'I have developed a new program to defragment RAID disc drives', saying 'My idea makes computers twice as efficient, and five times as powerful' is a lot more succinct and attention grabbing because it moves away from 'what the idea is' to 'what it can do'—which is what investors are interested in. If you have written a brilliant novel and are pitching to a publisher, you could say 'The story explores 20 something angst in the digital age'. If your solution improves existing anti-lock brake algorithms, then simply saying 'It improves automobile safety' will help communicate benefits quickly and without the use of technical jargon.

Elevator Pitch Format

Imagine the graphic below to be buttons in an elevator; where each floor presents an opportunity to deliver an aspect of your pitch. Starting from level 1, craft your responses and refine them in a manner such that they are succinct and impactful. Practise your delivery in front of a mirror and then in front of friends or colleagues, taking their feedback on board to perfect your 'elevator pitch' before delivery.

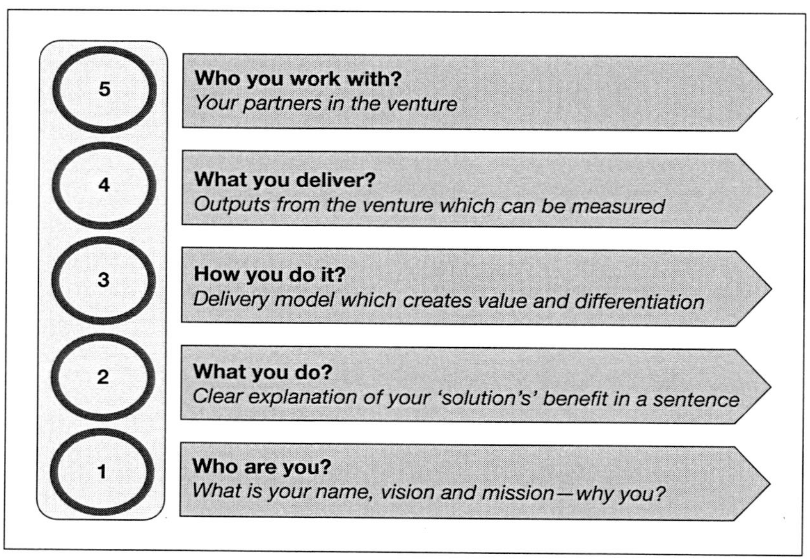

9.3. PREPARING FOR THE FORMAL PITCH

Based on their appeal in the elevator pitch, an entrepreneur might be invited to deliver a formal 'short-form' or 'long-form' pitch. The difference between these two pitch types lies primarily in the duration (but also in a less pronounced way—its content). Whereas, the short-form pitch is between 5 and 10 minutes, the long form lasts between 15 and 20 minutes. Both are followed by a session of question and answers.

Format of Formal Pitches as Seen on TV Shows

Dragon's Den (Kenya)

Shark Tank (Mexico)

Preparation for these formal pitches is crucial, which include (a) the compilation of content investors would need to make an informed investment decision; and (b) practising a confident and seamless delivery of such content. Both areas of preparation present different challenges. The content of your pitch should cover the following suggested areas[1]:

1. **Venture's identity:** Such as its logo and slogan; a good colour scheme and design along with a catchy phrase can add considerable appeal to your pitch and cast a positive impression right from the start.
2. **Business overview:** A brief explanation of what problem the venture aims to solve, and its VP—what specifically makes your venture better than other incumbents, and why. A timeline of progress to date can also be added here. The purpose here is to show investors that you have carefully thought about your venture's VP and that it has evolved through a process of trial and error over time; that it is not a bare bones idea that you have conjured up.
3. **Core team:** Photos and brief resume snapshots to showcase the talent you have attracted to your enterprise to make it a success. Investors know that new ventures need

[1] David S. Rose's presentation at the TED Conference on '10 Things to Know before You Pitch a VC for Investment' hosted on YouTube is acknowledged as an inspiration for the content in this chapter.

to be developed by not just one but a team of individuals who bring a variety of backgrounds, expertise and experience. The profiles of your core team must give investors the confidence that you have the right individuals supporting you and that they are committed to the success of the new venture.

4. **Market research:** Using data visualization and snippets of information describe the research you have undertaken yourself (primary research) and that which has been published (secondary research) to make the case for the market for your 'solution', estimate its size and potential. Your research should breakdown the 'problem' your potential customers face and as to what losses in productivity it leads to. The research's conclusions should be robust and believable. It should leave no doubts in the investors' minds that your venture, should it succeed, has the potential to unlock untapped new market potential.
5. **Solution:** Investors would want to know if you were 'reinvesting the wheel' or simply copying what already exists. Explain how the core offering solves a known 'problem' and how well does it do it, in other words, what are its performance metrics. To do this append photos or screenshots, especially of potential customers using the 'solution' to help bolster your claims. Good aesthetics in design will create a favourable impression. Essential here will be third-party validation. Why should investors believe what you have to say? They have no reason to —they do not know you personally, no historical relation would usually exist, and if it does, an investor might excuse themselves from the pitching citing 'conflict of interest'. Third-party validation—independent tests conducted on your solution by industry experts or agencies (like your country's National Testing Agency) to validate your claims or reviews by prominent potential customers—will afford your pitch credibility, and its value must not be underestimated.
6. **Business model:** How will the new venture generate value? This could be monetary value or other forms of value such as 'scale' or 'traction' (e.g., number of users registered on an online platform or a phone app). Overly complicated business models, with multiple lock-step stages and those reliant on too many externalities (e.g., seasonal demand) will confuse and ultimately put off investors. Think carefully about simplification (removing unnecessary stages to delivery) without slipping into over-simplification—which would be construed as lack of tact and nuance on your part.
7. **Strategic relationships:** Describe the nature of the key relationships you have built to enable the delivery of your 'solution'. Highlight the salient features of your agreements, for example, its term and respective roles and responsibilities. These relationships could be with a potential first customer who helped you test your solution and is now ready to use it; a supplier who can ensure timely delivery of a key component or ingredient or a delivery agency who have a good track record. Investors will recognize and appreciate the value of such relationships and you in turn will demonstrate commercial insight.
8. **Competition:** There will be a need to highlight which existing players in your industry and their competing 'solutions' would most likely create barriers of your market entry. There will be a need at your end to demonstrate foresight of their likely manoeuvres and your counter strategies to protect your commercial interests. Investors would like to know whether you have any clear strategic advantages over your competitors, who they would expect to do all they can to protect their own business and damage yours—such is the nature of market places. Investors would feel confident in a pitch if the entrepreneur demonstrates the ability to absorb competitive pressure, while pushing forward to claim their space in the market.

9. **Barriers to entry:** To judge the likelihood of your venture's success, investors would want to know if there are any significant hurdles ahead of you. For example, in certain industries (e.g., aviation, construction, pharmaceuticals) requisite government licenses are needed to legally operate. Acquiring such licenses can be a time-consuming and at times an expensive process, which does not always lead to the successful award of a license. Other barriers might include the need for heavy investment in marketing to create public awareness or privileged access to information (like citizens' personal medical records). You must be forthright and carefully think about all the important barriers that might hinder your venture's progress and cite these in the pitch along with your strategy to overcome them in due course. You can ask for the investors' help in overcoming some of these as well.
10. **Financial overview:** Ultimately, investors invest to derive returns and profitably exit from the deal they make with you (if they choose to). Explaining the upside (or the profit-making potential of your venture) will be fundamental to get investors excited about your offering and making an investment. Do this by citing sales projections and other (believable and achievable) figures such as numbers of new customers acquired and average sales volume per customer. Usually, a three-year sales projection is expected, with profit volumes and margins increasing year on year. Providing a return on investment calculation to the investors is also beneficial; in other words, should they choose to invest in your venture, by when can they expect to get their original sum back. Being realistic is very important; investors are business savvy individuals and can easily detect if the pitching entrepreneur is making up figures as they go along or offering commitments (s) he would not be able to fulfil.
11. **Use of proceeds:** A carefully thought out plan to highlight how the sums invested will be used must be shared. Investors would want to know if you are using their investment to pay yourself a hefty salary and buy yourself a car (not advisable) or would it be used to fund the development of the venture in such a way that their investment leads to the unlocking of new value. Highlight the specific areas where sums need to be invested; for example, in the purchase of specific assets (e.g., dry-cleaning machines, specialized software, tools), promotional activities, R&D, working capital (WC) and so on.
12. **Capital and valuation:** Finally, close by explaining the existing capital structure of the business and how much do you believe it is worth today (its valuation) and how much of it are you selling off to the investors. The capital structure should highlight your own investment and the investment of any other individual in the business to date. If you have no investment in the business, investors might object under the rationale: Why should we be asked to invest in a venture in which the pitching entrepreneur does not have confidence to invest themselves? If the entrepreneur has no capital investments made, investors feel that they take on the additional risk of the entrepreneur 'giving up' and exiting from the deal when difficult challenges arise in the future because they (the entrepreneur) have nothing monetary to lose should the venture fail. The valuation must be reasonable and based on justifiable grounds, such as IP, specialist expertise, and/or future sales potential based on past performance or existing deals (or orders) underway. Investors do not like being pitched an inflated valuation because ultimately that raises the cost per share that you are offering to them for buying in your venture.

Usually, formal pitches are facilitated by visual aids such as a Microsoft PowerPoint slide deck or a Prezi slideshow and props—your venture's merchandise, a product(s) display, artists' impressions or physical models. The quality and effort put on these will be judged by the investors and inconsistencies or oversights will give the wrong impression. Entrepreneurs should be prepared to invest between a 60 and 100 hours of time in preparing for a formal 15–20-minute pitch.

9.4. DOING THE FORMAL PITCH

A seamless and convincing delivery of the prepared content can mean the difference between attracting investment or being rejected by investors. The delivery task must not be underestimated; whereas, the content (described in the previous section) represents the tangible and verifiable aspects of the 'solution' being pitched, but such content does not provide information on the much-needed intangible and difficult-to-verify qualities in the 'person' behind the solution. Investors are actively judging both the 'solution' and the 'person'. It should be noted; judging the value of the 'solution' is easier for investors because of the ability of the entrepreneur to sign post investors to 'facts' and 'data' that support their claims, and also how such claims can be double-checked. However, convincing investors, in 15–20 minutes during a formal pitch, that an individual has the full range of qualities needed in a person that could multiply investments is, needless to say, quite difficult. Investors invest in 'solutions', but also 'individuals'—the solution being pitched is meaningless without the person behind it having the ability to take it forward and to make it a success.

Investors 'invest in people' with certain qualities. One cannot, realistically speaking, stand in front of a panel of investors and claim to possess these qualities, for example, say 'I am very *passionate*'. Anyone (with or without credentials) can make such a claim about themselves—who knows whether it is true or not. Therefore, such claims become clichés which in turn cannot be taken seriously. What is expected is that entrepreneurs 'show' passion in the time that they have in their pitch. This then becomes a content delivery problem; how does one 'show' passion to unacquainted individuals? Like passion, all the qualities investors are looking for (highlighted further), need to be demonstrated via non-verbal communication skills and using carefully selected examples that are relayed during critical junctures during the pitch. The pitch then becomes a carefully orchestrated and well-rehearsed theatrical performance.

Entrepreneurs must realize that when they enter the room where the pitch is taking place, the investors already seated there know nothing (or not very much) about them. You have about 10–20 seconds to gain their attention—and this can be done by starting the pitch with a neatly honed story, allowing the building of rapport quickly. Remember: it is your job to build rapport, not the investors. The pitch necessarily needs to have emotional highs and lows; however, everything that is said needs to elevate the energy level in the room and reinforce points already made, culminating in a final 'knock-out' close.

Provided further are the qualities that must be 'demonstrated' to entrepreneurs during the pitch.

1. **Integrity:** The single most important quality any investor is looking for in an entrepreneur is 'integrity'. They must know by the end of the pitch that the person in front of them is 'honest' and 'reliable' and that (s)he would look after their investors' interests; in fact, put the investors' interests before their own. They need to be sure that

you are the person who is going to remain committed to delivering on their promises, be honourable and uphold the highest standards of ethics in their dealings. Be fair and not end up in a situation which would harm reputations—the damage which is sometimes irreparable. Not disappear with their investment or try and cheat them out from future gains in value. If they remain unconvinced about your integrity, you could be pitching the next wonder gadget like a motor that runs perpetually without electricity, they will certainly not invest.

To demonstrate integrity, clearly say that you believe in professionalism and have had a strong upbringing right from schooling where principles discerning right from wrong were deeply imprinted on to your moral compass. Highlight any incidents in the past where you had the opportunity to take unfair advantage but did not or exposed foul play at work. You can say that 'I have never been accused of perjury or fraud and take my reputation and that of my investors very seriously'.

2. **Passion:** Being passionate is important because it is passion about and true belief in the value of the pitched solution that will make an entrepreneur take personal risks, work 16–18 hours a day, perhaps 7 days a week for a year or even more to make the venture a success. If the pitching entrepreneur does not show passion, why would the investors feel passionate about what is being pitched? Like some other social qualities, passion is infectious, it is contagious and can spread provided the initial vector/contagion (the entrepreneur) is energetic enough. Investors want to see if you have the right amount of passionate energy needed to go beyond the call of duty to make the venture a success and in the process multiply the net worth of their investments.

   Passion can be shown by an upward modulation of your voice along with strong eye contact when speaking about your background and the unique qualities of your solution. Explain how you truly believe in the merits of your solution and the way it can make a difference. Highlight examples from your past when you showed passion for something; it could be as simple as the desire to learn a new language or play a musical instrument or when you took initiative to correct, what you felt was a wrong, for example, lobbied your college administration to improve facilities for female students.

3. **Experience:** Investors want to know if you have relevant industry and work experience. If you have never worked in a restaurant before and you are pitching for investment in a new culinary venture, then very rightfully, investors will have serious doubts about your ability to set up and run one successfully. When one has had no experience and is doing something for the first time, then they are very likely to make mistakes, some of which might be very costly; and investors do not appreciate the idea of entrepreneurs making easily avoidable commercial mistakes with their money. You need to be able to claim with confidence that you know what it means to hire good employees and train them, to instruct accountant and legal professionals, to chase after creditors, to negotiate with customers and to deal with unscrupulous individuals who might want to exploit your success.

   It would be ideal if you have prior industry or business start-up experience before making a formal pitch for investment. Develop specific examples (by writing them down) from your professional and academic career where you successfully led a team, dealt with conflict, undertook a commercial negotiation, produced written communication and so on—aspects that you believe demonstrate your abilities as a future successful entrepreneur.

4. **Knowledge:** It would concern investors if an entrepreneur does not demonstrate general and specific knowledge on the industry and market in which their new venture would be embedded. Consider for example, an entrepreneur pitching to attract investment for a commercial real estate-based venture and is asked a question about recently announced regulation which requires real estate developers to undertake detailed environmental impact assessments as a part of the building control authority's approvals process. If the entrepreneur is not aware or does not fully comprehend the impact of this new regulation on the future performance of their new venture, they will demonstrate a lack of necessary knowledge. Not only are entrepreneurs expected to know their industry's and market's dynamics very well (such as size, growth, regulatory pressures and industrial associations), but also possess unique insights into market gaps and new opportunities in the industry that existing players would find it difficult to capitalize on.

   Demonstrate knowledge proactively by citing latest developments. This could be done by posing questions: 'I wonder if you saw the Minister of Environment's speech last night?' Wait for a response and continue along lines of: 'I believe the anticipated changes she announced in the approvals process are likely to lead to new opportunities in environmental consulting'.

5. **Skill:** The entrepreneur must possess the skills necessary to deliver the core service. Investors will lose faith in an entrepreneur, who for example, is pitching for a business based around running after-school football clubs for teenagers, if they themselves are not accomplished football players or trained coaches with an excellent track record (perhaps having won regional or national accolades in a recognized competition). An entrepreneur who is not skilled cannot be expected to ensure service quality or be expected to properly instruct and monitor those working for them. Investors will come to the conclusion that if you are not an accomplished coach yourself, how can you be expected to ensure that the coaches you employ are doing their best and servicing your clients professionally? What if, on a particular day when an employee coach is absent, can you take his place and run the club to a good standard?

   If you have created works of art, written software or are an expert in farming silk from worms and such skills are linked to your business, evidence it via photos and statements of praise made by your peers and mentors about the quality of your skill set. For evidencing general management skills, LinkedIn endorsements can be a helpful guide for investors to get third-party validation to confirm whether you are as skilled as you claim to be.

6. **Leadership:** An entrepreneur should be able to command the respect of their employees and shareholders and have external parties take them seriously. Investors would want to know whether you have the strength of character to deal with internal crises, which can manifest themselves unpredictably during the pre-start-up and start-up phases of new venture creation. They will be thinking to themselves, does this individual know what it means to deal with 'troublemakers', or when (s)he might face a sudden cash crunch, would they be able to make difficult decisions in time like letting go of employees. Do they have the psychological and emotional strength to put up a brave front in the face of serious problems (e.g., a large amount of customer returns due to product defects) and

take steps to ensure that they secure our investments? During the pitch, investors will be looking at your demeanour carefully, signs of nervousness and a show of low confidence in your responses will cast doubts in their mind about your ability to lead by example.

To reassure investors, highlight the times where you have faced adversity or difficult challenges and the way you resolved them. If you have taken a commanding role in the past, for example, won a college election or were nominated as president of a student society—speak about it candidly and explain that you felt comfortable and ready to take decisions on behalf of others after having held consultations to drive your agenda forward.

7. **Commitment:** A fervent concern for investors, when parting with their hard-earned residuals, are the thoughts: 'Is this investee, when the going gets tough, going to walk away and leave us in the lurch?'; 'Are they doing this just for a bit of fun on the side?' Investors want to feel confident that you will remain 100 per cent committed to the new venture and dedicate your full energies and potentials to make it a success. This means no distractions are allowed—which includes family commitments unfortunately. The amount of time and energy commitment needed for new venture success is phenomenal and if it is revealed during the pitch that the entrepreneur aims to run the new venture part-time after work hours and during the weekends, investors will instantly put off and are likely to immediately withdraw from discussions. If the entrepreneur is the primary carer for a disabled life partner or a parent, for example, their ability, once again, to offer the level of commitment needed to ensure the success of the new venture will be significantly diminished. Investors want to get the comfort that you will dedicate your fullest potential and energies, without any distractions, to the venture and that there are no distractions in your professional (like a lingering law suit) or personal life that could hamstring your ability to do so.

   During the pitch, highlight the amount of time and energy you have already dedicated to the pre-start-up trial and error phase. Make clear statements about your intent, be truthful and authentic, and claim that you are at a juncture in your life where you have the energy and mental space to dedicate yourself fully to the success of the new venture.

8. **Vision:** You should tell investors what your ultimate goal is for the new venture. They would want to know the scale and scope of your vision, is it only a single outlet, a city-wide chain or a national franchise. Are they investing in one artisanal bakery with potential revenues in the hundreds of thousands or a national chain with potential revenues in the millions? Investors invest to multiply their original investments. What gets them interested is the potential for future growth in the venture they are putting their hard earned cash in. You will have to help them envision what the new venture might become in three years and then five and beyond. A lack of a clear and attractive vision at the end of the entrepreneur will signal a lack of ambition and imagination; and investors understand that for the entrepreneur to keep their commitment levels high throughout the start-up-growth-scaling phases of a venture—a vision for what things might be is essential.

   Think carefully about your vision for the new venture and say it with confidence; use statements such as 'I believe' and 'I know' to ground yourself and take the investors on a mental journey through storytelling. For example, you could begin along the lines of 'Imagine yourself in 2025, and you are wanting to order a birthday cake for your best friend, the only name that comes to mind is my brand, you see the logo flash in your mind—you walk into one of our 50 outlets across the country, you are greeted by the manager, dressed in….' The rich detail you can add to the story, by adding descriptions of taste, sound and feel, can make the visioning exercise quite sensory for the investors. Remember: the investors are there to listen to what you have to say, and what you say needs to be interesting and memorable otherwise why would they remember it. Stories, out of all narrative forms, are the most memorable—practise telling your vision story prior to the pitch.

9. **Realism:** Investors are drawn to entrepreneurs who might have their heads in the clouds, but their feet firmly planted on the ground. They are wary of individuals who overcommit and underdeliver, and during the pitch, they will be paying attention to any verbal or non-verbal cues you put out on their 'over confidence' radar. Realism on the part of the entrepreneur investors invest in is important because it tells them that their agent will remain pragmatic and understand the real-world consequences of their actions and decisions. Realism is important for anticipating 'blowback', which are unintended consequences (the way medicines have unwanted side effects) emerging from any action. For example, if in a pitch an entrepreneur makes a statement 'The dating app I have designed will take majority market share in just one year and become bigger than Tinder—the market leader', investors would see this as unrealistic, a mere 'pipe dream'. There is a fine line between being visionary and ambitious and being quixotic. By being realistic entrepreneurs can give investors the confidence that they have the ability to set the correct pace of work, account for externalities and build contingency plans.

   To show realism, during the pitch acknowledge which factors have the potential, if left unchecked, to become limitations, what could potentially go wrong, under what conditions your plan may not work, and what contingencies have you built in your implementation strategy that will counter act against any 'worst case scenarios'.

10. **Coachability:** The final important quality investors look for in entrepreneurs is the ability to listen to and take the investors' advice on board. When investors put in money into a new venture, they do want to have some say in its development. They want to be able to positively intervene when the entrepreneur is about to make an expensive mistake. A majority of investors have been entrepreneurs themselves at some stage and believe that along with their investment they bring valuable connections, real-world experience and industry know-how to the investment mix. They do want to be able to 'mentor' the entrepreneur such that not only venture failure or losses could be prevented but that their investment—the new venture—grows quickly and sustainably. However, if they detect hesitation on the part of the entrepreneur to receive advice and to follow it, then they develop the necessary impression that the entrepreneur might be a 'rigid' or an 'uncoachable' individual. This means (s)he would be hard to work with—and no investor would want to have the trouble of dealing with an individual who refuses to listen to good advice when they need it the most.

Coachability can be shown by you proactively seeking the investors' assistance beyond the sums they put into your venture. If you are able to, research their backgrounds prior to the pitch and see what kinds of industries they have been a part of and what types of ventures are a part of their existing investment portfolio. Drawing on this information, you could make specific requests for assistance. For example, if you have developed a new range of frozen ready-made meals and want these stocked and sold at a large super market chain, then anticipate that you will have difficulty in setting up meetings with the procurement manager of this chain. Without pointing specifically to an investor in the panel (because doing so might alienate other investors) you could say that 'My taste trials have shown that people love my ready-made meals but the difficulty I am having is connections—if I could be introduced by a reputable person in the XYZ chain, then I am confident that I can get them to agree to stock my products—even if on a trial basis'.

To sum up, remaining true to the theatrical spirit of the pitch being propounded in this section, remain authentic and not utter things that are simply not true. If you are caught telling a lie or misquoting figures, you might not be found out then but it could happen after the pitch. Maintain eye contact and use Microsoft PowerPoint's 'Presentation Mode' to avoid having to look back at the slides. Do not read from the slides at any cost. No slide, as a rule should have more than four–five bullet points—better no text at all, instead images. Remember: the focus must remain on you; the investors should be looking at *you* and not the slides so they can judge the above non-tangible qualities.

Contrasting Presentation Styles

Bill Gates Presenting: Notice the Busy Slide

Steve Jobs Presenting: No Slides, Total Focus on Him

Avoid technical language with acronyms and jargon; the rule is to 'walk the investors through the pitch like 6th graders without being patronizing'. By using jargon, you would necessarily make them pause and think, which means that they would stop listening to you and start processing what you have just said, disrupting the pitch's flow in their minds. Avoid internal inconsistencies; for example, use standard units of measure and currency, stating figures in Saudi Riyal on one slide and Chinese Renminbi on another will cause irritation—because it might require investors to undertake mental arithmetic for currency conversion. Finally, review, re-review and re-re-review your materials for typographical or syntax errors because these will denote unpreparedness. If you show that you are incapable of doing a pitch properly, then how can you expect investors to believe that you are capable of running a new venture.

9.5. PITCHING ONLINE

Crowdsourcing platforms like Kickstarter.com are rapidly emerging in developing and emerging economies and new entrepreneurs can use these to pitch their idea to the 'crowd'. Each platform tends to operate under their own set of rules—the important thing to check before posting your pitch on any platform is to check the level of commission you will be asked to pay for your listing. The aspects discussed in the previous two sections also apply to pitching online—a considerable amount of preparatory work is needed to ensure that you raise your target funding. If you fail to achieve your target funding amount in a stipulated time period, then your pitch is deemed unsuccessful and is archived. Do your research on local and regional crowdsourcing platforms and check their track records, the number of backers registered and the average amount of funding raised. Especially, look at the pitches of the 'successful' posters.

Example Crowdsourcing Platforms in Developing and Emerging Economies

1. www.ideas.me: Latin America's crowdsourcing platform
2. www.indiegogo.com: Jumpstart Africa
3. www.fundstart.vn: Crowdsourcing in Vietnam
4. www.catapooolt.com: India's largest crowdsourcing platform

A number of elements worked in favour of Jide Ipaye when he pitched Keexs on Kickstarter. First, the quality of his promotional video—it was emotive, clearly spelled out the benefits of his product, described his background and vision and also put forth a socially conscious business ethos that went beyond the traditional profit motive. Second, the clarity of the narrative—information was presented succinctly and through the use of visual aids, it was personal and relatable and gave confidence to the backers about the genuine intent of the pitcher. Third, the promise of good rewards and recognition—a range of promised rewards to backers who pledged amounts in increasing amounts of value helps to generate interest. Fourth, Jide took out time to thank all his backers, irrespective of their pledged amount which generated viral interest. Finally, the pitch page was promoted beyond Kickstarter in the local press, via podcasts, bloggers, Instagrammers and other social media 'influencers' which drew in interest from Nigerian and other backers from around the world.

Remember: while creating the content for your online pitch, follow the guidelines in the previous two sections. Before you make your pitch 'live' on the platform of your choice, invite your colleagues to critically review your pitch and give feedback. It would be a good idea to also invite potential backers via social media requests who do not know you personally to undertake a review. Doing this will help—because once your listing goes 'live' you are not usually allowed to make changes to your content. If the pitch is unsuccessful on the first-choice platform, then it would be hard to get a listing on other platforms—because platforms are not interested in hosting pitches that are likely to fail (and have failed prior), doing so is risky, a repeat failure can negatively impact their reputations and performance statistics. Hence, it is important to get your pitch 'as right as possible' the *first time*, which is why it is being recommended that considerable pains be taken in its refinement prior to posting. World famous architect Frank Lloyd Wright once stated: 'You can take an eraser to the drafting table, or a sledge hammer to the construction site'. It is far simpler to make refinements and adjustments at the planning stage, but once you have built something then refining it would be quite costly and time-consuming. In this manner, once your live pitch is viewed and then you realize that mistakes have been made based on the comments you receive from potential backers, then regrettably, it might be too late to make changes.

9.6. SUMMARY AND APPLICATION

Pitching is an aspect of communication—which is an important enterprise skill (described in Chapter 1). By keeping the investors' view point at the fore, basing your preparation on the twin aspects of the 'idea' and 'you—the person behind the idea' and practising your delivery—provided that you have successfully tested and validated the idea—you are likely to succeed in attracting investment. Investors are always on the lookout for the 'next big idea' that they can back and cash on. They understand that not all of their investments are going to be 'hits'; in fact, research suggests that only 1 out of 25 venture capital backed investments leads to a successful 'exit'. This makes savvy investors very wary of 'cowboy entrepreneurs' and they use a whole variety of cognitive filters to pick up on and take apart information snippets relayed to them in pitches. Hence, in a pitch, you do have to present yourself and your idea as 'the total package'—a bulletproof case with such intuitive appeal that investors cannot wait for the pitch to end so that they can hand over their cash to you. To get investors to empty their pockets and to fill yours, you will need every ounce of your talent and apply all the learning from this chapter in your preparation and delivery. Be prepared to answer penetrating questions after the pitch. If you are asked the question: 'What will be your profit at the end of years 1, 2 and 3?', then investors will expect an answer quickly and without hesitation. If you can do this, then you will demonstrate both passion and knowledge. However, if you respond along the lines of 'Sorry! I do not remember the figures right now, I will have to speak to my friend who created the financial projections', then investors will develop concerns about your level of preparedness. Remember: investors have ample choices, there are hundreds if not thousands of aspiring entrepreneurs looking for their investment—if you have not adequately prepared to respond to their questions, then they have other options and can simply move on to the next entrepreneur in the queue. A good way to anticipate investors' questions is by watching clips of successful pitches on TV shows like *Dragon's Den* and its counterparts televised in various countries around the world. Watch as many pitches as you can and take note of the line of questioning by investors at the end of the pitch. Write down the 10 most frequently asked questions and rehearse your responses to these.

Pitching can also be done online; practise script writing, filming and video and sound editing skills, all of which should convince potential backers to pledge support. The best way to understand what might draw backers to your pitch page out of the hundreds live on the platform, is to put yourself in the backers' position and carefully look through the existing listings—which ones appeal to you to the extent that you would be willing to pledge cash to back them? Learn from their listings and attempt to mimic their most attractive elements—be careful not to wholly imitate, remain original while drawing inspiration. The last thing you want is potential backers accusing you of plagiarism.

Exercise 9.1. Watch between 8 and 10 pitches aired on famous TV shows like *Dragon's Den*. Take notes on the entrepreneurs' demeanour and the content covered. Pause the video after the pitch is complete and attempt to anticipate the investors' line of questioning. List down four–five questions you would want to ask the entrepreneur. Next, play the video again and follow the investors' line of questioning and assess the quality of the entrepreneur's responses. Did the entrepreneur secure the investment? If they did, then note down the reasons why. If not, what do you believe they could have done to secure investment?

Exercise 9.2. Practise creating a dummy pitch page for a crowdsourcing platform. With your business partners'/friends' help create a snapshot of your idea by writing a script for two–three minutes video promo. Watching promo videos hosted on various crowdsourcing platforms will be beneficial. Create the visualizations other successfully backed pitch pages contain. When writing the accompanying narrative, attempt to make it personal, ambitious and add a social dimension to idea. Next, either film yourself or direct the filming of original footage and use video and sound editing software to refine and clip the footage together. Add captions; perhaps even a translation in your local language. Once complete, showcase the developed promo to your classmates and get candid feedback on how many of those who watched video would like to pledge support.

10

Sales and Sales Management

LEARNING OUTCOMES

- Understand the various stages of the customer journey
- Become familiar with the design of a marketing communication and advertising campaign
- Be able to develop a sales strategy

10.1. DEVELOPING SALES SKILLS

Spotlight on Dong Nguyen, the Creator of the Mobile Game Flappy Bird

Dong Nguyen from Vietnam designed and published the immensely popular game Flappy Bird on the Apple iOS App Store in 2013. In the first eight months, his game did not attract much attention—it was one of the millions of applications on the App Store. However, by the end of 2013, Flappy Bird was ranked 74 in the App Store's 'Family' category and by January 2014, the game was one of the 10 most downloaded free apps in America and sixth most downloaded free game. The app's performance and popularity shocked not only mobile game players, but the tech world when it became the most popular App Store download in 53 countries one month later that year. Flappy Bird was reportedly earning Dong up to $50,000 per day, which was substantial for a young graduate student. The question to ask is: Why did Flappy Bird, an obscure game from an unknown developer in Vietnam, become so popular?

Dong became interested in coding at 16, he then proceeded to study computer science at the Vietnam National University. Soon after, he joined an internship programme at a game development firm in Ha Noi—this was when he discovered his talents and his unique game design philosophy. He knew that from over 600,000 games available for download on Google Play and the Apple App Store, only a very small proportion were played on a regular basis. Dong realized that his design philosophy ought to be different than other developers. He did not have the means to mass market or directly sell the game, except via traditional social media platforms. He figured that 'simplicity' and 'addictiveness' were the two qualities in game play that made people play mobile games over and over.

Traditionally, players enjoy games because of the connection they feel with their in-game characters, the beautifully designed graphics or intuitively complex gaming mechanics. Dong did the exact opposite when he created 'the most hated bird of all time'. While playing his Flappy Bird, gamers became frustrated within the first few minutes of playing yet would become overwhelmingly addicted—ignoring, or even enjoying, their frustration to better their scores. Gamers would think to themselves 'it is such a simple game, why am I so bad at it'. The truth was that the game was both simple and difficult at the same time. Simple in design and mechanics where players only need to tap their screen to control their 'bird', but the oppressively challenging factor was that if they mistimed their tapping, their 'bird' would collide with an obstacle and it would be *game over*.

Flappy Bird was doing exceedingly well and garnered substantial media attention—some of it negative, where claims were made about its 'addictive' nature. The media furore and the background work needed to keep the App active and to deal with the deluge of 'comment requests' overloaded Dong. On 8 February 2014, just over a year after launch, he decided to shut down Flappy Bird and pulled it from the Apple App Store. He gave his reasons for doing so: Flappy Bird was too *addictive*, perhaps even harmfully addictive for players. Further, he also commented that 'I cannot take this anymore' and 'I want to live in peace'.

'Selling' is a key entrepreneurship skill discussed in Chapter 1. As an entrepreneur, you will have to sell your offerings directly or indirectly. Indirect sales can be over online platforms where it is not usually possible to proactively approach prospective customers; here entrepreneurs are expected to create an attractive offering that would entice customers to trigger a sale. Dong Nguyen did just this—his game was so well designed that it sold itself—whoever played it, quickly understood it and wanted to keep on playing and told others about it. Since selling can be time-consuming and expensive, the task for the entrepreneur is to hook in customers with minimal effort such that they consume quickly and return for more without needing any reminding, again and again—*ad infinitum*.

In direct sales, you will have to proactively find and reach out to customers and meet with them face to face or talk to them over telephone to entice them to commit to buying. Direct sales approaches are used for selling to established businesses. For example, if your offering is a new type of commercial water dispenser or a fire alarm system, home or retail customers are not going to be your target market—it would be already existing businesses who you would need to reach out to. The first step will be to identify the right individual to speak to in that business, someone who has decision-making powers to authorize the purchase of the sort of products/services that you are looking to sell—a procurement, administration or facilities manager perhaps.

Be mindful, your target individual might already have an established network of suppliers and maybe reluctant to shift to a new one (you and your new venture), especially if you do not have an established track record. Hence, the second step is to research what *solution* and supplier they use existingly; what they might be paying on an ongoing basis to keep their existing product/service solution active and in working condition and the quality of customer care offered. Remember to use only ethical market intelligence gathering techniques for this investigative exercise. No solution is ever perfect, and if you can uncover your target customer's pain points and create alignment between these and your offering's 'value gaps' and VP, then you will be in a good position to hook this customer in. If you do not, then consider your sales call from your target customer's perspective—what incentive do they have to perform a potentially risky *shift-over* to your 'solution'?

Managers in large firms have busy schedules and they need a very good reason to find time to meet you. You need to establish connection with the 'gate keeper' in your target organization. For instance, an introduction from a common friend or through a social network like LinkedIn can be effective in breaking down initial barriers. After this initial introduction, the third step is to request a meeting time—offer a few days and times proactively for them to choose from. It is considered good practice to send in advance information about your venture, your track record (which you might have developed during pre-launch testing) and the features of the solution. Make sure you are well prepared to answer your customers' questions in the following areas: (a) how your product/service will help solve their problem; (b) back up your claims of benefits with customer testimonials and/or references; and (c) answer their objections on aspects such as pricing and features.

Expect your target customer to raise objections to your proposals. For instance, they might feel that some of the features of your service or product are not aligned to their pain points. To convince them, you need to be knowledgeable about their business and attempt to anticipate their future states, for example, if they were to expand in the next year with another branch or move into another line of business; in these scenarios the feature they might have a concern with now might just become relevant. Also expect the interested buyer to embark on negotiations by asking you to lower your price. You might counter price objections by either convincing the target customer that the price is value for money, offer discounts for a bulk purchase order or commit to a lower initial price for a strong commitment of future orders.

The final step is to close the sales deal, and this can be done using several approaches. You can attempt to get a 'trial close' by asking and confirming an expression of interest if you see buying signals from the manager. You could also force the customer to decide between two options by offering them options. For instance, you could ask 'do you want an initial order for 1,000 or 2,000 units?' You can also suggest a 'concession close' where you offer a discount on price to close the sale. This can be offered at the end of your meeting. For instance, you could say that 'if you place an order within this month, there is a special 5 per cent discount available'. Finally, you can try to have 'quotation close', that is, an opportunity to provide a formal quote at the end of your meeting.

Within the prevailing ways of doing business, because information is widely available (about your venture and its offerings), expect your target customer to have checked your online reviews or to have sought expert advice instead of relying on the information you would have provided. Your target customer might come to the meeting having partially made up their decision and after clarifications might straight away resort to price negotiation. As a salesperson, you need to see buying as a joint decision where your expert consultation can influence the sales process.

10.2. CREATING AWARENESS

Your new venture may offer a differentiated product or service with a distinct VP but that does not mean that customers are going to queue up to make purchases right from the start. First, prospective customers need to be made aware of your venture's existence. Then, you will need to convince these prospects to buy a new product or service that they have never tried before. Convincing customers to make a purchase is a challenging task for a new venture as the firm has little or no credibility and lacks a track record. Even if you are selling on behalf of an established brand in a new market through a franchise, it is possible that your customers might not be able to recognize the brand you represent. Thus, making your first sales or getting your first customer is a major milestone.

10.2.1. PERSUADING PROSPECTIVE CUSTOMERS

New ventures need to create awareness of their product or service and this often depends on the type of business and its customers' profile. For instance, if your business is a social enterprise, you would need to run a social awareness campaign. If you are introducing a radically new product or service, you would need to create genuine public interest. Prospective customers will need to be persuaded to make their first purchase from your new venture. There are a few approaches you could take to persuade customers to make initial purchases.

1. **Free trials or introductory offers:** To get new customers, you could offer a special deal, extra service or a lower price during a 'trial period'. You would need to set a time frame for the trial period like as 30 days. You can allow customers to return the product within that time frame and they would be billed if they decide to keep the product. You can also distribute free samples for food and beverage products or offer coupons as incentives for customers to try before they buy.
2. **Product demonstrations:** You can set up product demonstrations in high traffic areas in shopping malls or large retail stores to convince prospective customers that they need your offering because it solves a problem for them. During these demonstrations, you can

distribute flyers or brochures and have large posters and other visual displays that highlight the unique attributes of your offering(s).

3. **Communicate scarcity of products:** You can highlight scarcity by displaying with your offerings terms such as 'for one week only'; 'sales end today' and 'this offer ends in three days three hours and thirty seconds' (countdown timers).
4. **Recruiting affiliates:** Third parties or affiliates can be recruited to generate prospective customers for you. Affiliates usually charge a commission based on the sales they generate by promoting your product or service. For instance, when a visitor places an online order, the affiliate earns a commission.
5. **Launch event:** You can choose to organize a celebrity launch, and this could be done for free if you are able to leverage your personal social networks. Launch events can be especially effective if your new venture is a retail unit. Celebrities maybe persuaded to endorse your product, especially if it appeals to their values such as 'eco-friendliness', 'organic produce', and 'fair trade'. You can also get your entrepreneurial story published in print or other media as journalists and especially those that are local are often looking for inspiring stories. Developing and distributing a press release and organizing a press conference after the launch event to garner media attention can also be helpful. Product launches for radically new innovations do tend to attract media attention, but in case of incremental innovations or products/services that are generally familiar, you would need to become a lot more creative to get media publicity (like running carefully orchestrated public relations stunts).

Public Relations Stunts

An 8 ft fully animated polar bear let loose in London by Sky Atlantic. Citizens got a chance to interact with it and in return posted about their experiences on social media.

Felix Baumgartner, on behalf of Red Bull, became the first person to break the sound barrier—he fell 23 miles through the Earth's stratosphere. This stunt by Red Bull, captured the world's attention and led to 8 million live views on YouTube.

Italian fashion brand Diesel set up a 'fake' goods store in New York where merchandise were purposefully stamped 'Deisel'. This stunt attracted considerable attention ahead of Fashion week.

10.2.2. USING WOM

A new venture has a range of mass communication media available to initiate, develop and maintain relationships with prospective customers. However, none of the traditional media (TV, print, radio, film and so on) are interactive; social media on the other hand offers WOM-based sales communication and is a new channel to reach customers. As a new venture, you cannot afford to be *not* on social media—all your customers are most likely on social media; and they most likely spend most of their online time on social media platforms, in contrast to passively consuming content using traditional media.

WOM-based recommendations and networking are a significant way to promote a new venture and generate sales enquiries. WOM can also be a low-cost sales option; initially, it only requires the involvement of individuals from our personal/familial network and their recommendations of your venture to others within their networks. Many small enterprises such as wedding planners and catering firms start out by selling through familial networks. Once you are established, you need customer recommendations. For instance, every town and city has long established or innovative eateries that local people recommend to visitors.

Kayani Bakery, Pune, India

Kayani Bakery was founded in 1955 by two partners Homuz and Khodayar Iran. Overtime, this wholesale bakery has become a landmark in Pune which has over 50 other bakeries within its geographical vicinity. Kayani's signature products are its Shrewsbury biscuits and mawa cakes that have over time become a local favourite. The Bakery is highly recommended by Pune's residents to visitors as a 'must visit' local place. Despite its rustic layout and fairly limited range of products, the bakery has withstood competition from its contemporary competitors through strong WOM recommendations. Its success is reflected in the daily queues of buyers; and visitors to the city customarily return with gift packs of Kayani's signature products.

WOM recommendations are the most effective means for promotion. Customer recommendations are quite valuable for spreading your promotional messaging within a geographic location and later social networks can help you reach a wider audience. Hence, WOM marketing can be very effective and offers several benefits to the new venture. First, WOM is mostly personal and not influenced through monetary incentives. This can have a positive effect on an advertising or promotional campaign as consumers provide honest reviews about a product or service based on their use and motivation, therefore, other prospective customers get a 'genuine' and 'authentic' recommendation. However, there are disadvantages as well because electronic WOM can include not only positive reviews but also negative ones made by former customers. Further, if you recruit WOM agents, and customers find out, then they are likely to feel cheated because the person influencing them has gained monetary benefits to influence them 'unnaturally'—which can generate negative reviews and damage your brand's reputation.

WOM marketing differs from natural recommendations in that in case of the former, enterprises actively encourage or influence WOM promotions by rewarding regular customers to engage in WOM or appoint WOM agents like celebrities. To encourage WOM, you would need to first build trust and commitment among your regular consumers of the quality and consistency of your product or service. Then, you could launch customer club memberships and campaigns as indirect ways to encourage WOM.

Social media is a cost-effective way to initiate and garner WOM-based recommendations. You could use Facebook to promote your new venture by creating your business's page on the platform. The page can be customized to include information about your venture like contact details, product or service information and links to your venture's website. Make sure you add photos and visuals to reflect your business's operations and new product launches. You will need to do some 'offline' activities to gain followers online, for example, a launch event; otherwise, no one would know that you exist online on Facebook. Through regular updates on your activities, you could engage with your newly gained followers and gather customer feedback. Finally, you need to promote your page and build a following on Facebook. In your business cards and marketing materials like brochures, remember to provide links to your Facebook page. You can include a discount coupon on your

Facebook page and ask customers to like your page in order to get that concession. Finally, you can engage your customers through interactions using tools like polls or raising questions that followers would like to answer as a means of engaging via WOM marketing.

SELCO Solar Lights: Using Solar Power to Empower Rural Communities

SELCO is a for-profit social enterprise founded in 1995 by Dr Harish Hande in Bangalore, India. The enterprise aims to improve living standards for rural communities through social energy-based interventions. The company has developed products for the bottom of the pyramid households such as solar home lighting, solar water heaters and solar inverters. SELCO has successfully installed over 450,000 expensive solar solutions for the poor by using financing methods designed by SELCO and its financial partners. Local rural youth were employed to maintain the solar-based systems in rural areas and energy service centres were developed to cater to door-step servicing. By employing staff from local villages, SELCO was able to build trust and acceptance that is essential with its target beneficiaries/customers-marginalized communities in rural settlements.

SELCO's communication channels include its organizational website and a strong social media presence through Facebook and YouTube. Its public Facebook account, launched in 2010, provides an overview of the company, its products and news/product updates, while its YouTube account has dozens of videos uploaded to demonstrate its products and their benefits to end users—attracting comments and dialogue and approximately 2,000 subscribers.

YouTube is also an important platform for generating WOM. You can embed your videos' YouTube links on to your venture's website to ensure faster streaming by customers who visit your web page. You also need to take advantage of search engine optimization (SEO) and branding options offered by YouTube. Use every opportunity to create videos as it helps to build customer relationships. You could create a tutorial video on how to operate your product or use your service or create a 'behind the scenes' on product launches. It would be important though to monitor the comments and questions left behind and to respond in a timely way.

10.2.3. SOCIAL MEDIA INFLUENCERS

'Social media influencers' have been increasingly used for promoting products online. This type of marketing focuses on using 'influential' people online (bloggers and vloggers)—those who have a large following online and are considered 'celebrities' in their domains (like 'make-up' or 'travelling') to use your product and service and to authentically endorse it for their 'followers' to use. To effectively use social media influencers, you need to identify the right individuals who have influence over your potential customers and orient marketing activities around these influencers. Influencer content may be organized as testimonial advertising where they might play the role of a potential buyer or they may act as third parties like journalists, academics or industry experts.

MissMalini.com, India's Glamourous Digital Influencer

Malini Agarwal, now famous as Miss Malini, is one of India's most popular and pioneering digital influencers. She is a woman entrepreneur who founded a blog MissMalini.com in 2008. A former radio jockey, Malini cashed in on the popularity of Bollywood starting out as a hobby blogger as an extension of a weekly gossip column in the Mumbai tabloid *Mid-day*. These were early days in blogging and she continued working on her multiple jobs as both a radio jockey and column writer. It was only in 2010 that she focused full time on MissMalini.com and transformation to a social media influencer began that led to the creation of a media empire. The blog covers gossip and current events in Bollywood, Indian TV, fashion, beauty and lifestyle. The blog boasts of having over four million monthly visitors. In addition, MissMalini's social media presence is maintained through platforms such as Instagram, Facebook, Pinterest, YouTube and Twitter. By 2018, in total, MissMalini Entertainment Private Ltd has a social media outreach of over 10 million fans and followers making it one of India's top social influencers among the youth and millennials.

Due to her online influence, marketers realized her content's worth, worked out how it could be leveraged for integration with their own marketing campaigns. MissMalini Entertainment has partnered with the world's biggest fashion and cosmetics brands. For instance, it partnered with MAC and Bobbi Brown to co-create influencer campaigns with customized content advertising for the Indian market. Some of the recent successful partnerships with online fashion brands include Koovs, Myntra and LimeRoad. Malini has also anchored two seasons of her own show *MissMalini's World* on TLC.

10.2.4. ADVERTISING

Advertising involves promoting a new offering through a range of media such as print (magazines and newspapers); radio; TV, hoardings, direct mail and emails. Most start-ups have a small advertising budget, hence, advertising at the scale of large corporations who can spend significant sums to launch a new product (like smartphone) is simply not feasible. For a start-up, low cost advertising means such as flyers delivered to local residences and posters placed in strategic locations such as community clubs and shopping malls can be effective. If such advertising contains a message encouraging a trial purchase or a discount offering, then this can stimulate sales. Described further are different means through which you can advertise your venture and its offerings.

1. **Display advertising:** Display advertising uses text, logos, animations, videos and photos to target users with certain traits. Online advertisers frequently use cookies which can identify specific computers so that advertisers can decide which adverts would be most relevant for a particular visitor. Advertisers can use behavioural, contextual or geotargeting to target customers. For example, advertisers can use your location details on your mobile to display location-related links to restaurants and shops that you might search online. Web banners are display adverts that are graphical and can be displayed within a web page. News feed ads are those that are sponsored stories that exist on social media sites that offer news feeds. Some examples are promoted Twitter tweets and LinkedIn's sponsored updates.
2. **Online advertising:** To help prospective customers find you online using search engines, you can bid on keyword phrases that are relevant to your target market. You can increase your organizational website's visibility in search engine result pages through sponsorship. Sponsored results have visual cues to differentiate from non-sponsored or organic results. You can attempt to improve your new venture's organic search rankings by increasing the website content's relevance to search terms. Using sponsored search to advertise a new venture can also be helpful; search engines rank sponsored listings based on several factors such as bid price, keyword relevance and site quality.
3. **Pay-per-click advertising (PPC):** This is a more focused approach to advertising and can be cost-effective for a new venture. Examples of PPC advertising on search engines include Google AdWords and Microsoft Bing Ads. Content sites like news aggregators also offer PPC advertising—a relevant ad is displayed when a user searches for a particular keyword. PPC advertisers may use any of these methods to charge per click: (a) a flat rate based on a published rate card which is common on comparison websites or (b) bid-based rate where advertisers bid for an ad spot through some form of online auction.
4. **Online classified advertising:** This requires the creation of a categorical listing of specific products or services that you offer on classified web portals such as online job boards, auctions, OLX and Gumtree. Alibaba is an example of online classified listing.
5. **Mobile advertising:** This involves use of mobile gadgets like smartphones or tablets for advertisement. It can be done through SMS or MMS or mobile search advertisements. In recent years, mobile advertising has grown exponentially as the number of smartphone users has increased. Smartphone-based advertising is rapidly advancing, and mobile advertisers have become technically proficient to target potential customers within

geographical confines. Emerging and developing countries now have tech start-ups using mobile advertising to promote everything from health care services to online food delivery.

6. **Email advertising:** This involves sending an entire email or a part of the email message to potential customers. Most marketers provide an opt-in option which involves getting a recipient's consent prior to emailing or providing the recipient with an option to opt out of future marketing communication over email.

10.2.5. FEEDBACK AND LOYALTY

Customers who purchase your product or service will evaluate whether they actually deliver the VP promised by you. Every aspect of your marketing mix (product, price, place and promotion) will be examined including after-sales service. If your customers are satisfied, then they might be willing to provide testimonials endorsing the venture and its offerings with positive feedback, which would be essential for further WOM marketing. There are several ways of collecting customer feedback.

1. **Customer feedback from your website:** Websites can be embedded with an on-site widget like Beacon to collect customer feedback in real time without customers having to answer survey questions.
2. **Using analytics for on-site activity:** You can use reporting tools to understand which web pages on your website are most frequently visited so that you could focus your interface and other refinements; which could trigger the submission of positive feedback.
3. **Social media:** You can gather customer feedback through social media from direct comments or use features like quick poll on Facebook to collect customer feedback in a cost-effective manner.
4. **Exploratory customer interviews:** You can conduct either face-to-face interviews or use tools like Zoom to conduct one-to-one interviews with customers and publish a compilation of these on your YouTube channel.
5. **Email and customer contact information:** You can use email to assure customers of a timely response and to send follow-up emails. At the end of their complaint's resolution you could request feedback.

Existing customers can be persuaded to place repeat orders and becoming regular customers. For instance, you can develop a customer loyalty programme by using loyalty cards that encourage existing customers to make regular, repeat purchases using incentives or points that could be redeemed for special rewards. Loyal customers would be willing to recommend your product or service to others and they might even help you in product development. You can incentivize loyal customers by offering them monetary incentives like discounts or commissions.

10.3. DEVELOPING A SALES STRATEGY

The sales strategy plan of a new venture details how you propose to achieve the sales targets you have set out. Discussed further are the essential components of a sales strategy plan.

10.3.1. SALES TARGETS

Your sales projections must be realistic and achievable (more details on this topic appear in the next chapter). In case your new venture is introducing a radically new product or service, then it might be difficult to forecast sales accurately. Market research has limited utility in estimating sales demand for radical innovations as customers do not understand the new product or service being offered. In such cases, it is best to launch the business with minimum risks and develop a persuasive argument to attract customers. In case of traditional and well-known offerings, sales forecasts can be justified by showing that there is sufficient market demand and that your venture has operational capacity to achieve set targets.

10.3.2. MEASURING SALES PERFORMANCE

This section should highlight the specific sales metrics that you and your sales team intend to use to measure performance. To measure sales performance, you can create a sales performance measurement system that tracks the performance of your new venture. In terms of sales management practices, sales measurement can take the form of weekly dashboards, monthly reviews or the development of quarterly key performance indicators.

10.3.3. CUSTOMER PROFILE

This section entails the development of a detailed profile of your target customers including the various market segments, psychographics and the buying process. Provided in Table 10.1 is an

TABLE 10.1 Customer Profile Example: City Cakes, Bangkok

	Morning Regulars	Event Celebrators	One-time Weddings
Description	Frequent visits; low spend. Most common customer stops for coffee and pastries in morning	Middle-aged, moderate spend; catering their celebrations. Small segment biggest contribution to turnover	Newly-weds, tiny customer segment contributes 20 per cent to turnover
Age range	25–40	40–55	20–40
Priority	Fast service; freshly baked pastries and freshly brewed coffee	Customized menus to make celebrations unique	Unique flavours; customer service; delivery options
Marketing channels	Loyalty rewards card; sidewalk posters and email coupons	Email marketing with seasonal promotions; social media promotions of latest creations	Facebook ads; Pinterest posts; Instagram; wedding newsletter
Preference	Email and mobile app	Email; direct mail; Facebook/Instagram	Facebook; email; Pinterest

Source: The authors.

example of what a completed customer profile looks like. City Cakes is a bakery in Bangkok that serves three main types of customers who are profiled along a number of descriptors.

10.3.4. PRODUCT OFFERINGS

The product offering section should outline the product benefits and features with emphasis on those that meet the target customer needs. There are three levels of a product:

1. **Core product:** This is the core or basic customer benefit your product or service offers.
2. **Actual product:** This relates to tangible aspects of product appearance such as quality, colour, styling, packaging and features. These aspects differentiate your product from those offered by your competitors.
3. **Augmented or extended product:** This includes product-related service aspects such as customer support, credit terms, delivery, warranty and brand name image.

GMW Electric Smart Auto: Product Offerings

Gayam Motor works (GMW) offers two versions of its electric three wheelers: Urban ET and Taskman.

Core Product

The core benefit of the product is that these electric vehicles (EVs) produce zero emission, require little maintenance and are cheap to recharge. The vehicles are fitted with lithium-ion (Li-ion) batteries that can be swapped easily using proprietary technology developed by GMW.

Actual Product

Economical: Running costs are very low per kilometre, saving fuel costs of up to 400 per cent.
Performance: Powered by high performance Li-ion batteries and powerful electric motors. Zero emissions.
Design: Aerodynamic body for maximum efficiency. Torsion resistant suspension, compact wheel base, wide body cabin seat for four people and low centre of gravity for stability.
Low cost and eco-friendly: High performance battery with a lifespan of more than 200,000 kilometres.

Augmented Product

Smart and connected: Can be synched with your mobile allowing you to track your vehicle's battery health, mileage, location and pollution levels.

10.4. GROWING YOUR MARKET SHARE

The early adopters of your product or services are generally those people who choose new products and services after a thorough evaluation of your offerings. As the number of customers adopting your offerings increases, you will gain reputation and acceptance in the market. This will also alert and attract your competitors. Your rivals are likely to respond in direct competition by either modifying their marketing strategy or changing their product and service offerings. Expect this to happen; therefore, you will need to adapt and change your sales and marketing strategy to overcome threats from competitor responses and in the process grow your own venture. Your sales and marketing strategy will depend on whether you have a stronger or weaker competitive position in the market.

10.4.1. WEAK MARKET POSITION

You will need to be more careful in case you have a weak competitive position—in other words, your offerings are not superior to existing offerings. In such a scenario, you ought to identify a niche within a competitive marketplace. New ventures are more suited to operate within a niche market as they can charge premium prices at a lower volume of sales. In comparison, catering to the mass markets requires huge fixed costs to achieve economies of scale.

10.4.2. STRONG MARKET POSITION

If your venture introduces a radically new offering, then you will have a relatively strong position in the market. This represents an opportunity to exploit your first mover advantage before competitors imitate your new idea. Accordingly, to benefit from your strong competitive position and low levels of competition, you will need to adopt a growth and expansion strategy. This would help you to expand quickly by investing in developing your VP and establishing your brand identity.

10.4.3. DIFFERENTIATION

By differentiating yourself from competition you can charge a premium price for your offerings right from the launch of your new venture. However, competitors will soon emerge who will imitate your innovation. Their imitations will lead you to either reduce your offering's price driving, down your profits or to invest in further enhancement of product attributes through incremental innovation. However, this incurs significant R&D costs that can stifle the venture's growth or even threaten its existence.

Bakeys, Edible Cutlery from India

Bakeys was founded in 2010 by Narayana Peesapaty in Hyderabad, India, as an edible cutlery manufacturing unit. This start-up's mission was to provide an eco-friendly option to disposable cutlery made from plastics, paper and wood. Tons of plastic cutlery and utensils fill up landfills. Plastic pollution is a worldwide phenomenon threatening our environment and endangering wildlife and fishes in oceans. It is estimated that 40 billion tons of plastic utensils are used in the USA within a single year.

Bakeys edible spoons, coffee stirrers and chopsticks are vegetarian and can be eaten after their use. The flours used for manufacturing edible cutlery are jowar, wheat, rice and millet with a shelf life of two years. The edible cutlery is 100 per cent natural without any preservatives. Unlike plastic cutlery that pollutes the environment, edible cutlery decomposes naturally if not consumed by insects, animals or birds within 3–7 days. The edible spoons are available in natural flavours such as cumin, mint-ginger, carrot-beetroot and sugar. Thus, Bakeys edible cutlery is a radical product innovation that uses natural ingredients and is an eco-friendly option to disposable utensils.

Bakeys marketed its products in India by appointing distributors of disposable utensils and is seeking overseas resellers. Growth was slow as the founder of Bakeys struggled to raise finance. In 2016, Bakeys was able to raise $35,000—on the Ketto crowdfunding platform from over 1,500 investors. This round of funding has helped the company grow its domestic sales. The company's successful financing round led it to launch a new financing campaign on the international crowdfunding platform Kickstarter which raised $250,000.

In the case of Bakeys above, the venture introduced edible spoons manufactured from natural ingredients that were biodegradable to differentiate itself from competition. The firm had to invest in R&D in order to develop new products such as edible coffee stirrers and chopsticks as well as introduce product variations. This differentiation helped the firm to grow its market; however, this growth required finance. The founder of Bakeys struggled to raise finance for a significant time and the company has reportedly since struggled to dispatch its overseas shipments as per orders from Kickstarter started to come through.

10.4.4. COST LEADERSHIP

If your growth strategy is to compete on the basis of low prices, then you would need to achieve economies of scale rapidly to gain a strong market position. This would require you to adopt an aggressive marketing strategy to expand market share; and invest in ways of keeping your costs down like in automation. In both cases, your venture's success would depend on how well you develop your customer relationships, attract customers through promotional activities and expand your distribution channels. You can also choose to appoint agents and distributors to expand into new geographical areas. By expanding into new markets—nationally and internationally—a new venture can compete from a strong competitive position.

10.5. SUMMARY AND APPLICATION

Your sales and marketing plan details customer segments and specific marketing strategies for each segment. First, you need to convert prospective customers to existing customers by finding ways to encourage them to make an initial purchase. Then, customers will evaluate their initial purchase to see if you have succeeded in delivering your venture's promised VP. If they are satisfied, they can be persuaded to place repeat orders and provide testimonials or further leads to other customers through positive WOM. Building strong relationships with customers is essential for the success and growth of your new venture. As it has been explained in this chapter, strong customer relationships can be built through regular communication such as face-to-face interactions, internet and social media.

Exercise 10.1. Develop a sales and marketing strategy for the launch of your new venture.

1. Identify your customer segments and list the ways in which you intend to create awareness.

	Segment 1	**Segment 2**	**Segment 3**
Awareness-building approach 1			
Awareness-building approach 2			
Awareness-building approach 3			
Awareness-building approach 'n'			

2. How will you find prospective customers?
3. How will you encourage prospects to make a trial purchase?
4. How will you make existing customers repeat their purchase?
5. Estimate the costs associated with sales and marketing of your new venture.

11

Entrepreneurial Finance

LEARNING OUTCOMES

- Become familiar with different sources for finance for new venture creation within an emerging economy
- Understand how to estimate your new venture's start-up costs
- Be able to evaluate your company for shareholders and financers based on a financial plan

11.1. ESTIMATING THE FINANCIAL NEEDS OF A NEW VENTURE

Spotlight on Sumita Ghose, Indian Social Entrepreneur and Founder of Rangsutra

Social entrepreneur Sumita Ghowse has a postgraduate degree in economics from Mumbai University. She was also a Fulbright scholar in the USA and completed another postgraduate in conflict resolution. She has also been a recipient of the MacArthur Fellowship for leadership and is among the first batch of the Aspen India Fellows. She worked for several years in rural India for NGOs like the 'URMUL Trust' engaging with rural communities in the western Indian state of Rajasthan for social change and economic development.

Her experiences made her realize that rural communities had latent skills in India's ancient craft heritage of embroidery and craftsmanship that could be leveraged to create sustainable livelihood opportunities. These artisanal rural communities, unfortunately, were steeped in poverty and suffered from social marginalization. With a mission to set up a new enterprise that would be based on collective bargaining power and give rural artisans recognition for their talents and a respectable income from their produce, Sumita began searching for investors and approached several banks for loans.

However, raising finance proved to be a major challenge and bankers were reluctant to give loans to a former social worker with no track record in managing a business. This rejection from the formal credit sector made her think about alternative sources for raising finance. Hence, in 2005, Sumita set up Rangsutra Crafts as a 'community-based social enterprise' with £10,000 of her own savings and a shareholder capital raised from over 1,000 of her target rural beneficiaries—the artisans, where each contributed what they could afford—a capital sum of £10 each. The artisans of Rangsutra are organized into production groups in remote rural regions of India from Kashmir to Bengal. Marketing professionals and fashion designers organize production on bulk orders received from large retailers like Fabindia and from overseas like IKEA. The inclusive business model of Rangsutra, therefore, empowers its artisan members, most of them women, to gain sustainable employment through shared ownership.

In 2007, Sumita approached Aavishkaar, a social venture capital (SVC) fund in Mumbai that invested in social innovations to support inclusive development opportunities in rural and semi-urban India. Rangsutra received an investment from Aavishkaar to develop computer-based information systems and to build their marketing networks. Aavishkaar's equity investment and mentoring helped the business to grow exponentially from an annual sales turnover of £26,000 in 2006–2007 to over £480,000 in 2008–2009. Following Aavishkaar's successful investment, a number of formal financial institutions funded Rangsutra's growth including EXIM Bank, NABARD, The World Bank and Asian Development Bank. In 2012, Aavishkaar 'exited' the firm, and for them Rangsutra was a very successful investment. By 2018, nearly 2,000 artisan shareholders were organized into independent production groups in remote rural regions of India such as the deserts of Rajasthan and the Himalayan state of Uttarakhand.

Before you try to raise finance, the first logical step is to determine what proportion of the entire amount needed, you wish to raise from sources other than 'friends and family'. Raising finance is an ongoing concern for every new enterprise and it is likely that your new venture would need to go through several stages of financing that reflect its growth from a newly launched business to a going concern. Broadly, you need to identify both the 'start-up costs' and 'working capital requirements'.

Start-up costs are non-recurring (expenditures you make only once to set up your new venture) and can include legal fees, company registration expenses, initial advertising, promotional activities and employee training. These costs are not to be confused with 'pre-start-up costs'—which are costs associated with proofing the business idea, initial R&D, prototyping, customer testing and other 'market scoping' activities (like travelling to meet with potential clients/customers or researching competitors by visiting their retail locations). Recall Chapter 4 and the 'affordable loss' principle. The idea is to keep these pre-start-up costs at 'zero' or 'very low'; thereby, keeping the net financial impact on you negligible should the idea not be deemed viable for implementation. Once you do decide to move forward, then adapt the following template to calculate your 'start-up' costs (Table 11.1):

TABLE 11.1 Start-up Costs Estimation Template

Registrations - Business registration - Licences/Permits - Accountant/Lawyers' fees - Phone/Internet connection	**Capital** - Business purchase price - Franchise purchase fees - Start-up cash
Insurance - Building and contents - Vehicle(s) - Public liability	**Plant, Equipment and Office** - Real estate/space acquisition - Shop fitting and decor - Vehicles - Machinery - Security system - Office equipment
Marketing - Branding and merchandising - Website development - SEO - Social media promotion - Initial advertising	**Total Cost**

Source: The authors.

In addition to start-up costs, you will also need to estimate your WC requirements. WC is a financial measure that represents operational liquidity available to an enterprise. In other words, WC includes the recurring costs that need to be incurred for the running of your enterprise. These can include:

1. Utility bills payment
2. Employee salaries
3. Any loan repayments and interest accrued on such loans or other financing
4. Real estate or property taxes accrued
5. Payments to be made to suppliers of your stock or raw materials and its conversion into finished goods
6. Stock that you need to sell on to your customers
7. Diesel fuel (if you require backup power)
8. Ongoing marketing and advertising, including social media content development
9. Ongoing R&D for new product development
10. Website maintenance and updates

The basic formula for calculating your WC needs is as follows:

$$\text{Working capital} = \text{Current assets} - \text{Current liabilities}$$

If the 'current assets' (cash and other assets that can be expected to be converted to cash within a year) are less than the 'current liabilities' (amounts due to be paid within 12 months, like the recurring costs described above), then the enterprise is said to be WC deficit—which will be a problem.

Recall from Chapter 1, 'estimation' is a key entrepreneurship skill—exercise it cautiously, because miscalculations can have financial consequences. It is advisable that you remain 'liberal' in estimating start-up and WC expenditures, therefore, build contingencies and reasonably inflate expected costs.

11.2. THINKING ABOUT SOURCES OF FINANCE

Entrepreneurs need finance beyond 'friends and family' to launch their new ventures and to fund their growth. Sources of finance can be categorized in several ways. Based on the 'duration' of finance—long, medium or short terms depending on whether the duration is five years for long-term to a year for a short-term source. Table 11.2 gives an overview of sources of entrepreneurial finance.

We can also classify finance as either 'debt' or 'equity'. Debt finance or borrowings refers to cash injections into a venture by commercial entities such as moneylenders and banks. Debt finance usually requires a 'collateral' (something pledged as security, like papers of a property or bonds/ shares owned) and 'guarantees'. Most commonly, founder entrepreneurs use their personal assets as collateral and their well-known contacts as guarantors. Debt financiers who make a cash injection in your new venture, do so in the hope of receiving a financial return in the form of 'interest' charged on the sum borrowed. 'Interest' plus 'principle' (the actual amount borrowed)

TABLE 11.2 Sources of Entrepreneurial Finance

Duration	Source of Finance
Long and medium term	*Equity* – Personal savings, family and friends' investment – Venture capital finance – Business angels finance *Debt* – Personal, family and friends' borrowing – Banks and microfinance institutions *Crowdfunding/Peer lending platforms* *Lease and hire/Purchase* *Government loans and grants* – Soft loans; grants with zero interest
Short term	Short-term loans Personal, family, friends Bank loans like WC loan

Source: The authors.

needs to be paid irrespective of how well the venture performs. If repayments cease, then the lending entities can convert your deposited collateral to cash to recover the amounts owed or initiate legal proceedings to cease your venture's assets (and/or your personal assets, depending on the legal format of your business—see Chapter 13), if the deposited collateral is deemed unviable. In emerging and developing countries, your access to debt finance will most likely be highly restricted—most formal sector lenders do not consider the 'start-up' and 'small and medium enterprise' (SME) sectors as a 'viable' return on investment; their lending operations are usually targeted to large corporations, industries, listed companies and governments.

For equity investors, financial returns are in the form of 'dividends' rather than 'interest'. Dividends is a sum paid (typically annually) to the owners/shareholders/investors of a venture out of its profits (or reserves). The key difference between 'debt' and 'equity' finance is that 'dividends' or drawings from a business like in the form of salaries for owner-directors or profit distribution are *optional*. The amounts 'drawn' are determined by the extent of financial success the venture achieves—if the venture performs well and set revenue targets are met, then profits are paid out in the form of 'dividends' in proportion to share of ownership. In the initial stages of start-up (years 1 and 2), it is possible that the owners/shareholders/investors may agree to *not* draw down a salary or take minimal salary payments and not claim the share of their profits. Instead, they might exercise the option to re-invest profits accumulated back into the venture to build up its value for a future sell-off to other investors or a buyer. A sustainable, profit generating venture with meaningful cash reserves would be quite attractive to sell. The sale of the venture would mean a profitable 'exit' for the investors, who would then be able to generate more substantive returns from their equity invested.

Remember two important things about equity finance: first, each time you will raise equity finance, you will dilute your ownership or stake in your own venture. You *sell* your ownership stake in your firm to equity financiers, who buy a chunk of your venture for an agreed 'price'. If you sell off too much stake, say over 50 per cent, then you will most likely lose control of your venture—which means your financiers will have the option to force your hand—replace you if they are not happy with your performance or win a majority vote to sell the company, perhaps against your wishes. Second, equity investors usually look for a clean 'exit' in a few years post the investment. Their decision to invest (see Chapter 9 for more details) will be based on your ability to deliver on the profit generation commitments you make. You need to have a plan in place right from the very onset, perhaps before you even pitch for equity finance, on how you will ensure their 'exit' so you can regain full ownership and control of your own venture (if that is what you wish). Take legal advice and negotiate in clauses to protect your ownership and control.

11.3. INTERNAL SOURCES OF FINANCE

At the start-up stage, founder entrepreneurs commonly raise finance by using their personal savings, borrow money from friends and family or resort to 'bootstrapping' which involves using other people's assets for as long and as often as possible (like a 'rent-free' location). If you have reasonable savings, then these could be used to fund your start-up. This is the most common source of finance for most new ventures in emerging economies. By using your personal savings, you benefit from avoiding borrowing costs (interest payments). However, you will need to consider the opportunity lost in being able to earn interest from those savings (if invested) and associated personal risks should the venture fail.

Eventually over time as your venture grows, savings may be insufficient to meet the venture's entire financing needs. Your network of friends, immediate and extended family can be another source of funds you could tap into. Accessing your personal networks can be beneficial as individuals with whom you have close ties may lend you money with a 0 per cent interest rate and without the requirement of any guarantees because of the trust they have in you. Family ties have traditionally been used to develop family businesses in most emerging economies in South Asia and Africa.

Mast Kalandar, a Quick-Service Restaurant Chain

In 2005, Pallavi Gupta and her husband Gaurav Jain co-founded Mast Kalandar in South India. They both left their high paying corporate jobs as software professionals to set up the venture even though neither had prior experience in the hospitality sector. Gaurav was driven by an inspiration to serve home-cooked North Indian vegetarian food at affordable prices in the city of Bangalore—India's Silicon Valley. He spent nearly a year conducting market research, deciding on various operational aspects such as suppliers, the venue and their business's model for generating revenue. After deciding on the quick-service restaurant format, the husband–wife team invested £18,000 of their personal savings and the first Mast Kalandar outlet was inaugurated in the suburbs of Bangalore.

The pair had to get hands-on experience in restaurant operations. Learning from scratch the requirements of running a commercial kitchen, Pallavi carefully designed the menu and sourced fresh ingredients from North India to ensure authentic flavours. Chefs from North India were hired and trained to prepare food as per Pallavi's proprietary recipes to ensure consistency and to standardize the customer experience. With little money for advertising, the venture fully relied on WOM sales. Within a year, the first Mast Kalandar outlet had achieved its break even and opened its second branch in the city.

The owners soon developed their website to allow customers to order food online. Later, the chain launched the acclaimed 'MK Dabbawala' phone app which gave their customers the option to order food based on a menu refreshed daily for home delivery. The venture's app launch meant that the orders increased exponentially making the chain a market leader in food app segment.

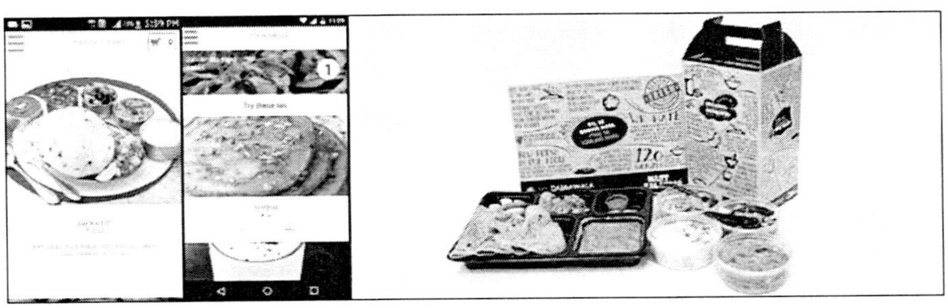

In order to scale, Mast Kalandar had to go beyond funding raised from personal savings, friends and family to external sources of finance. Gaurav and Pallavi have had three successful funding rounds in 2008 and 2010 from venture capitalists (VCs) Helio Venture Partners and Footprint Ventures, respectively. In total, through these rounds, Mast Kalandar raised a total of US$11 million to fund growth plans. The chain has grown significantly as a result, and currently employs 600 staff and operates 45 outlets in four Indian large cities—Bangalore, Chennai, Hyderabad and Pune. Plans are under way to use the latest round of funding to grow the food chain to 100 outlets over the next two years spreading to other regions such as Delhi, Mumbai and other Indian states.

You can also raise finance by pooling financial resources from a community by using an inclusive approach to doing business, like setting up a 'cooperative' or 'community-based enterprise'. To illustrate, in the spotlight case of Rangstura, the founder Sumita Ghose raised capital from over a thousand artisans, each of them contributing what they could afford. By organizing a new venture as a cooperative, like Sumita, you too can raise funding from the target beneficiary community who might be working members of your enterprise such as rural farmers, flower growers and bee keepers. Collective forms of entrepreneurship have been very successful in emerging and developing countries as they allow individuals to pool their financial resources in the scenario where there is very limited access to formal sources of start-up finance.

11.4. EXTERNAL SOURCES OF FINANCE

As explained earlier in this Chapter, one way to differentiate between external sources of finance is to categorize them as either 'equity'- or 'debt'-based. In this section, we will understand the value of the various types of external finance sources within these two categories—each source has its associated risks and rewards and the entrepreneur needs to choose carefully, because once finance is raised using a method, it would be difficult to undo that decision and choose another mode. To hedge their risks, at times, entrepreneurs choose a mix of approaches.

11.4.1. BANKS AND MICROFINANCE INSTITUTIONS

Start-ups in emerging and developing countries find it difficult to borrow money from banks and other financial institutions as new ventures are perceived to be risky borrowers. Given the high failure rates of new businesses, banks generally expect much lower rates of return from loans made to start-ups compared to larger businesses with an established track record.

Lending decisions of banks are influenced by their lending policies as well as general economic conditions. If you understand how a bank would evaluate an application (their process of 'due diligence') for a start-up loan, then you could 'tweak' and 'fine-tune' your documents to meet their general criteria (obviously remaining transparent and above board). Banks will require a detailed business plan of your venture with your loan application form (Chapter 13 outlines the components of a business plan). The bank will first assess the purpose for borrowing. Then, an evaluation is done to check whether the amount being sought is appropriate enough—too little or too much? Are the costs estimates adequate? Is there a contingency? The bank would also want to ensure that interest is regularly paid and that the loan capital is repaid in full on the due date. For this, they would analyse the submitted 'cash flow forecast' to check if enough cash would be generated by the business to not only meet its own operating expenses but enough to pay back what it would owe to the bank, while remaining profitable. Finally, the bank wants to ensure that the repayment terms are realistic. To make this judgement, the bank would need to understand the business's finer details to see if it is in fact viable.

Banks expect that interest is paid first over any capital expenditures or personal drawings by the entrepreneur. Bankers are also interested in the business's break-even point and 'margin of safety' (how much of its sales level could fall before a business reaches its break-even point)—indicating operating risks. Besides finances, bankers also make judgements on the personal character of the borrower by evaluating their credit history, education, business experience and previous track record.

A final point to note is that bank borrowings are often backed by a collateral or the additional security demanded in case there is a default on a loan. Collaterals can come from business assets or the applicant entrepreneur(s) might be asked to deposit a personal collateral or provide guarantees for the loan. While valuing business collaterals, it should be noted that the bank assumes that business assets would be sold at scrap value which lowers their valuation.

Due to the above requirements and the nature of debt finance itself which puts the interest of the lender before the venture, entrepreneurs struggle to convince bankers to lend. However, in the last three decades, microfinance institutions MFIs have emerged to cater to the credit needs of willing customers who do not constitute banks' target market, for example, impoverished individuals/families, rural populations, micro and small business owners and *new entrepreneurs*. Most of these agents and entities do not operate a bank account or have any recorded credit history. It should be noted that a vast proportion of developing country populations do not bank—in Bangladesh, for example, research suggests that in 2018 only 50 per cent of Bangladeshis, aged 15 or above, operated an account, either through a financial institution or a mobile money provider. Therefore, MFIs, to cater to such non-banking customers' requirements, introduced 'microcredit' in numerous developing countries. Microcredit is small loans disbursed without adherence to the strict banking due diligence procedure described above. Instead, they use a *different* set of criteria that their target customers can fulfil. Generating interest income though remains MFIs' major focus.

The microcredit social innovation has played a significant role in the setting up of millions of microenterprises in the emerging and developing world from Latin America to Asia. The concept was pioneered by Professor Muhammad Yunus, founder of the Grameen Bank, Bangladesh (featured in Chapter 2). The concept has since spread to other parts of the world. For instance, the MFI in Nigeria, although had a late start, but by 2002 AB Microfinance Bank was set up by foreign investors in Lagos followed by Altitude Microfinance Bank in 2004. In 2005, the Nigerian government launched the microfinance banking scheme to reduce poverty and provide finance to millions of poor excluded from financing. In India, microfinance has had a long and successful history. Self Employed Women's Association (SEWA) Bank was set up in Ahmedabad in the western state of Gujarat in 1974. Other prominent Indian MFIs include Ujiivan Financial Services, Bandhan Bank and SKS Microfinance. More recently in 2016, the Micro Units Development and Refinance Agency Bank (MUDRA Bank) was set up by the Indian government to refinance MFIs and encourage entrepreneurship.

Whether your loan is approved by a bank or an MFI, as an entrepreneur, you ought to make your debt financing decision after having carefully understood all the repayment requirements, and making an honest judgement about whether you and your new venture would be realistically able to repay your outstanding loan(s) with interest in the time you are being asked to agree to. It must be a very seriously thought-out decision. Your debtors will under no circumstances forego their claims—you will have to pay back the money you borrow, you will be legally obliged to and if you fail to, there will undoubtedly be serious personal consequences. Even late repayments will be penalized with fines and accrued interest payments. Consequences for a loan default could include all or a combination of the following: the need to declare personal and/or business bankruptcy which would impact your ability to start new businesses in the future, blacklisting for life to apply for further credit, prosecution leading to imprisonment and the ceasing of your personal (in some cases family, if they are guarantors) assets.

11.4.2. CROWDFUNDING

A new source for external finance, relying on internet-based platforms, has of late emerged for entrepreneurs. Crowdfunding allows entrepreneurs tap into small or micro amounts either donated or invested, via the internet, by thousands or even hundreds of thousands of single individuals. A crowdfunding platform acts as an intermediary to connect small or micro investors (or lenders) while charging a percentage on the funds raised for the applicant entrepreneur. *Equity c*rowdfunding platforms enable entrepreneurs to offer a proportion of their venture's shares to the 'crowd'—a large group of individual investors registered on the crowdfunding platform. These platforms enable founder entrepreneurs to pitch their ideas through social media to attract the crowd's interest. In return for shares (or other securities), the investors can expect a potential return should the pitched venture come to fruition and perform well. Good performance by the venture also means that the value of the venture increases and alongside the value of shares that individual investors have purchased. The opposite also holds true. Start-ups looking for smaller scale investments have been historically more successful in raising equity with follow-up funding being raised from other sources.

Another form of crowdfunding is peer-to-peer (P2P) *lending*. This involves use of online platforms to *lend* money to entrepreneurs, where the platform acts as an intermediary between lenders and borrowers. Since the P2P lending platforms operate online and have lower overheads when compared to mainstream financial institutions, they are able to offer lower interest rates to applicant entrepreneurs. P2P lenders generally earn higher returns compared to savings and other investment products offered by banks. While borrower entrepreneurs are lent money at lower interest rates even after paying the platforms compulsory fees, the platforms do require the pledging of business (or other) assets as collaterals when offering loans.

Example Crowdfunding Platforms Operating in India

In 2010, Anoj Viswanathan, Sourabh Sharma and Mayukh Choudhry founded Milaap, an online fund-raising platform with its headquarters in Singapore and an office based in Bangalore, India. The platform was organized as a microlending platform with partner MFIS to enable both international and domestic investors to fund and positively impact marginalized communities in India. Milaap loans enable people to access basic needs such as clean water and sanitation as well as to fund skills development training that leads to sustainable livelihoods. By sourcing funds from investors across the world, Milaap's partner MFIs do not rely on borrowings from other banks, thereby, enabling end borrowers to access loans at a lower cost. As of 2018, the platform had raised over $64 million charging a flat fee of 5 per cent of funds raised without any upfront fees.

In 2012, Varun Sheth, Zaheer Aderwala and Bollywood actor Kunal Kapoor launched Ketto—a crowdfunding platform to raise impact investment for the social sector in India. Its fundraising campaigns range from raising funds for a new animal shelter to raising funds for the Indian state of Kerala's flood victims. Ketto charges 5–6 per cent fees on the funds raised or an upfront fee of £20, whichever higher. As of 2018, the platform had over 80,000 investors registered and had raised over $45 million.

In 2012, two women entrepreneurs—Anshulika Dubey and Priyanka Agarwal—founded India's first crowdfunding platform for funding creative projects exclusively. As of 2018, the platform had funded 250 creative projects across films, music and dance raising over US$1 million from over 11,000 registered investors. Wishberry works on a rewards-based system. Funders do not get any monetary return (such as profits and equity) for their investment in creative projects. They are asked for micro-investments in return for intangible rewards such as early bird or special access to the project they funded (invite to film premiers), limited edition merchandise and experience in the making of the project.

11.4.3. GOVERNMENT SCHEMES

In recent years, governments in emerging and developing countries have launched schemes to encourage self-employment and entrepreneurship among their youth populations within identified priority sectors such as tourism and agri-technology. Government loans, grants and support schemes vary across countries and are usually in two different categories: first, *start-up loans*—these are 'soft loans' offered with much lower interest rates than those prevailing in formal lending markets to citizens who wish to start a business. The terms of these loans are also less stringent, and the award takes the form of a personal unsecured loan (compared to a secured business loan). Second, *government grants*—these are provided by the local, state or national government to an eligible applicant, and the amount granted is not expected to be repaid. The grant also does not require the applicant to meet any other criteria like to provide guarantees, pay interest or share revenue. Such schemes usually have stringent eligibility criteria and attract a large number of applicants, therefore, are quite competitive. Often the entanglements of bureaucracy mean that would-be entrepreneurs find that it takes too long to obtain their 'won' finance.

Example Government Schemes in Developing Countries

Nigeria

The Government of Nigeria supports several initiatives to support entrepreneurship and financial access for small and medium-sized businesses in the form of grants and 'soft' loans. For instance, the YouWIN connect programme; this is an annual initiative launched by the Federal Government of Nigeria that invites young citizens to submit business plans for new business ideas and undertake training and mentorship. A second programme, Youth Entrepreneurship Support was launched by the Nigerian Bank of Industry (BOI) to build the capacity of youth aged 18–35 with innovative business ideas through skills development and seed funding.

India

Start-up India is a flagship initiative of the Indian government launched in 2016 to promote entrepreneurship by mentoring and supporting existing start-ups in the smaller cities of India. A start-up in this scheme is defined as an entity that is headquartered in India that had been in existence for less than seven years, and with annual turnover of less than US$3.5 million. Some of the initiatives under this scheme are: (a) the I-MADE programme to help Indian entrepreneurs create new mobile app-based start-ups and (b) the MUDRA banks scheme, a US$2.8 billion initiative which provides low interest loans to entrepreneurs from marginalized socio-economic backgrounds.

'Make in India' is another government initiative launched in 2014 that called for Indian citizens, business leaders and investors to centralize information about opportunities in the manufacturing sector. Finally, the Atal Innovation Mission (AIM) of the Indian government aims to promote a culture of innovation and entrepreneurship by setting up innovation hubs, grand challenges, supporting start-ups and creating self-employment opportunities in the technology sectors.

Vietnam

The Vietnamese government has launched several initiatives since 2015 to help start-ups in Vietnam including the facilitating of tie-ups with foreign investors like those from Finland within the Finland-Vietnam Innovation partnership. The National Technology Innovation Fund (NATIF) was launched by the Ministry of Science and Technology, Vietnam with US$47 million—half of this fund is used for science and technology research and technology transfer from overseas, whereas the rest is used to provide guarantees for commercial loans or lent as soft loans to start-ups.

11.4.4. BUSINESS ANGELS AND VCS

New ventures with high growth potential can raise equity from business angels or VCs. Business angels are often high net worth individuals, often successful serial entrepreneurs themselves who invest smaller amounts of money than VCs in new ventures; in the range of £10,000–£150,000. They prefer to invest in ventures targeting those sectors in which they have personal expertise. Investment from angel investor has a number of advantages: first, as they are entrepreneurs themselves, business angels understand risks and are willing to support a good idea if they think it has growth potential. Second, the capital invested by the angel is not a loan that needs to be repaid. In exchange for the capital funds invested, the business angel receives an ownership stake in your venture so that if the business succeeds both you the entrepreneur and the angel reap financial rewards. However, if the business fails, the angel investor does not expect you to return the funds offered. Third, the business angel brings with him or her years of entrepreneurial experience and networks that increase the odds of success for a venture under their mentorship.

The disadvantages of angel investment are that the business angels expect very high rates of return as they are taking on large risks on your behalf. They could expect returns that are 10 times the original investment in a span of 5–7 years. Hence, the entrepreneur would have to adopt a high growth strategy to meet their expectations. Also, the entrepreneur gives up a percentage of ownership in their venture to the angel investor depending on how much investment they make. Finally, angel investors tend to adopt a hands-on approach; they take an active part in strategic decision and exercise control through a directorial position in the new venture. This can be intimidating and seen as losing of influence at the end of the entrepreneur.

An Angel Investor in Pakistan

CresVentures, founded by Humayun Mazhar—a technology entrepreneur, is an angel finance firm in Pakistan that helps early-stage entrepreneurs with financial resources, strategic advice, contacts and mentoring support to get off the ground. The firm funds technology start-ups and its prominent investee companies include:

Sukoon: Now Pakistan's largest online platform that allows customers to hire pre-screened, trained and insured technicians for homes and offices.

Perkup: An online platform that provides tools to SMEs to develop customized customer loyalty and marketing programmes.

VCs are not individuals but a type of financing institution that provides large value equity finance for very high growth potential new ventures. The start-ups they invest in operate within high-tech industries such as information technology, clean technology and bio technology. VC funding usually begins with an initial seed amount and with this financing the aim is to generate substantial returns through an eventual 'exit' event like an initial public offering (listing on a stock exchange), a trade sale or through a merger and acquisition of the enterprise. Like business angels, VCs too take on risks associated in investing in start-up companies in return for an ownership stake and control over their investee's strategic decision-making. Besides investment capital, VCs also give their investee entrepreneurs access to technical expertise, mentoring and marketing knowledge. For these privileges, at times, after several rounds of funding, their ownership stake in the new venture can be greater than the entrepreneur's—up to 70–80 per cent, with the entrepreneur left with the mere remainder. In this scenario of inequitable ownership, the VC can exercise a tremendous amount of control and sometimes force the venture (using directorial powers) to take a direction where the VC can profitably 'exit' at the cost of the venture's long-term sustainability and the entrepreneur's overall personal gains.

In developing countries, in recent years 'impact investment' or 'social venture capital' has emerged as a new source for start-up finance. Like VCs these equity investors invest in high growth ventures often within a social mission. The following case is illustrative of the growing importance of SVC to micro-and small entrepreneurs in marginalized communities.

Aavishkaar: A SVC Fund Based in Mumbai, India

Vineet Rai, while at a Gujarat government initiative in India—Gujarat GIAN as CEO, realized that high-growth rural enterprises lacked access to finance in comparison to their urban counterparts. He quit GIAN and began searching for investors to set up a Silicon Valley styled venture capital fund for these ventures. In the late 1990s, the average investment in the commercial venture capital industry of India was to the tune of $1 million. In comparison, the microfinance sector (whose target was primarily rural populations) loaned out $10,000–$15,000. The market gap identified by Vineet was to provide a mid-range financial provision of $30,000–$50,000—micro-venture capital for rural enterprises. However, raising funds for his SVC fund—Aavishkaar (which means 'invention' in Hindi)—proved to be quite challenging. After a long and arduous network building journey, Aavishkaar was finally set up in 2001.

The initial funds raised were $200,000 from Singapore-based investors but these were far short of the estimated two million that were needed. The founder and senior management of Aavishkaar adopted financial prudence and frugal practices to overcome the limitations due to their meagre resources. A rigorous approach to investing was adopted with high-levels of due diligence and strong investee accountability. In 2002, the first investment was made in Servals Automation, a social enterprise pursuing sustainable rural energy products such as energy efficient cooking stoves and kerosene/biomass/plant oil stoves. The innovative products developed by Servals were designed to cater to the energy needs of the 'bottom of the pyramid' (poorest) consumers. A second investment was made in 2003 in SKEPL, a social venture that provided automated dairy systems to rural dairy cooperatives. In 2004, Aavishkaar invested in Craftsbridge India, a Pune-based cross-channel design and marketing organization in the handicrafts industry offering products like home furnishing; collectibles such as paintings and sculptures; personal accessories such as bags and purses as well as ethnic jewellery. By 2005, due to good returns and growing experience, two investments were made: (a) Naveen Gram Agrotechnologies, a marketing and distribution organization in Jodhpur that dealt with agriproducts for small enterprises and (b) NSystems a firm that aimed to enhance accessibility for the disabled by creating IT infrastructure, including new hardware and software-based applications.

In 2006, three investments were made in (a) Tide Technocrats that provided micro hydel installations for rural electrification; (b) CK Technologies that built multilingual software applications to bridge the digital divide and (c) Vortex Engineering, who manufactured low cost ATMs for the rural market. In 2007, Aavishkaar invested in two handicraft-based ventures providing sustainable livelihoods to thousands of rural artisans and farmers. One of these was Rangsutra (the Chapter's spotlight case) and Desert Artisan Handicrafts, a Rajasthan-based not-for-profit trust that produced traditional crafts like embroidery, tie and dye to produce handmade fabric and other traditional accessories. In 2009, investments were made in (a) BASIX, an MFI aimed at providing credit to microenterprises and (b) B2R, a rural business process outsourcing organization based in the Himalayan state of Uttarakhand. In 2010, Aavishkaar invested in (a) Swas Healthcare, a Gujarat-based firm that ran clinics and hospitals based on naturopathy, Ayurveda and Yoga with an aim to provide affordable health care solutions and (b) Utkarsh Microfinance. Between 2012 and 2013, Aavishkaar exited from Rangsutra, Desert Artisans and Craftsbridge successfully.

Over the span of a decade, Aavishkaar invested over $100 million in high growth social ventures in sectors ranging from agriculture, energy, handicrafts and ICTs for development.

11.5. COMPONENTS OF A FINANCIAL PLAN

Entrepreneurs must develop a financial plan to be able to attract investment/external capital. This essential document will allow prospective investors or lenders to assess the risks, revenue generation potential and 'value' of your venture. In this section, the various components or sections that must be included in your financial plan are explained.

11.5.1. FINANCIAL INDICATORS

To be an attractive proposition for an entrepreneur or an investor, the following *financial* indicators of a venture need to be carefully assessed: (a) profitability; (b) liquidity and (c) risks. We will now consider each of these indicators and their related measures.

11.5.1.1. Profitability

The difference between your 'sales' or 'turnover' and 'costs' of doing business determine your 'profits'; in other words, Profit = Sales – Costs. Profitability is revealed in the 'profit and loss' or 'income statement' of the venture. Profits measure how your venture's assets have increased through day-to-day trading activities. However, profit is not equal to cash. For instance, you might not have received the cash payment for your credit sales. In time, profits should translate into cash depending on your credit terms. Further, you would need to pay cash for salaries and other expenses even if you do not receive cash payments from your debtors. If you are unable to pay cash for your recurring expenses, then this persisting lack of cash can make you go out of business. Hence, it is possible for a *profitable* enterprise to be 'illiquid' (cash poor) or vice versa.

11.5.1.2. Liquidity

Liquidity measures a venture's ability to pay for its routine, short-term financial obligations. Cash is the most liquid of all business assets, whereas inventory or stocks are the least. Cash levels are detailed in the 'cash flow statement' of a venture. This statement shows how *quickly* cash will flow into an enterprise from sales and the cash outflows that reflect payments made for expenses and any capital purchases. By analysing the cash flow statement, cash deficits can be determined and avoided.

11.5.1.3. Risks

Financial statements can be used to determine two main types of risks: first, operating risks—which are determined by measuring the level of your venture's 'fixed operating costs' in comparison to its 'profitability'. Operating risk levels are determined by the venture's 'break-even point', which is the point at which total costs of doing business and total revenue generated are equal or 'even'; there are neither any losses or gains. A venture's break-even point is calculated using the following steps:

$$\text{Break-even point} = \text{Fixed costs } (\div) \text{ Contribution margin}$$

$$\text{Contribution per unit} = \text{Sales price} - \text{Variable cost of each unit sold}$$

$$\text{Contribution margin} = \text{Contribution per unit } (\div) \text{ Sales price}$$

Break-even Calculation Illustration

ABC Ltd has total fixed costs of $15,000. Each unit produced by ABC sells for $15 with $7.5 in variable costs per unit. To calculate ABC Ltd's break-even point, you will need to work through the following calculations:

Contribution margin per unit = $15 (selling price) – $7.5 (variable costs) = $7.5

Break-even point = $15,000 (fixed costs) (÷) $7.5 (contribution margin per unit) = 2,000 units or 2,000 × $15 = $30,000

ABC Ltd will need to sell 2,000 units and generate $30,000 in income to reach its break-even point.

The second category of risk is financial risks. Investors would want to know if any existing loans or repayments might impact your venture's performance. Financing risks increase when you borrow money to increase sales volume, for example, a loan to buy bigger and better equipment to increase production. Although it may increase your profits for the time being if you are able to profitably sell what you produce, however, if the demand for what you are producing reduces, then you might have difficulty paying back what you borrowed—which can be a risky situation for an investor. Financial risk, thus, represents the risk of default when an entrepreneur increases their amount of debt to fund growth. By measuring the degree to which a venture relies on borrowed money/loans for growth, provides a useful way for assessing it financial risk. To highlight such risks, present 'gearing ratios' in your financial plan. Commonly used gearing ratios are:

Debt-to-equity ratio – Total debt (÷) Total equity

Times interest earned – Earnings before interest and taxes (EBIT) (÷) Total interest

Debt ratio – Total debt (÷) Total assets

Equity ratio – Equity (÷) Assets

The financial objectives of an enterprise involve being highly profitable with sufficient liquidity so that the operational and financial risks are minimized. To present objective measure of these objectives, we need to develop financial forecasts for our financial plan. These include forecasts of sales, income, balance sheet and cash flow—discussed in the following sections.

11.5.2. SALES FORECAST

Financial forecasts usually start by the forecasting of sales or the turnover of your venture, considering the costs incurred while generating such sales and the resulting profits. *Monthly* sales need to be

TABLE 11.3 Sample Sales Forecast

	Jan	Feb	Mar
Unit Sales			
Lunches	72	90	150
Lunch Bvg	124	160	250
Dinners	537	700	825
Dinner Bvg	323	500	600
Other	68	40	50
Total Unit Sales	1,124	1,490	1,875
Unit Prices	Jan	Feb	Mar
Lunches	$11.90	$12.00	$12.00
Lunch Bvg	$2.59	$2.75	$2.75
Dinners	$19.85	$20.00	$20.00
Dinner Bvg	$7.17	$7.00	$7.00
Other	$1.21	$1.25	$1.25
Sales			
Lunches	$857	$1,080	$1,800
Lunch Bvg	$321	$440	$688
Dinners	$10,657	$14,000	$16,500
Dinner Bvg	$2,316	$3,500	$4,200
Other	$82	$50	$63
Total Sales	**$14,233**	**$19,070**	**$23,250**

Source: https://articles.bplans.com/a-detailed-sample-restaurant-sales-forecast/(accessed on 14 June 2019).

forecasted for at least two years, although three is considered the norm. The sales forecast needs to be realistic and achievable as it can be the starting point for the remainder forecasts. To project demand for your product or service, you would need to conduct market research (see Section B, especially Chapter 8). To investors, you would need to demonstrate that (a) there exists enough market demand for your product or service and (b) the targets set are achievable within the resource constraints of the venture. It is important that your forecasts are consistent and convincing, hence, detailing the assumptions which form their basis would be vital. Investors will scrutinize these assumptions carefully to check if you are being unrealistic or inflating your projections only to entice them to make an investment. They will most likely check your forecasts against industry averages.

Consider a restaurant, for example, to develop its sales forecast we might look at the number of covers and the average spend per cover to check whether sales estimates are realistic. In Table 11.3, within 'unit sales', the entrepreneur has good assumptions to forecast that in January, they would be able to sell 72 covers for lunches, 124 for lunch beverages and so on. The numbers of covers

FIGURE 11.1 Sample Income Statement

			Amount	Percent
Sales:	Food		$2,000,000	74.1%
	Beverage		700,000	25.9
		Total	$2,700,000	100.0
Cost of Sales:	Food		690,000	34.5
	Beverage		206,500	29.5
		Total	896,500	33.2
Gross Profit			1,803,500	66.8
Other Income			35,000	1.3
Total Income			1,838,500	68.1
Controllable Expenses:	Salaries and Wages		755,000	28.0
	Employee Benefits		130,000	4.8
	Direct Operating Expenses		140,000	5.2
	Marketing		78,000	2.9
	Utility Services		70,000	2.6
	Repairs and Maintenance		46,000	1.7
	General Administration		130,000	4.8
		Total	1,349,000	50.0
Income before Occupancy Costs			489,500	18.1
Occupancy Costs:	Rent		162,000	6.0
	Property Taxes		24,000	0.9
	Property Insurance		13,000	0.5
Earnings before Income, Taxes, Depreciation and Amortization			$290,500	10.7%

Source: The authors.

steadily increase in February and March. By multiplying unit sales (number of covers) by the unit prices, total sales can be estimated. The entrepreneur might forecast a dip in revenue during June–July, for example, due to seasonal fluctuations.

11.5.3. INCOME STATEMENT

After you have estimated the monthly sales and recurring costs for your venture, you can develop a forecasted income statement. You would need to use an accepted template for this statement, the one provided in Figure 11.1 is for restaurant:

First, the gross profit is calculated by adding revenue from various categories of sales. From the gross profit, all controllable expenses such as salaries, marketing and utility services are deducted to arrive at the operating profit. Next, occupancy costs are deducted to arrive at earnings before income taxes. From these, any financing costs that are interest payable are deducted to arrive at the net profit before dividends. To keep the basic structure of the income statement in mind, refer to the following formula:

$$\text{Gross profit} = \text{Total sales} - \text{Cost of sales}$$

$$\text{Operating profit} = \text{Gross profit} - \text{Operating costs}$$

$$\text{Net profit} = \text{Operating profit} - \text{Interest}$$

Create the projected income statement for the end of Years 1, 2 and 3 based on your sales forecast and your estimation of the fluctuation in your venture's running/recurring costs.

11.5.4. BALANCE SHEET

The balance sheet will provide a snapshot of (a) assets and liabilities of your business and (b) the source of these assets or liabilities. The two sides of the balance sheet are 'assets' and 'liabilities' and must always balance. Assets of a business include cash, receivables, inventory and fixed assets such as equipment, IP (patents, goodwill and so on), premises and machinery. Sources of funds for these assets could be overdrafts, loans, creditors, share capital and accumulated profits. The following is a standard template for a balance sheet. Consider the balance sheet in Figure 11.2, on the assets side, all the various classes of assets owned by the venture are listed along with their respective values. The total value of all assets must be equal to the total owed liabilities (shareholder's equity is treated as the venture's liability). Like the income statement, the balance sheet would also need to be created to depict the assets vs. liabilities position of the venture at the end of Years 1, 2 and 3.

11.5.5. CASH FLOW STATEMENT

You need to develop an accurate cash flow forecast that outlines the total *monthly* inflows and outflows for your enterprise. Like the previous forecasts, the cash flow for your venture too would need to be projected for a two–three-year period. The cash inflows would illustrate how soon you are able to receive cash from your sales; accounting for those made on cash and also on credit. Cash outflows represent cash expenses associated with rent or purchase of premises, buying machinery and other equipment and purchasing stock or inventory. By calculating net cash flows, that is, cash outflows less cash inflows for each month, an entrepreneur can forecast periods where cash might be in shortfall (see the following formula).

$$\text{Cash flow} = \text{Total cash receipts} - \text{Total cash payments}$$

Projected cash deficits would need to be financed through borrowings (e.g., from a bank) or via equity injections. The format of the cash flow forecast is quite typical for a new venture and includes the following information:

FIGURE 11.2 Sample Balance Sheet

Assets		Liabilities and Shareholders' Equity	
Current assets		**Current liabilities**	
Cash and cash equivalents	$100,000	Accounts payable	$30,000
Accounts receivable	20,000	Notes payable	10,000
Inventory	15,000	Accrued expenses	5,000
Prepaid expense	4,000	Deferred revenue	2,000
Investments	10,000	Total current liabilities	47,000
Total current assets	149,000	Long-term debt	200,000
Property and equipment		**Total labilities**	247,000
Land	24,300		
Buildings and improvements	250,000	**Shareholders' equity**	
Equipment	50,000	Common stock	10,000
Less accumulated depreciation	(5,000)	Additional paid-in capital	20,000
Other assets		Retained earnings	197,100
Intangible assets	4,000	Treasury stock	(2,000)
Less accumulated Amortization	(200)	**Total liabilities and shareholders' equity**	**$472,100**
Total assets	**$472,100**		

Source: https://www.templatesdoc.com/wp-content/uploads/2016/04/balance-sheet-sample-594.png (accessed on 14 June 2019).

1. **Cash inflows:** Includes all the cash receipts into the business. Investment (from the entrepreneur or from external sources) is a one-off cash inflow, whereas payments from customers are regular sources of cash.
2. **Cash outflows:** Includes all movements of cash out of the business. When estimating cash outflows, one must take a conservative approach and include contingencies, that is, unexpected costs or higher than expected payments.
3. **Net cash flow:** This is the difference between the total cash inflows and total cash outflows. If there is a cash deficit, an entrepreneur will need to consider whether they would need access to a bank overdraft.
4. **Opening balance:** This is the cash balance at the beginning of a period.
5. **Closing balance:** This is the amount left at the end of a period.

To better understand the manner in which a cash flow statement is prepared, consider the case study as follows.

Cash Flow Statement Illustration: Noor and Kareena's

Experienced interior designers Noor and Kareena decided to start a business together in a residential area of Bangalore, India, by entering into a partnership. Each partner agreed to invest $5,000. They expected to attract two interior design assignments per month for the first six months of operations. Each assignment would average $1,500. According to their 'terms and conditions', customers were expected to pay 25 per cent of the assignment's value as an advance and the balance was to be paid on completion. They estimated that the average time to complete an assignment would be approximately one month. Monthly costs associated with this new venture were as follows:

1. Marketing: $100 per month
2. Equipment $2,500 in January (first month) and then again in April (fourth month) totalling $5,000
3. Project materials: $300 per month (two assignments). Suppliers would need a 30-day payment period
4. Legal and accounting costs: $200 (first month only)
5. Sub-contracted labour (other tradesmen): $400 per month
6. Noor and Kareena's monthly salaries: $1,000 per month
7. Other miscellaneous costs: $50 per month

Based on the above assumptions, a cash flow statement can be produced:

	Jan	Feb	Mar	Apr	May	Jun	Total
Cash Inflows							
Investment	10,000						**10,000**
Sales (Cash)	750	750	750	750	750	750	**4,500**
Credit sales		2,250	2,250	2,250	2,250	2,250	**11,250**
Total Cash Inflows	**10,750**	**3,000**	**3,000**	**3,000**	**3,000**	**3,000**	**25,750**
Cash Outflows							
Project materials		300	300	300	300	300	1,500
Sub-contract labour	400	400	400	400	400	400	2,400
Marketing	100	100	100	100	100	100	600
Legal and accounting	200						200
Equipment	2,500			2,500			5,000
Noor and Kareena's salaries	1,000	1,000	1,000	1,000	1,000	1,000	6,000
Other costs	50	50	50	50	50	50	300
Total Cash Outflows	**4,250**	**1,850**	**1,850**	**4,350**	**1,850**	**1,850**	**16,000**
Net Cash Flow	6,500	1,150	1,150	**−1,350**	1,150	1,150	**9,750**
Opening Balance		6,500	7,650	8,800	7,450	8,600	
Closing Balance	6,500	7,650	8,800	7,450	8,600	9,750	

11.5.6. BUSINESS VALUATION

Valuing a start-up business is more difficult than valuing an established business because of the associated uncertainties and lack of a traceable track record for the venture. Before seeking equity investment, you need to value your business first—how much do you assess your venture to be worth today? Before making an equity offer, investors too would assess the value of your business—they would expect you to have overvalued your venture, while you should expect the investors to somewhat undervalue your business. This tension between entrepreneurs and investors is based on the 'price' or value of your business. Investors can buy more of your business with the amount they would like to invest if it is valued lower than general expectations; whereas, you would want to get the highest possible amount of investment without giving up too much ownership.

For example, if you were offered $50,000 for a 25 per cent stake in your business by an investor, they have valued your business at $200,000. In comparison, your evaluation could be much higher. You may think $50,000 is worth only 10 per cent, which means that you believe your business is worth $500,000. You will then have to convince investors to improve their evaluation by divulging more information about your venture and its potential which the investors might be unaware of.

There are the following three ways of valuing a business:

1. **Determining the market value of your assets:** Asset-rich enterprises with tangible and intangible assets such as premises and land can be valued at prevailing market rates. Tangible assets that can be valued include inventory, equipment, furniture and fittings as well as account receivables. Intangible assets (IP) are much harder to value—it would be best to seek expert advice to arrive at a fair valuation. Asset values at the market rate will provide a minimum valuation for your venture and this valuation will be useful in starting negotiations with investors.
2. **In terms of profits:** Enterprises that have a few tangible assets (e.g., technology-based ventures) can be valued in multiples of their annual net profit. For example, a venture with annual sales of $100,000 with a profit 'multiple' of 3 maybe valued at $300,000. Similarly, if the venture's multiples were 10, then the same enterprise would be valued at $1,000,000. Your sales, profit and loss, and balance sheet forecasts would prove helpful here to make your case.
3. **Mix of 1 and 2:** Enterprises may be valued by mixing both the above methods. For tangible assets market values might be used, whereas intangibles maybe valued in terms of profit. In the case of start-up ventures, only forecasted profits would be available to act as a starting point for the valuation. For estimating the *multiple*, you can look at (a) the track record of the venture, (b) the sustainability of its earnings, (c) factors that enhance the credibility of the forecasts such as the experience of the management team or advance orders received before the launch of the venture and (d) industry benchmarks that reflect the existing risks in that sector. Needless to say, a start-up with no record will have a lower multiple than an established enterprise, and ventures that are perceived as *risky* will have a lower multiple rather than those considered as less risky. New ventures that introduce new technologies or new ways of doing business that can be expected to earn high profits may have a higher multiple even though they might be perceived to be highly risky.

From the above, determining the *multiple* is a difficult task. The price of *anything* (including that of your business) requires a willing buyer and a willing seller. Single figure multiples are normal for a new venture. However, a larger multiple could be used in case your venture is involved in an interesting niche sector with few competitors and an offering that is hard to copy and proven through research to be of much customer demand. The valuation can also be much higher if a large corporation perceives the venture as strategically important for their own operations. For example, Daraz.pk, a Pakistani start-up founded in 2012, is an online store for branded products for men and women in clothing, footwear and jewellery. Daraz.pk was acquired by China's Alibaba, the online retailer, in 2018 for $55.6 million because through Daraz.pk's acquisition Alibaba can more quickly and seamlessly enter the lucrative Pakistani domestic customer.

11.6. SUMMARY AND APPLICATION

The cases of Sumita Ghose, Vineet Rai and Pallavi and Gaurav show that entrepreneurs in developing countries often have to use their personal savings and other creative approaches to raise finance. Millions of individuals who had no access to formal lending services and were financially excluded were empowered through microfinance. However, microfinance like finance from any formal banking institution will need to be paid back in full with interest over a stipulated term—be mindful of the overall repayment costs levied on to you and the penalties for default.

Before you approach MFIs, banks or investors, you need to have a good idea of how much finance you need in the first place; careful calculations would be required to justify the amount being sought. Once the start-up cost figure becomes available, you can start to think about the channels which might be most viable to target to get your venture's start-up funded. Country-specific crowdfunding platforms are emerging rapidly; if you find none that operate within your country, then you have the option of pitching the venture on the dozens of platforms that operate on a global basis. Use the internet to research whether any government schemes are available to fund new ventures in your country which you might be eligible for. National-level business plan competitions are now common in most emerging and developing countries, participating entrepreneurs, even if they do not win the usually attractive prize monies, get excellent exposure. If you do not win any government grant funding or are successful in their 'soft loan' applications, then look for business or technology *incubation services* in your city. Usually, academic institutions house business and technology incubators—their role is to provide entrepreneurs with the *right* conditions to grow their venture. Being inducted into an 'incubation' programme can mean savings on a variety of start-up costs, such as office rental and utilities payments, while enjoying many intangible benefits such as mentoring, advice on legal and tax matters, registration of your IP, sales leads and introductions to investors.

At some stage, you might choose to pitch your venture (see Chapter 9) to investors; for your pitch to succeed, it would be important to have a valid and reliable 'financial plan' with realistic forecasts and accompanying assumptions. Forecasting can be quite difficult, remember: be conservative in your sales estimates to avoid the pitfalls of over committing and under delivering. Investors will try and negotiate up their ownership stake while valuing down your business; practise negotiation skills before your pitch—if you are unsure what equity to give away for what amount of investment, you can always request for time to revert with a counter offer.

Exercise 11.1. Using the Noor and Kareena cash flow template, develop a cash flow forecast for the first year of your venture's operations. Think about the amount of cash you can inject at start-up, your monthly cash outgoings and realistic monthly incomings. The difference between outgoings and incomings should highlight surpluses or shortfalls. If you have monthly shortfalls, then determine how much external finance you will need to sustain yourself till the time you achieve 'break-even'. For this you will need to perform a 'break-even' calculation. Think about the internal and external sources of finance you could target to fund your cash shortfall till break-even. What category of finance would you choose—internal or external and debt or equity. Explain your choices and your strategy to pitch your venture.

12

Ethics and Professional Practice

LEARNING OUTCOMES

- Understand the link between values, mission and vision statements
- Become familiar with the ways ethics and corporate social responsibility create brand value
- Learn how to create a values-based identity for your new venture

12.1. VALUES, VISION AND MISSION

Spotlight on Rivigo, 'Making Logistics Human' from India

Although the Indian road freight market is worth an astounding 150 billion dollars and is growing at about 12 per cent; the trucking industry is known to be an unorganized and fragmented industry. Fleet owners' main aim is to ensure maximum capacity utilization for their vehicles, because losses are borne if a truck is not linked to a delivery order. Such a system is heavily time bound, the shipper generally requires a transport vehicle on short notice and requires deliveries promptly.

The pressure to perform, keep fuel costs low, deal with emergencies, to be prompt, ultimately, falls on the individuals who are doing the job—the truck drivers. What increases pressure is the fact that they are traditionally paid based on the number of kilometres driven and not a fixed monthly salary. Long journeys coupled with time away from home as well as long driving hours very negatively impact truck drivers' well-being. India's one million truck drivers encounter a harsh lifestyle and become susceptible to drug use, disease, a poor diet and poor health.

In 2014, Deepak Garg—who had an engineering qualification and extensive work experience in management consulting in the USA—took notice of the above problems and set up Rivigo (portmanteau of 'river' and 'on the go'). He wanted to ensure the well-being of his truck drivers and simultaneously reduce delivery time to increase profitability. He solved both problems via a 'driver relay system'. Rivigo set up about 70 pit stops all across the country, each driver drives about 4.5 hours to a company pit stop and hands over to another driver who drives for another 4.5 hours till the next stop, this 'relay' continues till the truck reaches its destination.

This relay system has cut delivery time from Delhi to Chennai, for example, from 96 hours to 48 hours, while maximizing truck utilization. The driver who gets off at the pit stop catches a truck going back in the direction of origin. This method helps improve the drivers' lifestyle and allows them to earn better wages when compared to industry norms. Based on the relay system, Rivigo also offers the 'full truck load' service which promises delivery anywhere in India in three days compared to the industry average of seven–eight days.

Their proprietary software tracks a truck from its journey's start to finish and informs the driver when and where to refuel based on cheapest diesel prices. Rivigo also offers its drivers training which focuses on mindset, well-being, behavioural and disciplinary issues as well as driving for mileage efficiency. In its first three years, Rivigo reached a valuation of nearly US$1 billion and has an annual revenue of about US$200 million.

It is important that your new venture reflects your values and beliefs as it is an extension of you and your personality. Your values and beliefs lay the foundation for the ongoing development of your start-up, and a well-grounded and deeply embedded *ethics* system can add value to your new venture and create a coherent identity for your brand.

In general, ethics is a branch of philosophy that seeks to answer the questions of human morality by defining concepts such as *right* and *wrong* or *good* and *evil*. More specifically, business or corporate ethics, refers to examining ethical principles, morals or problems which arise in the course of doing business. Business ethics help businesses to connect with its stakeholders on mutually agreeable terms.

Business ethics cover all aspects of a venture's operations and have a wide-ranging influence on employees, managers and owners. Business ethics include norms of behaviour, decision-making priorities and principles of governance that constitute a framework within which an organization's constituents act. These have their origins in a legal-cultural-economic-social system and/or from the founder entrepreneur's devised and stated values, vision and mission.

As a new entrepreneur, you ought to consider participating in ethics training yourself and also arranging the same for your partners and employees. Such training can help, in general, to make ethical decisions, especially in scenarios where answers are less than clear or involve ethical dilemmas. The most direct benefit of ethics training is to reduce the likelihood of corruption, penalties and a damaged reputation for breaching laws or moral norms accepted in society.

12.1.1. VALUES

Values refer to your core beliefs and the degree of significance you give to something or action; they help you determine what actions are most suitable to take and the significance of those actions when compared to other possible actions you choose to not take. Values are essentially operating philosophies or principles that guide internal conduct within an organization as well as its external relationships with customers, partners and shareholders. Your venture's values would usually be summarized in your 'mission statement' or in the venture's 'statement of core values'. Values can be derived from religious or cultural affiliations as well as philosophical systems of ethics and morality—deriving or forming the basis for what is believed to be 'goodness'. Their purpose is to create an internal organizational culture where all members act in unison promoting 'goodness', which could be *goodness* for the organization, its customers, employees and/or the wider community. For instance, in the spotlight case, Rivigo has outlined 10 values summarized in their 'Rivigo Way of Life' (see Table 12.1). These values are an extension of Deepak's personality and provide the normative rules which orient all Rivigo employees towards a common purpose.

TABLE 12.1 Rivigo Way of Life

Ownership	I am an owner. Not an employee. I act on behalf of the entire company.
Hire better people	I hire people better than myself. I mentor and coach to make them better.
Technology obsession	I use technology to solve problems. I always ask how technology can bring efficiency or reduce effort in whatever I do.
Data driven	I like to get into depth. I like to measure everything through numbers and believe it is the only source of truth.
Boundless energy	I deeply connect with my source of energy every day and bring that energy to everything I do in life.
Think big	I think big. I think bold. I do not say no to challenges and do not fear failures.
1 per cent improvement every day	I constantly better myself and my work every day. I believe in learning from mistakes to ensure I do not repeat them.
Respectfully disagree and commit	I respectfully challenge the decisions of my team members when I have a better solution.
Frugality	I am sensitive to wastage and inefficiency. I do not overspend. I am resourceful.
Say/Do=100 per cent	I do what I say. Not less. It helps me build a cycle of trust with everyone around me.

Source: https://www.rivigo.com/careers/the-rivigo-way-of-life (accessed on 14 June 2019).

Organizations that hold strong values find it easier to recruit staff, because they get an apt selection criterion to choose from among applicants; those applicants are preferred who show that they identify with established values. Shared values will create solidarity and build bonds which will act as a social glue aligning and motivating people within your venture. Without core values, it would be nearly impossible to create an identity for your venture and without an identity you cannot explain 'what your venture is' to any interested stakeholders.

Powerful values and affirmative ethical stances that can bind a venture's employees and promote cohesive action can be derived from world religions. For instance, in the following case, the venture's value system is based on the philosophy of 'Karma'—a core belief in Hinduism that reflects the adage 'what goes around comes around'. This core value helps the venture create close relationships with its customers and suppliers, eventually leading to a strong brand identity.

Karma Recycling, India: Venture's Name Reflects Its Core Value System

Karma Recycling was founded in New Delhi, India, in 2013 by Aamir Jariwala and Akshat Ghiya as a trade in operator and redistributor of mobile devices in India. The start-up was based on the philosophy that 'a useless device for someone can turn into a useful device for someone else'. By recycling and encouraging reuse of devices, the start-up reduces the negative impact of e-waste filling up landfills.

Karma Recycling has an online electronics trade-in services portal that allows users to sell over 3,000 models of used smartphones, laptops or tablets with instant online quotes for devices in any condition. In addition, customers can also use Karma's in-store exchange programmes in retail stores where customers can get in store value out of their old devices against purchases of new devices.

Once a device is purchased, Karma conducts a complete data wipe off as well as a software reboot, undertakes any needed repairs, conducts a 50+ step check of the device, repackages the device for sales and then resells the device at a fraction of its original price. The refreshed devices are resold with a 15-day money back guarantee.

Non-repairable devices are stripped for spare parts and are recycled back into metals and plastics. Similar recycling services are available to corporations where Karma acts as a government-approved electronic waste collector and segregator. Since inception, the start-up has recycled over 100,000 mobile devices and redistributed these across India saving tons of e-waste from filling landfills and enabling those who could not afford to buy a new smartphone to buy a recycled one at a much lower cost.

Core values help derive a 'vision' and 'mission' for your venture. These statements are not to be taken lightly; and very careful thought ought to go into their formulation. A well-formulated vision and mission can help steer the venture onward to what you believe is its destiny or destination; and can also pull you back on to the 'correct path', if you believe you might be losing your way. If you take the analogy of a ship with you as its captain, then vision and mission answer the important questions 'where are we going' and 'how are we getting there'; murky answers to these questions mean risking getting lost at sea.

12.1.2. VISION

You need to create a vision for your new venture that indicates what the business might be in the future. This vision should be 'living' and 'breathing'—aspirational and motivate you and all the other involved stakeholders. The vision for your venture defines its purpose and creates a shared mental image of a desired future state for the enterprise. It should describe how your venture is going to leave an impact on customers and the greater community. Your values would influence the vision of your business and these can be captured in the form of a vision statement.

The vision statement should be emotionally grounded rather than being based on rationality and logic. Emotion dictates that we circumvent the outcomes of rational–deductive thinking and take action which might seem wholly illogical. For example, when someone risks their own life, overcome fear and jump overboard to save an unrelated person who might be drowning, then they are said to be acting on emotion and not rationality. A purely rational individual in the above scenario would weigh their own life and well-being first, because of the rule of 'self-preservation' over everything else. Consider Rivigo, their vision is captured in the following aspirational statements: 'Transform 100,000 lives by creating meaningful livelihood for truck drivers'; 'Create *The Hero's Hermitage* at RIVIGO'; and 'Make India a top name in the logistics sector'.

12.1.3. MISSION

The mission statement is the formal statement of the venture's purpose. It states what the business aims to achieve and how it will go about achieving it. It usually defines the scope of the business by including references to its offerings, VP, market segments and the benefits customers derive. The mission statement needs to be consistent with your values just like the vision statement and must be a clear and succinct declaration of your strategy. It should be written in a manner such that you and your employees have a framework to guide action and an orienting purpose.

The four essential questions your venture's mission statement must answer include: What do we do? How do we do it? Whom do we do it for? And why you do what you do? For example, consider the mission statement of M-KOPA Solar from Kenya (their case is illustrated in Chapter 3):

'To upgrade lives by making high-quality solutions affordable to everyone'.

What we do: *create solutions*; how do we do it: *by making them affordable and of high quality*; whom do we do it for: *everyone*; and why you do what you do: *to upgrade lives.*

We became familiar with M-KOPA in Chapter 3. The following excerpt is an extension of that case to highlight how values, and the vision and mission statements can be configured under a socially conscientious ethos.

M-KOPA Solar, Kenya: Bringing Electricity to East Africa

M-KOPA is a solar energy company which was founded in 2012 in Nairobi, Kenya, by Nick Hughes, Chad Larson and Jesse Moore. The start-up sells home solar-based systems in Kenya, Tanzania and Uganda. Its mission and values are:

Mission:

'To upgrade lives by making high-quality solutions affordable to everyone'

Values:

Maendeleo (progress): We have an appetite for advancement and our customers do too. Our aim is to get better every day, improving our business operations, while our customers better their lives.

Umilki (ownership): We help low-income consumers acquire and own high quality, affordable energy solutions, and we gain pride knowing that our customers gain independence through ownership.

Uwazi (clarity): We aim to make life easier for our customers, and we value straightforward, common-sense solutions. We make our business decisions based on a clear and honest assessment of facts. We believe that good ideas and straight insights come from all directions—from our customers, our partners and our staff.

M-KOPA has introduced a proprietary and patented technology platform that combines embedded GSM and mobile payments to revolutionize asset financing in emerging markets. The off-the-grid household customer pays a deposit to take the solar-based system home, pay a daily sum through M-Pesa for a year, after which they own the system.

As of 2018, M-KOPA had connected over 600,000 homes in East Africa to affordable solar power saving customers a projected $405 million over the next 4 years.

12.2. VALUES-BASED IDENTITY

Your venture's *identity* is influenced by the values, vision and mission you set for it. A venture's identity can add value and fuel its growth by attracting a certain type of discerning customer who might associate with what the venture proclaims to stand for. A clear identity for the business means that customers are inspired to make purchases and if they *believe* in the underlying values themselves, then they may make repeat purchases.

By developing a brand identity that is based on positive values, you can develop a closer relationship with customers and targeting those purposefully who identify with your values. Customers make purchases from social enterprises like Adorn Online because they believe in its mission of 'empowering artisans and preserving indigenous crafts'.

Adorn Online, Supporting and Nurturing the Work of Artisans

Adorn Online is a social enterprise based out of Pakistan that was set up by two women professionals Najia Siddiqui and Rosie Pannell. The social enterprise promotes products crafted by individual artisans and other NGOs who support artisans. The artisans are mostly women from marginalized communities and deprived regions of rural and urban Pakistan. The enterprise's mission is to promote the work of talented women and organizations and to encourage better pay and working conditions in the handicrafts sector.

Each artisan is given design training and all the necessary inputs required to carry out their work. They are paid immediately upon receipt of the finished product, rather than to wait for compensation until the item is purchased by a customer. The artisans are home-based and due to their association with Adorn reap advantages such as flexibility of schedules and a safe working environment.

These benefits allow women with added responsibilities such as farm, domestic and/or child care work, the ability to balance priorities and earn supplemental income. Adorn rates of work are significantly higher than normative market rates which protects them from exploitative practices.

Adorn set up its online store as a platform to market its produce both locally and internationally. Items listed for sale are examples of exquisite craftsmanship done by Pakistani artisans. The collection includes women shirts, salwars or pants, scarves and shawls, quilts, cushions, sofa throws and tableware. The problem, however, is competition from traditional businesses. Adorn's base costs are higher than those of a mass-produced, machine-made product, accounting for the higher labour rates it pays to its artisan workers to ensure a better livelihood for them.

Although a majority of customers are price conscious, Adorn, over the years, has built up a group of clients who buy from them because of their social mission. These clients became acquainted with Adorn's products via their Facebook, Instagram and Pinterest posts and through their participation at trade shows in London, New Jersey, Dubai and Jordan.

12.3. TAKING SOCIAL RESPONSIBILITY

Social responsibility is a broad term that refers to an enterprise's commitment to social issues such as employment opportunities for marginalized individuals and communities; or offering products or services for those at the bottom of pyramid (the most poor and marginalized). It is estimated that over four billion people in the developing world have unmet needs in the areas of health care, education, transport, communication, credit, electricity, drinking water and other areas which are usually taken for granted in developed or industrialized nations.

Taking social responsibility is now expected of all existing and new ventures. As an entrepreneur, you will be expected by your customers, the government and media to not only earn profits but to use your skills and the venture to give back to society. In order to do this, you can adopt 'corporate social responsibility' (CSR) principles in the manner you conduct your business. CSR is a form of private business self-regulation which helps an organization configure its 'socially conscious' identity visible to its stakeholders.

There are a number of recognized CSR standards and approaches which you can study when configuring your venture's values, vision and mission. These include 'ISO 26000', an international standard for adopting CSR and 'triple bottom line'. Your new venture's CSR-derived identity can yield several known and valuable benefits.

12.3.1. BRAND AWARENESS AND INCREASED SALES

A social responsibility-based identity can help in building brand awareness and equity. It gives new ventures an opportunity to attract media coverage helping them with public relations, especially if such ventures are introducing radical new offerings. Customers are increasingly aware of environmental and social issues and take exception about unethical work practices. This awareness can influence their purchase decisions. A growing number of consumers prefer businesses that are willing to work on global, social and environmental issues. And it is well documented that such consumers are willing to pay a higher price for product offerings that are driven by social responsibility concerns.

For instance, Thrive Agric, the online agri-tech platform in Nigeria (illustrative case appears as follows), banked on the rising concern among Nigerians to reduce food imports (and make the country more self-reliant) to create a unique business model that linked farmers with investors wanting to invest in sustainable agricultural production. Due to this 'socially responsible' identity, Thrive Agric has received considerable media attention, public interest and also investment. It is now well established, new ventures with an identity that is based on social responsibility are attractive to investors.

Thrive Agric, Empowering Farmers in Nigeria

Thrive Agric (www.thriveagric.com) based in Nigeria is a technology-driven agriculture company set up in 2017 that allows investors to sponsor farmers with a predictable return on investment on their harvests. The venture's mission is to ensure food security and is backed by Telefonica's Wayra, Ventures Platform. Its launch was facilitated by Google Launchpad and Y Combinator's start-up school based in Silicon Valley, USA.

The online platform acts as an intermediary between farmers and those interested in investing in farming. Investors can get an assured return on investment each year, whereas cash-strapped farmers, who have no access to formal credit, get funding for their operations. Since inception, the start-up has sold more than 200 hectares of farmland.

To begin, interested investors create an online account and choose a farm or farms and the quantity of harvest they need by paying a subscription fee. Next, the subscribers get regular online updates of developments on the farm and production events from start to finish. Once a harvest is successful, the produce is sold, and the returns are distributed to the subscribers within a set time limit.

Thus, Thrive Agric is a technology-enabled start-up that empowers farmers in Nigeria by raising funds to finance agricultural operations in farms. Such a solution is desirable as it curbs Nigeria's high food import bill and culture which has an adverse impact on local farming, leading to the benefits of farmers who are currently out priced by imported produce.

12.3.2. DEVELOPMENT OF NEW PRODUCTS

By truly adopting the notion of 'social responsibility', a new venture can develop very original new products and services that not only derive profits but also address a pressing social need. Emerging and developing countries are afflicted by a vast array of socio-economic problems; and cash-strapped governments of such countries are usually not in a position to effectively resolve them in full (though short-term measures are often in place). This gap between socio-economic needs and public serves creates an immense opportunity for innovative entrepreneurs. For example, life-style diseases due to obesity are reaching epidemic levels in a number developing countries. This would be a public health issue within the purview of national governments. However, to capitalize on the opportunity to present innovative cures for life-style diseases, a number of start-ups in developing countries are focusing on developing new products and services to tackle health problems such as obesity and type 2 diabetes.

HealthifyMe, India: A Digital Weight Loss Platform

In 2012, Tushar Vashisht, Mathew Cherian and Sachin Shenoy founded HealthifyMe in Bangalore, India. HealthifyMe is a digital weight loss platform that has been developed for both the iOS and Android platforms which provide calorie tracking, water intake tracking and cloud-based fitness coaching using a gamified approach to motivate users.

Users with a premium subscription can choose from an array of in-house nutritionists, fitness trainers and certified Yoga coaches to work on their personal health goals. The start-up provides access to the world's largest Indian food database with a calorie counter for regional foods of India along with an exercise tracker for logging in physical activities. In 2015, Healthify partnered with Godrej's Nature Basket, Manipal Hospitals, Medanta and the Apollo Centre to launch the 'Healthify India Movement' which aimed to pledge Indians to a healthy lifestyle, while paying attention to lifestyle disorders such as obesity and diabetes.

This movement garnered considerable public and investor interest in the venture such that in 2016, HealthifyMe successfully raised $6 million from IDG Ventures, Inventus Capital Partners and Blume Ventures. In 2017, the start-up launched Ria—a new product. Ria is an artificial intelligence powered virtual nutritionist that has learnt from the 150 million food logs and 50 million workout logs on the platform.

In 2018, HealthifyMe raised $12 million from a number of international investors such as Sistema Asia Fund, Samsung's AI focused fund NEXT and Atlas Asset Management.

Now consider the case of Embrace Innovations, a social enterprise in India. Embrace's focus on 'social responsibility' has led it to develop health care technologies that aim to reduce the number of infant and maternal deaths that afflict poor and marginalized communities in emerging and developing countries. Developing affordable health care for such 'bottom-of-the-pyramid' markets represents an as-of-yet untapped entrepreneurial opportunity.

Embrace Innovations, India: Improving Infant and Maternal Mortality

In 2008, four former Stanford University students—Jane Chen, Linus Liang, Naganand Murty and Rahul Panicker—founded Embrace Innovations—a for-profit social enterprise in India. The founders had previously participated and won a design challenge at their university to develop an infant incubator. This new incubator's cost was 99 per cent lower than traditional ones, which are roughly priced at US$20,000. This university project led to the Embrace Infant Warmer and a few found mission to develop health care technologies focused on reducing infant and maternal deaths in emerging and developing countries.

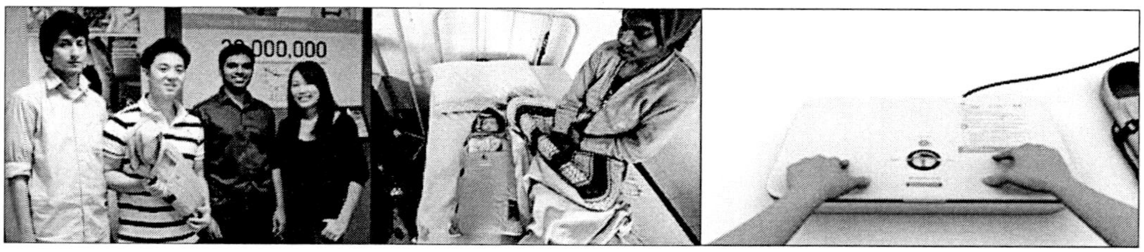

It took four years of R&D and testing, but in April 2011, the first Embrace Infant Warmer was delivered to the Little Flower Hospital in Bangalore, India, and by late 2011, it was introduced in Africa. The company has since developed two versions of the Embrace Infant Warmer, each with three components—an infant-sized sleeping bag, a pouch of phase change material and a heater. The pouch, when heated, can maintain the body temperature for premature babies for up to eight hours. Another product, the Embrace Nest was designed for hospitals that suffer from intermittent electricity supply. This product is simple and portable enough that it can be used by a health care worker or a village mother. Embrace's distribution channels and global partnership with GE Healthcare are helping them popularize the socially conscientious products.

In 2012, Embrace's the non-profit arm began developing a new programme to augment the Infant Warmer with education on hypothermia and neonatal health. By 2013, this programme had been introduced in 10 countries and had benefitted 5,000 mothers. By 2018, Embrace had reached out to 300,000 in 22 countries and had grown to serve 10 states in India.

12.3.3. NEW OPPORTUNITIES FROM SUSTAINABLE EMPLOYMENT

Sustainable employment is the idea that a new venture exclusively recruits individuals from excluded or marginalized communities who might be un- or underemployed. Committed employees are the backbone of any new venture, and finding, training and retaining them can be exceptionally difficult. Relying on disadvantaged communities to supply your venture's labour force can be exceedingly rewarding and motivating, whose benefits are incalculable. Evidence suggests that staff from such communities is eager to learn, adaptable, loyal and dedicated to their employers.

Several start-ups in developing countries are committed to running their operations by creating sustainable employment opportunities for marginalized individuals, like those with hearing disabilities. It is estimated that in India alone, there are over eight million deaf adults of which only 67 per cent are gainfully employed. Mirakle Couriers' mission to empower hearing impaired individuals through sustainable employment in a courier business reflects its commitment to social responsibility.

Mirakle Couriers, the Silent Couriers of Mumbai

Mirakle Couriers is an award-winning courier agency in Mumbai that was founded in 2009 by Dhruv Lakra as a for-profit social enterprise. The enterprise aims to generate employment opportunities for low-income hearing-impaired men and women and empowers them to gain financial independence.

Dhruv had a chance encounter with a hearing-impaired boy while travelling on a bus journey and this led him to realize the challenges faced by such people on a day-to-day basis. Curious to learn more, he began to research and realized that hearing impairment was an 'invisible disability' with little public awareness and empathy in India. Employment opportunities too for such individuals were limited as people lacked the patience or foresight to learn sign language. Dhruv spent months learning the Indian sign language and decided to focus on the courier business as it primarily required visual skills with little or no need for verbal communication. He realized that individuals with hearing disabilities are excellent at reading maps and in readily recalling roads and buildings because of their enhanced visual inclination which acts to compensate for their impaired hearing.

Mirakle Couriers' office opens early at 8 am where Dhruv's team couriers divide-up the day's deliveries—mostly e-commerce parcel deliveries for Amazon. The heavier packages are delivered by the hearing abled delivery men on motorcycles. As the hearing impaired were banned from driving motorcycles in India until recently, they instead used the city's bus network to deliver their packages, with each round lasting around eight hours. The delivery men hand over parcels and get signatures from recipients without uttering a single word. When they face problems, they use a WhatsApp video call using sign language to explain their problem to hearing impaired female employees at the company's headquarters.

Currently, Mirakle Couriers has two branches in Mumbai employing 64 hearing impaired staff and deliver over 65,000 monthly shipments. The back office is run by 20 hearing impaired women who have been trained on the job in data entry and manipulation, tracking and scanning, sorting and other day-to-day branch operations.

Mirakle's clientele includes large Indian multinational corporations such as Mahindra, Godrej and Aditya Birla Group as well as the retail giant, Amazon. The average income of each courier is $220 per month which is well above India's current per capita monthly income.

In developing countries, a major social problem is the lack of employment opportunities for women from lower income groups. Women from poor households often lack education or technical skills and confidence to take up job opportunities. However, if adequately trained and provided a safe work environment, women can be as productive, if not more, as their male counterparts due to their work ethic, commitment and pronounced abilities in multi-tasking and maintaining focus for extended durations.

Consider the following two illustrative cases from India: Sakha Cabs recruits exclusively women, due to which they are able to tap into a growing market niche exclusively, which traditional taxi cab firms are not able to. While Jayaashree Industries have designed equipment that manufacturers an affordable solution to a women's only problem; the equipment and solution are exclusively operated and sold by self-employed rural women.

Sakha Cabs, India: Safe Transport Solutions for Women by Women

In 2008, Sakha Cabs was launched in New Delhi, India, by social entrepreneur Meenu Vadera who has pioneered the idea of 'Women on Wheels'. Women on Wheels has received several recognitions and awards for its innovative business model as well as for the transformative impact made on lives of resource poor women. Since inception, Sakha Cabs has become a pioneering social enterprise that provides women with safe transport solutions.

It offers two broad types of services. First, its Chauffeur Placement Services places women chauffeurs on both short-term daily duty as well as on full-time contracts with individuals and organizations. Second, cab hire services which are a premium cab hire service for women where the taxi cabs are driven by women drivers on fixed rates (hence, no haggling required).

Sakha cabs has partnered with the Azad Foundation—a non-profit institution—to provide women from lower-income background a sustainable livelihood solution through driving. Training and development of women from marginalized sections of society is sponsored by the Azad Foundation. The foundation's in-house trainers and those from the Maruti Institute of Driving and Technology Research impart driving skills. In addition to this, Delhi Police trains the women drivers in self-defence and their Crime against Women cell equips them to deal with adverse road incidents and violence.

To date, Sakha cabs has enabled 700 women to become employable as professional drivers or chauffeurs in Delhi, Jaipur, Kolkata and Indore.

Jayaashree Industries, India: Low-cost Sanitary Napkins for Women by Women

In 2006, after four years of re-engineering, Arunachalam Muruganantham, a college dropout from Coimbatore, South India, made a breakthrough. He had developed a sanitary napkin manufacturing machine costing just \$931 compared to \$635,000 for similar imported machines. The social entrepreneur won several accolades for his invention (which received patent protection) from institutions like Indian Institute of Technology Madras, Chennai. Lack of access to affordable products for menstrual hygiene is a pressing social problem for women; and is one of the major reasons why girls miss vital schooling and are not able to actively participate in the labour market.

Arunachalam's machine used purely mechanical processes such as grinding and defibration, and pressing and sealing to convert the raw material—high quality pine wood pulp (instead of unviable cotton used in industrially produced sanitary napkins)—into a sanitary napkin. The sanitary napkins produced through this process are low cost and hence affordable by women from low-income backgrounds.

To commercialize his invention, Arunachalam set up Jayaashree Industries. The venture has to date sold more than 1,300 machines across 27 states in India and in seven other countries. This social enterprise sells its low-cost machines directly to rural women through the support of micro-credit institutions and in partnership with other non-profits whose beneficiaries are poor women. The woman machine operator is trained in the full napkin-making process in just three hours and who can then employ three other women to help with processing and distribution of the low-cost product. Hence, the venture creates both self-employment and direct employment for rural women. Further, the model proposed reduced start-up costs and enabled local production saving on transportation and distribution costs because the produce, though voluminous, was light weight.

Arunachalam's vision was to create a million livelihoods for poor women and making India a 100 per cent sanitary napkin using country from its current level of just 2 per cent use in rural India.

12.3.4. HIGHER PROFITABILITY FROM ENVIRONMENTAL MITIGATION

Being environmentally conscious is a part of taking 'social responsibility'; and contrary to popular belief, considering the environmental impact of doing business will not adversely impact your venture's start-up or operating costs. In fact, evidence suggests that business processes designed to reduce a venture's negative environmental footprint improve efficiency and increase bottom-line profit margins. Being environmentally conscious can include an enterprise's efforts to eliminate waste and emissions, while maximizing the efficient use of resources. As with other 'social responsibilities', governments in emerging and developing countries are keen to encourage entrepreneurs to their environmental responsibilities seriously through supportive policies and other interventions.

As a new venture, you can develop an environmental policy that shows your commitment to reducing your environmental impact and these can be communicated in your communication and marketing campaigns which can have public relations benefits and drawn in new customers, a growing majority whom now hold environmentally conscious views. Using recycled materials as raw material or for packaging is also shown to bring down production costs and increase profit margins.

New start-ups in emerging and developing countries are making clean technology their focus; designing, producing and distributing products and services that are environmentally friendly. These new ventures often conduct an 'environmental audit' and publish results on their environmental performance in monetary terms to reflect their environmental ethos's bottom-line impact. To illustrate, consider the model of HPS—the social enterprise discussed in Chapter 4. Rural communities in developing countries lack electrification which is capital intensive and relies on public sector investment, which unfortunately, due to a vast array of reasons is sparingly made to benefit marginalized communities. It is estimated that billions of people worldwide lack access to electricity; to enable sustainable and environmental friendly access of poor rural communities, HPS uses rice husk rather than fossil fuel to power its generation plants. Rice husk is significantly cheaper than its traditional counterparts and its burning process produces much fewer harmful emissions. As a result, the electricity produced is carbon neutral and much cheaper than what might be supplied through the national grid.

The following three cases further dis-spell the myth that being environmentally conscious for venture increases its costs of doing business.

Vortex Engineering, India: Solar Powered ATMs

Vortex Engineering was founded in 2001 by Indian Institute of Technology Madras, Chennai, alumnus L. Kannan in the southern Indian city of Chennai. By 2005, the venture had started focusing on developing self-service transaction systems such as ATMs for banks and services for ATM management. Vortex specifically designed ATMs that consume very less mechanical and electrical components compared to conventional ATMs. This helps reduce their costs substantially when compared to imported options, which remain largely unaffordable. The ATMs also come with solar power options, which means they can be set up and operated in areas with severe power shortages—primarily rural communities. Further, unlike expensive imported ATMs, these consumed less than 100 watts of power and did not require a temperature-controlled operating environment. All these features and benefits made the machines ideally suited for serving marginalized communities.

In 2010, Vortex had a breakthrough when it received a bulk order of 545 ATMs including 300 solar-powered ATMs from the State Bank of India. By 2011, Vortex ATMs were being sold in several developing countries in Asia and Africa such as Nepal, Bangladesh and Madagascar.

Vortex was backed by a number of investors such as Tata Capital, Aavishkaar (featured in Chapter 11), Ventureast and Oasis. In 2016, a special biometric technique was incorporated in the ATMs which enabled rural folk with little literacy to remember four-digit PIN numbers to operate their accounts. By reading their thumbprint, the ATMs enabled rural banking customers to withdraw cash.

Vortex Engineering is now regarded as the world's lowest power consuming ATM and leading provider of solar ATMs. The company has won a number of accolades like World Economic Forum Technology Pioneer in 2011 for empowering rural communities.

Berman-Kalil Housing Concepts: South Africa, Innovative and Affordable Housing

In 2015, Brad Berman and Alicia Kalil founded Berman-Kalil Housing Concepts in Cape Town, South Africa. In South Africa alone, it is estimated that there is a shortage of 2.3 million family homes. The founders wanted to create innovative, sustainable housing solutions by 'recycling' decommissioned shipping containers into low-cost homes for modular worldwide distribution.

The start-up has converted shipping containers into a range of products such as homes, offices, restaurants and kitchens, medical facilities, community centres, classrooms and childcare facilities. The founders of Berman-Kalil estimate that their converted homes are 40–60 per cent cheaper than brick and mortar homes which can be manufactured and delivered to low-income consumers in just three weeks.

For just $7,910, the start-up offers bachelor units with a bathroom, kitchenette and built-in cupboards. The home is fully finished with windows, flooring, a door and different exterior cladding options. On the higher end of the spectrum, a two-bedroom home with additional extras such as oven and extractor fan costs about $14,250.

By upcycling shipping containers—which are very inexpensive to acquire and are plentiful—Berman-Kalil is solving a pressing social problem with a viable solution with environmental benefits; because otherwise the shipping containers would have been scrapped and smelted—contributing to carbon emissions. Its product addresses a problem for which there is a growing market of consumers who can afford to pay the prices Berman-Kalil has set.

WaterWalla, India: Improving Access to Clean Water

In 2009, a group of students—Anshu Vaish, Neil Parikh, Amer Hassanally, Soaib Grewal and Rayna Chandaria—from Brown University, USA, launched WaterWalla in Dharavi, (Asia's largest slum), Mumbai. WaterWalla's mission is to improve access to clean water for underserved communities worldwide by engaging academics, non-profits and business communities. Access to potable, clean drinking water is a basic human right; unfortunately, in developing countries, most surface and underground water bodies suffer from high levels of bacterial and chemical contamination. With little access to piped, filtered and treated water due to high cost and public sector negligence, excluded communities have no choice but to consume contaminated water. As a result, the incidence of easily preventable water borne diseases in such communities is very high, leading to poor health and even mortality.

WaterWalla champions market-based solutions (which would be profit-making) to the water crisis, with an emphasis on financial and operational sustainability. WaterWalla sources affordable purification technologies from its technology partners, promotes these through their resource network and finally introduces solutions through local micro-entrepreneurs into excluded communities impacted by poor quality drinking water. The solutions are introduced through entrepreneurship, education and links with technology partners.

WaterWalla works with a network of partners and advisors including non-profits and research organizations from across the globe such as Tata Institute of Social Sciences (India), Brown University (USA) and Medentech (Ireland/USA). The start-up has launched a WaterWalla fellowship that provides seed funding to fellows working to develop solutions for clean water for marginalized communities.

12.4. REPORTING ETHICAL VALUES

Internal reporting (or whistleblowing) of a breach of ethical values refers to a situation when an existing or former member tells someone internal about an illegal or immoral practice. This kind of reporting is especially done with the purpose of seeing the practice change. For example, exploitation, corrupt practices or public breach-of-trust. Usually, employees in a venture want to be able to tell someone within the organization and do not necessarily wish to harm their employer's reputation. As an entrepreneur, if you do not punish or discourage unethical and immoral practices, then they would typically get worse, until an employee or any other stakeholder—often motivated by conscience—believes that they must notify the press or a government agency, which can be very detrimental. This is known as external reporting or whistleblowing.

Whistleblowing is vital to the sustainability of organizations. Ventures that make it difficult for their employees to report ethical and moral problems internally are likely to find themselves facing much larger problems externally. However, often it is the case that employees who speak up, even internally, are sometimes seen as traitors, or as people who are 'not team players'. Right from the very onset, as an entrepreneur, you ought to set up systems which will allow your employees, customers and other stakeholders to report any problems. Once reported, these should be logged, investigated and settled promptly.

Externally reporting your ethical values and progress on any initiatives that promote such values is important. Such reporting offers credible promotional and brand building opportunities for your venture, and if done well, can attract significant, and most importantly, *free* media publicity. There are several ways in which ventures can report their ethical values and initiatives in CSR to stakeholders.

12.4.1. SOCIAL ACCOUNTING

Social accounting involves communicating social and environmental impact of a company's economic actions to stakeholders and society at large. Reporting guidelines and standards serve as frameworks for social accounting, auditing and reporting. The Social Audit Network (SAN) is a non-profit that facilitates the exchange of information between practitioners of social accounting and audit in the social economy and voluntary sectors. Their manual and guidelines are available for purchase.[1]

12.4.2. SUSTAINABILITY REPORTING GUIDELINES

The Global Reporting Initiative is an independent, international standards organization that helps businesses, governments and other organizations understand and communicate their impacts on issues such as climate change, human rights and corruption. Their 'Sustainability Reporting Guidelines' can be accessed for free.[2]

12.5. SUMMARY AND APPLICATION

Your new venture needs to reflect your values and beliefs. These set guidelines are for how your venture would behave with various stakeholders-customers, suppliers, distributors and employees. You also need to develop vision statement that reflect the future state of your business, and a mission statement that outlines the purpose of your new venture—both of which should ideally reflect your values, beliefs and ethical stances.

Being socially responsible means access to new opportunities for designing products and services for customers, who do have a capacity to pay, but their requirements are often not understood or

[1] Please refer to: http://www.socialauditnetwork.org.uk/getting-started/new-guide-tosocial-accounting-and-audit/.

[2] Please refer to: https://www.globalreporting.org/standards/gri-standards-download-center/.

simply ignored by mainstream corporations and the public sector. Being environmentally conscientious will make your venture more efficient and robust and will attract more public admiration and interest from investors. Finally, take any breaches of trust and ethics violations exceedingly seriously. There will be a need to subscribe to internal and external reporting standards fostered within a culture that encourages those with information about such breaches and violations to come forward and to bring these to your notice.

Exercise 12.1. Values and Beliefs

1. List your social concerns, philosophies, core values and beliefs.
2. Develop a mission statement for your new venture. You can look up the examples mentioned in this chapter.
3. Develop a vision statement for your new venture that is in line with your mission statement.
4. Propose a name for your new venture that is consistent with a 'socially responsible' brand identity.
5. Design a logo for your new venture reflecting the above identity.

13

Implementation and Operations Management

LEARNING OUTCOMES

- Be able to choose the appropriate legal form for your venture
- Identify the key activities you need to do for launching your venture
- Create an operating plan for your venture and identify critical success factors

13.1. SETTING LEGAL FOUNDATIONS

Spotlight on ELEME, Gigantic Chinese Food Delivery Platform

ELEME Inc. (www.ele.me) is the largest online Chinese food delivery platform founded in 2008 by two computer game fans Mark Zhang and Jack Kang while in their early 20s, studying at Shanghai Jiao Tong University. ELEME's mission is 'everything 30 minutes'. The online business has successfully exploited Chinese consumers' growing preference for takeaways by creating a local platform which allows food delivery from thousands of restaurants in cities across China.

ELEME Inc operates as an O2O platform whose name roughly translates as 'Hungry Now'. It has two categories of customers—people who wish to order food and restaurants who wish to attract customers. The platform provides benefits to its customer categories—it enhances people's choices and access to food delivery while allowing restaurants to increase their income.

The founders of ELEME Inc tested and validated their core offering by testing their 'solution' on their own university's students. Initially, they provided lunch and dinner choices; most students live in dormitories that lack catering facilities and they tend to order food from the university canteen or restaurants in the vicinity of their university dormitory. ELEME Inc took orders by telephone, acting as an intermediary between students and restaurants while charging a small commission for each order delivered. Promotion was done using leaflets sent out to student dormitories. Mark and Jack noticed that the response from students was very positive—students appreciated the increase in choices, reviews and ratings to help them decide and the efficient 30-minute delivery service. Restaurants too wanted to be on the platform because ELEME had its own delivery teams. Restaurants could avoid costs associated with delivery such as owning and operating food delivery vehicles and staff. Mark and Jack became convinced that online food delivery was a real opportunity. Shanghai proved to be a good target market given the large number of universities and businesses in the city—they could target both students and white-collar workers in the city's commercial districts.

The platform has grown exponentially from Chinese Yuan 0.15 billion in 2010 to Yuan 44.2 billion in 2015. The new ELEME Inc app allows people to choose and order food from thousands of restaurants by filtering their options based on a variety of parameters such as location and reviewer comments. In addition, a new system—'NAPOS'—for restaurants which enables them to manage orders, update menus and view financial reports. In this manner, from an 'operations' standpoint, the platform integrates customer relationship management, customer analysis and food delivery with marketing.

From small beginnings, the company spread to various sized cities in China. By the end of 2016, ELEME Inc was doing deliveries in 2,000 cities with over one million restaurants registered, a staff of over 15,000 and nine million orders processed daily. The delivery arm of ELEME Inc 'Fengniao Delivery' employed over three million riders. Much of this growth was achieved through their unique franchising model and two successful rounds of financing in 2015. Mark and Jack raised $350 million early in the year and then $630 million in the latter half by investors CITIC Holding, Tencent Holdings and Hongshan Capital. In 2018, ELEME Inc was acquired by the Alibaba Group in a deal worth approximately $9.8 billion. The e-commerce giant Alibaba plans to leverage ELEME Inc's delivery network to blend physical retail with online shopping where consumers visit shops but place orders through their phones with goods being delivered to their homes within 30 minutes. If Alibaba's model works, customers would not need to carry handbags anywhere.

Once you have tested and validated your idea and feedback clearly suggests that you have a scalable model; then it is time to think carefully about your business's 'operational' aspects. Often, entrepreneurs find it exceedingly hard to shift their thinking and approach from 'entrepreneurial' to 'managerial'. At some point in the life-cycle of a venture, its founder(s) need to stop being entrepreneurial and become managers—because the skills required to *start* a new venture are very different from the skills needed to *grow* and *scale* a venture. Mark and Jack made the transition from *entrepreneurial* to *managerial* readily; they were able to test and validate their idea but then were also able to grow and scale it, by focusing on introducing operational efficiencies to the way they conducted business right from the very start. The very first thing, from an operations standpoint, entrepreneurs need to consider choices about their venture's legal foundations—discussed in the following sub-sections.

13.1.1. PROTECTING YOUR BUSINESS IDEA

As a founder entrepreneur, you need to think of whether you want to protect the IP of your business idea. IP is the real 'value' in your business, besides any other assets that you put into it (a building, vehicles and so on). Your IP could be a unique recipe (like Coke's or KFC's), a piece of software, a new method or product, a new plant or animal variety, your brand name and artistic compositions such as music, graphics and video. There are numerous ways in which you can protect your IP so that you have legal grounds to take action against anyone else copying it or using it without your explicit permission. In all countries around the world, IP laws exist, but they must be enforced by the entrepreneur. Your government will not usually police IP theft, you will need to keep an eye on who might be infringing on your IP rights. If you find any perpetrators, and you have legal IP protection, you will have the option to act through the courts of law and the police to stop the infringing party and claim damages. If you have no legal IP protection, like trademarking your business's name, and if anyone else starts using it, then it would be very hard, from a legal standpoint, to prove your case in court that you came up with the name first and have first right to it. By registering your business (its various forms are discussed later in this chapter), you do not automatically protect the name of your business. To protect your business's name, brand or trademark, you need to register it separately. By doing this, you will also ensure that you are not unintentionally infringing on someone else's IP. It might very well be that the name you have come up with, is already trademarked. In this case, you will have no choice but to come up with another name (you could also think about buying the trademark from its registered owner if you really want it). The lesson, therefore, is protect your IP immediately, at the very instance you create it—do not wait.

You can protect your IP by filing for patents, trademarks, copyrights and industrial design rights. Patents are used to protect inventions which are wholly new and original—usually physical products, pharmaceutical compositions or engineering methods. Trademark refers to a sign made up of words or a logo or both which distinguish goods and services from those offered by your rivals. Registered designs refer to protecting how the product design you are creating is unique from anything else registered. Copyright, which is traditionally an unregistered right, allows you to protect your original material across any media such as literary works, dramatic works, musical works and sounds. Figure 13.1 summarizes the broad classes of intellectual property.

FIGURE 13.1 **Broad Classes of IP (Country-specific Variations Will Exist)**

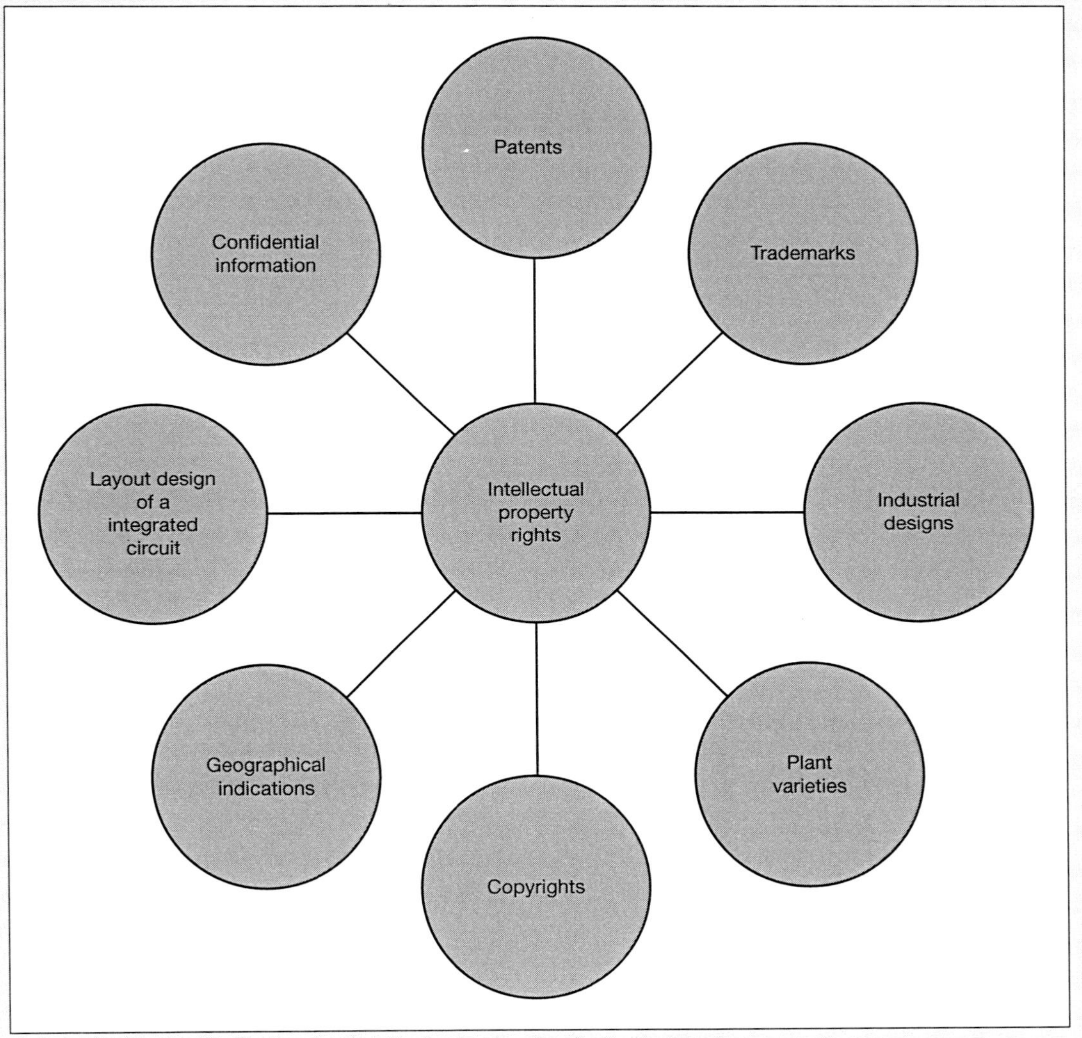

Source: http://trademarkyourbiz.com.sg/wp-content/uploads/IP-Rights.png (accessed on 14 June 2019).

Each country has its own IP filing procedures. IP registration processes can also have several disadvantages: patent applications take a considerable amount of time to get approved averaging over two years as well as significant costs. Once a patent is awarded, it is published by the government, and anyone can view it. The patent owner has an approximate 20-year monopoly to use the proceeds from their invention—they have the right to license their patent out to someone else, use it themselves or even sell it. After 20 years though (or the expiry date set by the awarding body), the patent automatically becomes public property, which means anyone can use it. If you neglect to pay the yearly patent fees, then your patent will also become null and void. Due to these problems, especially a patent's maximum allowed lifespan, corporations such as Coke and KFC choose to not 'patent' their recipes/formulations—they remain, to this day, 'trade secrets'; that is, the corporations take responsibility of keeping their IP safe through internal means and procedures.

In practice, for most start-ups, because of resource limitations, getting first to market might be the most effective way to gain competitive advantage rather than safeguarding IP via patenting or other strategies. IP infringement is rife in most developing and emerging economies because of high enforcement costs and weak policing mechanisms. A trademark registration, however, would be essential and must not be ignored under any circumstance. Alternative ways to safeguarding your IP is to consider putting in place 'secrecy' or 'non-disclosure' agreements when sharing your idea with others like investors.

13.2. LEGAL FORMS OF BUSINESS

Starting a new venture can be risky for you personally. You can limit your personal risk by choosing your business's legal form carefully. There are three common legal forms for a business—sole traders, partnerships and limited liability companies. Becoming a 'sole trader' is the simplest form of business; a single individual is owner-manager. Its main disadvantages are that as a sole trader you will have unlimited personal liability (which means that you would be personally liable to pay off any debts owed and your personal assets could be seized by the lender to settle your business's debts), it would be more difficult to borrow money from the formal financial sector and as owner you would have to pay personal tax. Partnerships are common in some professions such as accountants, lawyers and doctors. Its disadvantages are similar to sole traders and partnerships may need to cease trading when partners change. Limited liability firms have limited liability—which means that in the event you declare bankruptcy, you will no longer be personally liable to pay off your business's debts and your personal assets cannot be seized and liquidated by the lender. The limited liability company form makes it easier to borrow money, but it has disadvantages linked to stronger regulation, administrative requirements and disclosure of information to government authorities on a regular basis.

13.3. LEGAL FORMS OF SOCIAL ENTERPRISE

You can choose to form a business as a social enterprise that is a start-up with a clearly defined social mission and all the profits are ploughed back to support the mission. There can be several types of legal social enterprises: (a) *unincorporated associations*—similar to sole traders and partnerships where informal associations of individuals can come together an incorporate the form quickly; (b) *trusts*—these are run as per the social objectives articulated in a 'trust deed'—they are common in the education and health care sector and (c) *community-based enterprises*—different countries have different types of community-based enterprises including cooperatives governed by cooperative regulations.

13.4. TAXATION

All commercial enterprises are liable for tax and there are several taxes that businesses need to pay depending on the country where they operate in. All new businesses must inform their relevant tax authorities of their existence; particularly those with employees where arrangements have to be made to deduct income tax from salaries. It is very important that entrepreneurs take the matter of paying their taxes due seriously and consider the burden of taxation before they decide to move forward and implement their business idea. Tax avoidance is a crime in most countries, and if caught, hefty fines and even jail sentences can be levied on business owners. Explained further are the different kinds of taxes you and your business might be liable for:

Corporation tax: The rate of corporation tax varies across countries and can increase with taxable profit. There are different rules on how profit is calculated for taxation purposes.

Income tax for sole traders and partnerships: Personal income taxes are usually higher than the rate of corporation taxes. Income tax on business profits are calculated after deducting expenses as codified in within national regulations.

Income tax on employees: In many countries, businesses are responsible for deducting income tax from their employees on behalf of the government.

Sales tax or value added tax (VAT): This refers to a form of tax on businesses whose turnover is over a certain stipulated amount. VAT or its equivalent has been introduced in most countries; in some countries it might be titled general sales tax (GST). Some goods and services may be exempted from VAT/GST.

13.5. SEEKING LEGAL ADVICE

You should take formal advice from an expert to decide which form of legal incorporation is best for the sort of business you wish to set up—it is best to not decide on your own because any wrong initial choices could have negative unintended consequences later which could cost you a lot of money to undo. In most countries, the IP office and the various registrars of legal incorporation have free advice clinics or public help windows. Do not be intimidated; walk into these outfits' offices and ask questions persistently and with confidence; as public servants, they are obliged to answer and give accurate information. However, double check everything you are told with someone else in the same organization or an external expert.

Company registration is essential and different countries have different procedures for registering firms. Many governments in emerging and developing economies now provide services (such as company registration, applying for licenses and trademark registration) via e-government portals. You need to account for the amount of time it takes on average to gain the necessary permissions and to formally register when starting your business.

13.6. FRANCHISING

Kathi Junction, an Indian Quick-Service Restaurant Franchise

India is one of the largest franchising markets in the world. Franchising had a late start in India with the first franchising exhibition happening in 2009. Since then, the growth in franchising has been phenomenal, especially for local Indian companies. Franchise agreements in India are covered with two commercial laws: the Contract Act, 1872 and the Specific Relief Act, 1963 which cover both enforcement and remedies for breach of contract.

In the last decade, franchising has emerged as a favourable business model supported by a growing network of India-focused VCs and business angels. Some of the sectors that have seen a surge in Indian companies adopting the franchisor business models are: (a) restaurants; (b) education; (c) salon and spa and (d) pharmacy. Some of the largest Indian franchisors are: Pind Balluchi in restaurants sector; Junior DPS in education; Monsoon Salon and Spa; Apollo Diagnostics and Big Mart Retail in the groceries sector.

Kathi Junction, set up by Navneet Sajwan in 2009, is an Indian quick-service restaurant serving vegetarian and non-vegetarian Mughlai wraps. The menu offers affordable value-for-money fast food options. The restaurant was first launched in Thane, near Mumbai. Kathi Junction has since become the largest Kathi roll and shawarma company selling over 14,000 rolls and 4,000 shawarmas every day. The company has developed its own spice mixes that ensures standardization and uniformity in taste. The low-cost business model attracted a large number of customers and Navneet chose the franchise model for his business's future growth. Kathi Junction now offers three franchise models with royalty rate at just 4 per cent. Model A—a food court express costing £6,000; Model B—a dining restaurant at £8,000–10,000 and a Model C—restaurant at £15,000–18,000.

A franchisee of Kathi Junction will have several benefits from associating with the brand of the parent franchisor. First, the brand is widely recognized and the operational system is well established, hence, a franchisee would not face teething problems common with start-ups. Second, the products and services of the parent franchisor are well developed such as product recipes and spice mixes that ensure standardization and uniformity. Third, Kathi Junction provides trained chefs from its pool and runs regular training and development programmes—which means that the franchisee would not be at risk from staff turnover. Fourth, group advertising and marketing at national levels allows the business to get wider exposure and minimizes marketing costs. Fifth, the parent franchisor supports with the outlet's design, saving the franchisee architectural design costs. The franchising model allowed Kathi Junction to grow significantly, as of 2015, it had outlets in 23 locations with 53 stores.

Purchasing a franchise can be a quicker way for you to start up a new venture. Franchising is a concept of business expansion that is governed by a detailed franchise agreement between two parties—a 'franchisor' and a 'franchisee'—that usually lasts for a fixed time period ranging from five to thirty years. The agreement serves a specific territory or geographical area; however, some franchisees might be allowed to manage several locations. Large franchises are common in sectors such as hotels, spas and hospitals. Medium-sized franchises involving significant investments and involvement of the entrepreneur are seen in sectors such as restaurants, petrol stations, grocery stores and more recently in the technology sector.

The franchisor licenses their know-how, IP, use of its business model and rights to sell its branded products and services to the franchisee. The franchisor provides several tangibles and intangibles such as national and international advertising, training and other support services to the franchisee. The franchisee in return pays the franchisor an upfront franchise purchase fee and agrees to comply with obligations as set out in the franchise agreement. In addition, the franchisee is also required to make some or all of the following payments to a franchisor: (a) disclosure fees; (b) a recurring royalty for using the trademark; (c) a specified percentage of the business sales and (d) reimbursement of training and advisory services provided by franchisor.

13.7. BENEFITS AND RISKS OF FRANCHISING

Franchising could offer you many benefits. First, the risk of business failure is reduced since the franchisor licenses a business based on a proven idea and you can review the experience of existing franchisees before committing. Second, you would be representing an established widely recognized brand name that would reduce your initial 'awareness creating' cost. Third, you would benefit from advertising done by the franchisor both at the national and international levels. Fourth, you will receive support in the form of training, help with setting up the business, manuals and standard procedures to follow. Fifth, you would have exclusive rights to your territory. Sixth, obtaining start-up finance maybe easier as banks are likely to lend money to buy a franchise that has an established track record and a good reputation. Seventh, relationships with suppliers would have been established by the franchisor so that procurement of quality raw materials would be easy. Finally, failure rates are much lower for franchise business than independent business start-ups.

There are several risks for the entrepreneur looking to buy a franchise. First, franchisor rules imposed by franchising authorities are becoming increasingly strict. Some franchisors could use minor rule violations to terminate contracts and seize the franchise without any reimbursement to the entrepreneur. Second, there could be hidden fees. In addition to receiving a percentage of revenue, a franchise may have additional costs such as fees for training and marketing. You need to read the franchise disclosure documents carefully to understand all the fees that you would need to pay as a franchisee. Third, franchises have strict rules on how you run your franchise, prices charged and the layout of your business—these may be too restrictive to respond to your local market conditions. Fourth, misleading average income figures. When conducting market research, calculate profitability based on median figures of franchisees in your location. This is because some franchisees have good skill sets, backgrounds and quality locations, whereas others may not benefit from these advantages. Further, estimated gross sales figures provided by franchisors can be misleading because if sales are high, the associated costs could also be high too, resulting in disappointing net sales figures. Therefore, while researching a franchising opportunity, care needs to be taken that revenue and costs of doing business figures are not overestimated.

13.8. SEARCHING FOR AND NEGOTIATING FRANCHISING OPPORTUNITIES

There are several ways for entrepreneurs to search for franchise opportunities. You can approach franchise brokers that help franchisors find appropriate franchisees. For instance, within the financial industry, franchising opportunities exist in consulting, accountancy and financial advising. Increasingly, franchising opportunities are being posted online on dedicated country-specific platforms, for instance in India—franchiseindia.org. Franchise India enlists a variety of finance advisors and broker franchise opportunities across different sectors ranging from automotive to education. Try and negotiate a 'master franchisee' deal where you will get rights to sell sub-franchises within a geographical location or territory. For instance, Modern Montessori International (MMI), London, is one of the largest Montessori franchises offering Montessori-based childcare services and teacher training franchises worldwide. Chelis Education Consult Ltd is its master franchisee for Nigeria that is authorized to sell sub-franchises for MMI in Nigeria.

13.9. KEY IMPLEMENTATION AND OPERATIONS ACTIVITIES OF DIFFERENT TYPES OF BUSINESSES

The implementation stage of a venture requires the performing of a range of key activities. Some of these need to be accomplished to launch the business and some need to be performed continuously to run its operations. The one common activity is any category of venture under launch is 'marketing', especially using social media to promote the new venture online. You can choose from a range of social media platforms to reach out to your target customers. These include the following:

Twitter: Twitter allows companies to promote their products and services through short messages or tweets that can contain text, or links to product websites and other social media profiles. Some companies provide customer assistance through their Twitter accounts and by quick responses they try to build brand loyalty.

Facebook: Facebook pages can be more detailed as they allow companies to upload videos, photos and testimonials which allows followers to comment and see a range of information as well as the sentiment of others who have visited your page. Most companies use Facebook to promote their brands and for new ventures this can be a low-cost marketing option.

LinkedIn: LinkedIn is a business and professional networking site which allows companies to create profiles and network through use of widgets and company pages. It is especially been useful for companies looking for new employees to recruit.

WhatsApp: WhatsApp started as an alternative to SMS and has grown to having a customer base of over a billion people in over 180 countries. WhatsApp can be used to send bulk messages to targeted customers using the broadcast option that is cost-effective. WhatsApp does not allow businesses to place advertisement in their application yet.

Instagram: Instagram has millions of users with higher user engagement than Facebook and Twitter. Instagram provides a platform where a company can communicate publicly through messages and pictures with its current and potential customers. The platform is well supported by Apple and Android mobile systems.

YouTube: YouTube is a popular avenue where advertisements can be designed to suit the target audience. Advertisements become dynamic with animation and video content, which are tagged to videos which your target market would be interested in watching. YouTube enables publishers to earn money through its YouTube partner programme. Companies can pay YouTube for a channel that they can use to promote their products and services.

Social Bookmarking: Websites such as Delicious and Reddit are popular social bookmarking sites used extensively for social media promotion. These sites are dedicated to the collection and organization of links to other websites that users deem to be of good quality. These sites allow for user-generated promotion and offer advertisements for individual user communities. These sites have an ability to redirect large volumes of web traffic and target specific and relevant audiences.

The specific set of 'implementation' and 'operations' activities will depend largely on whether your business is (a) online; (b) manufacturing-based or (c) a service. Discussed further are these two sets of activities for the aforementioned business categories:

13.9.1. AN ONLINE BUSINESS

13.9.1.1. Implementation Activities

Many ventures trade exclusively on the internet; and most bricks and mortar businesses these days have an internet presence. If your business is internet based, you will need an online presence (a website, a listing on Amazon or eBay, and/or via social media) that attracts customers, is easy to navigate and enables order placement with ease. You could choose to have your website built by a third-party for as little as £250 to as much as £20,000. Platforms like Freelancer.com can be used to get quotations. Alternatively, you can use free web design services like Wix.com or GoDaddy.com which have basic designs and customizable themes so that you can create your website on a DIY basis. Use existing e-retail platforms such as Alibaba, eBay and Amazon to sell your offerings is also viable; however, these platforms will charge you for their services.

In addition to web design, you would need to work on SEO and website advertising to promote your website. If people do not know you exist, they would not search for you online. SEO increases the online visibility of your web presence. While conducting a search, the more sooner and frequently a website appears in a search list, the more likely it would be that visitors would be attracted to it who could potentially be converted into customers. SEO can be used for optimizing different kinds of searches including images, videos and academic research. SEO differs from local search engine optimization, also very important, which focuses on optimizing a business's online presence when a user conducts a 'local search' for a business or for the category of its products/services. Finally, security should be a key priority in the design phase, your customers will expect secure online transactions and assurances that their data would be stored safely.

13.9.1.2. Operational Activities

Once your website has been tested and is made 'live', you need to create a plan to launch your online venture. Your launch plan should include well thought-out answers to the following questions:

1. What would be your ideal or planned launch date?
2. Which content do you want your first customers to see on your launch date?
3. What will your pre-launch 'coming soon' teaser website landing page look like?
4. How will you create a viral effect to attract visitors?
5. Will you create a Google Alert for your brand and use features like 'share page' on social media?
6. Which relationships will you use to create a sense of excitement or buzz on your launch day, especially on social media marketing channels?

Following the website launch, you will need to update and maintain the content of your website regularly and ensure that all content is current and not dated. For doing this, you could use digital content management (DCM). DCM refers to the processes and technologies that lead to the management and publishing of information that is stored or accessed via computers. Digital content includes textual content as well as multimedia files—audio and video. Software vendors including Microsoft and Interwoven offer DCM software to help automate the collection, management and publishing of information on websites. DCM would require a designated individual, who would assign (or assume) the following roles, allocating responsibilities accordingly:

1. **Creator:** Creating and editing content on the website
2. **Editor:** Tuning the content and style of delivery
3. **Publisher:** Releasing the content on the website
4. **Administrator:** Managing access permissions

A big part of your operations would be marketing and promotion, and the 'channel' (or medium) for such activities for online ventures is social media. Social media marketing or digital marketing involves promoting your products or services using social media platforms such as Twitter, Facebook, Instagram and Snapchat. In the past decade, social media marketing has become exceedingly important among small businesses owners due to the following reasons. First, these platforms provide data analytics which help venture owners to track the success of their ad campaigns. Second, these platforms can address a wide number of a new venture's stakeholders such as customers, employees and journalists. Third, social media allows customers to post reviews, thereby, generating user-generated content rather than relying on market-generated advertisements for promotion.

A more active approach to social media marketing can involve using social media 'influencers' and 'vloggers' to endorse your product or service or to target advertisements to specific demographics interested in specific aspects like video gaming. When a celebrity, for example, endorses a cosmetics brand through their Twitter, Instagram and Facebook accounts, they help bring in the support of millions of their supporters.

If in your online venture you sell physical products, then inventory management (IM) would be a key operational function. IM includes the process of procuring, storing and utilizing materials for manufacturing into finished goods or selling finished goods (physical products) via online sales. Inventory is an important part of a venture's assets, and represents an investment by the entrepreneur that generates returns when the finished goods/products in inventory are finally sold. Inventory creation costs can be significant with associated costs such as storage, tracking and insurance. Mismanagement of inventories can cause substantial financial losses for a new venture and therefore your operations plan should include strategies for optimizing your inventory levels based on accurately projected customer demand.

13.9.2. A MANUFACTURING BUSINESS

GMW, an Indian EV Manufacturer

GMW was established in 2010 by the Gayam brothers—Raja and Rahul Gayam—in the southern Indian state of Andhra Pradesh. They took over their father's bus body building unit with a vision to manufacture EVs. The company has since introduced significant technological developments with limited resources. GMW has pioneered the world's first electric three wheeler using the Li-ion battery and supplies smart autos to the Swedish furniture maker IKEA for its delivery services in India. Their other major clients being Uber, Bigbasket, Flipkart, Grofers, Gati, Chittoor Police, the Andhra Pradesh and Telangana governments. The company also exports smart and electric three wheelers and four wheelers to over 15 emerging economies.

It was in 2015 when GMW introduced India's first electric three-wheeler vehicle. India is the biggest producer and exporter of auto-rickshaws across the globe. EVs provide a pollution-free alternative to fossil fuel-based three wheelers as emissions from the latter have been attributed to the millions of premature deaths each year in emerging economies such as India and China. The Gayam brothers felt that they could combine their expertise in clean energy and automobile manufacturing to manufacture EVs. They spent years of intense R&D work to create vehicles that can run on Li-ion batteries, a Quadra-drive system, a smart-battery management system and an integrated cooling system. However, once their 'smart auto' was built, the duo faced two major challenges: first, to run e-rickshaws that are as powerful as theirs, a government order had to be obtained from the various state governments in India. The brothers did obtain approvals from Gurugram in North India and a number of other states; however, the provision did not exist in other states such as Andhra Pradesh, Telangana and Karnataka in south India. This process of obtaining clearances across India was quite challenging and time-consuming for the management of GMW.

Another major challenge for the brothers was the lack of proper charging infrastructure in India unlike in industrialized nations, where there has been a government-backed drive to set up a national e-vehicle charging infrastructure. Hence, the Gayam brothers created battery swapping stations. A battery swapping station, usually located at conventional petrol stations, is kiosk where a GMW vehicle's discharged battery or battery pack can be immediately swapped for a fully charged one, eliminating the delay involved in waiting for the vehicle's battery to charge. These stations have become one of GMW's core offerings. The process appears simple in theory but is actually quite complicated to deliver efficiently to the extent that even well-established competitors like Tesla have only just tested and not yet made 'battery swapping' commercially available.

13.9.2.1. Implementation Activities

Manufacturing businesses are involved in converting (or assembling) components, parts or raw materials into finished goods or products that can be either directly sold to consumers or to other businesses. Manufacturing businesses need to purchase or lease machinery and equipment and employ people with technical skills to work in production. Manufacturing processes involve fabrication of raw materials, and the use of machinery and transportation to move inventory throughout the production system.

Manufacturing often calls for a heavy upfront financial investment in specialized facilities, such as land, a factory, manufacturing equipment and raw materials. Thus, a manufacturing start-up usually requires very careful initial planning. The manufacturing industry tends to be heavily regulated, and the obtaining of one or several government licenses and/or permits would be necessary before operations begin. Keeping the timeline and the various steps in the process of acquiring these licenses/permits would be important. Beginning operations without obtaining these licenses/permits first would be breaking the law, and if caught doing so, heavy fines and penalties maybe levied against you. You would also need to ensure that safety procedures that are prescribed as mandatory by the law of the land are being adhered to. In terms of staffing, you will need to recruit and train staff members and check compliance with employment laws. Finally, you would need to ensure that raw materials are procured in time, and stocks are adequate to meet initial customer demand.

13.9.2.2. Operational Activities

Manufacturing operations can be quite complex and are divided into four categories: (a) management; (b) production; (c) procurement and (d) quality control.

Management: A small management team is needed depending on the size of your manufacturing operations to manage specific tasks, assign work to the team, track and control costs, implement policies, strategies and procedures.

Production: For the manufacturing of products and organizing the production process, you might need to appoint a production manager or supervisor with the responsibility of overseeing employees. For a small operation, you might only need a single manager supervising a small production team; however, in cases where different items are being manufactured in large quantities, production teams with team leaders are need to streamline each part of the production process.

Procurement: In case your manufacturing assembles products, you will need to procure components, raw materials and store these as inventory. Procurement and inventory control are key functions performed by a procurement manager—whose job is to oversee purchasing clerks and warehousing staff.

Quality assurance: Manufacturing inevitably requires a quality assurance function to evaluate whether the specifications of finished goods meet required guidelines (set both by the government and your customers). In relation to these specifications, manufacturing businesses, at times, must meet the requirements set by international quality management standards such as ISO 9000. Quality assurance is usually the responsibility of a quality assurance manager.

13.9.3. A SERVICE BUSINESS

13.9.3.1. Implementation Activities

A service business which might serve either individual customers or business customers is relatively simpler when compared to manufacturing businesses to implement. This is since no upfront investment in plant, equipment, land and machinery are traditionally needed. A service business provides intangible services to individual customers (like as a beauty salon or a private tuition provider) or to industries, like banking or hospitality (commercial cleaning, for instance). As a service business owner, when implementing your business, you could choose to operate from (a) your home; (b) a commercial office; or (c) sell your services through an online platform. Depending on your choice of location, you might need to obtain a commercial lease or rental agreement for your premises and arrange for insurance.

If yours is a retail business such as a shop, café and restaurant, a basic activity which would need to be completed prior to launching your venture would be choosing its 'location'. Your location needs to be such that you could ensure good 'footfall' (customers walking-in) via easy access for the average customer. There are several factors you need to consider while deciding on location—including, the size of the local population, accessibility of the site, parking, site costs and availability of public transport. You might choose a shopping mall or shopping district/street but such prime locations can be expensive to acquire. You could choose a site which might generate lower footfall in case you sell products like furniture that customers seek out on their own and are willing to. Retailers sometimes cluster together in an area such as restaurants and cafés which attracts customers to a particular location. Once you have decided on the location, you will need to obtain commercial leases and licenses which can take considerable time, which you should account for in your implementation plan.

The service-creation environment needs to be planned with the customer in focus, especially if you are going to expect 'walk-in' customers. Here the layout of your facilities and the décor used would play an important role when *converting* a 'walk-in' to a 'paying customer'. The spaces, textures, look, colours and 'feel' of the place of the service are important to service customers; these aspects help potential customers decide whether you are trustable, reliable, skilled and quality conscious. The way you design the physical space of service delivery will elicit a certain *emotional* response from your customers. You must ask yourself the question: What do you want your customers to 'feel' about your venture and your brand identity? Do you want them to feel that your venture is 'traditional' and rooted in a particular culture, for example, or is hi-tech and futuristic? Getting experts to help you design your service delivery space by keeping the 'experience' of the customer at the heart of the design process will help you avoid costly mistakes and differentiate you from other similar businesses.

The service retail unit would have to be designed and fitted out which can take a while. The design and layout need to be in line with your brand's identity and values. As you would be dealing with walk-in sales, you would need to invest in a good security system to prevent shoplifting. Undoubtedly, you will need some web presence with a secure payment system. A credit/debit merchant account would also need to be set up. The ordering of your merchandise and stock would need to be done in time for launch, so that you can adequately tag your items with prices and add any in-store descriptions. You would also need to recruit and train your sales and other staff.

A launch event would need to be organized to promote a retail outlet and attract customers. You could offer products or samples at a lower price as a part of your opening sales strategy, and promote the event with hoardings, banners, flyers and via media promotions in local radio, newspaper or through social medial channels.

In terms of staffing, you would need to check compliance with local employment laws. You would also need to formulate policies and procedures to guide employees through various aspects of your service delivery operations.

13.9.3.2. Operational Activities

In a service operation, operations managers usually schedule employees to handle customer demand, which could vary from hour to hour in a typical day or might be impacted by seasonal trends. Further, coaching and training employees is necessary to ensure the delivery of quality services to customers. Managers need to consider staff turnover, while planning operations as this can be a major issue in most kinds of services. Retaining employees is a major concern for a service venture's operations manager. Service firms can use a range of methods to create employee loyalty such as conducting peer reviews, doing timely performance appraisals, training and other forms of recognition for good performance.

Service operations that sell tangible goods like restaurants also face inventory issues, therefore, procurement and stock control would become central to their operations. Finally, service operations require quality control and safety checks to ensure compliance and ongoing qualitative improvements.

As a part of everyday operations of a retail service unit, you would need to have regular promotions advertised through various media channels (print, social media, radio, TV and so on). You will need to control the service operations and maintain security at your retail unit. At the same time, maintaining inventories to an optimum level would be important to keep up with customer demand.

13.10. DEVELOPING A BUSINESS PLAN

In the previous sections, we went through the different kinds of activities that entrepreneurs launching either online, manufacturing or service-based ventures need to undertake for implementing and running their businesses. Usually, these activities are described in a 'business plan'. The business plan is a formal document that is generally used for raising finance through formal channels like banks or (individual or institutional) equity investors. This plan is the outcome of your business planning process as it sets out the goals for your venture, how you intend to achieve these goals and the time frame within which such goals are required to be achieved. It also includes a description of the nature of the business, provides background information, financial projections and finally detailed 'implementation' and 'operations' plans.

Business plans vary in length and complexity depending on the scale of your new venture as well as the purpose for which the plan is being developed. For instance, it can be quite brief—a mere 10 pages or less—in case it is intended for you alone, as a blueprint with milestones that provide a clear direction for your start-up activities. If the plan is intended for external use like to raise finance, then it would be more comprehensive and longer, up to 20 pages, with detailed financials and other elements as described in the sub-sections further. Finally, the document must be prepared like a report with vital information that can be used for taking decisions.

A general business plan structure is outlined as follows, you can omit some or add other sections depending on the nature of your new venture and the purposes for which you are developing it:

1. Cover
2. Table of contents

3. Executive summary
4. Business description
5. Industry analysis and market research
6. VP and customer profile
7. Marketing plan
8. Operations plan
9. Management team
10. Financing
11. Financial projections
12. Risks and mitigation strategies
13. Implementation plan
14. Appendices

Cover: The cover of your business plan provides the name of the venture, contact details and marked as confidential.

Table of contents: This outlines the contents with page numbers.

Executive summary (one–two pages): This is a very important section of the business plan, especially if you are seeking external finance as investors, with limited time, often look at this section first and then decide whether it would be worth their time to read the entire document. The summary should be written upright at the end when the entire business plan has been compiled and edited. This section should highlight the nature of your product/service, target customers, VP and competitive advantage. You should include financial highlights like expected returns on the equity investment you seek, or the manner in which you will pay back your loan—in case you are seeking debt investment from a bank. The executive summary must be focused and written in a concise manner, while being appealing to the reader. It must be written as a summary and not an introduction.

Business description (one page): This section includes basic information such as the name of your business, address, legal form and ownership. It should include a description of your product/service, a mission and vision statement and its objectives that you have formulated.

Industry analysis and market research (two–four pages): This section provides background information about your industry sector and the market segments. You can choose models like a PESTLE analysis to present finer details. PESTLE stands for the following: P for Political, E for Economic, S for Social, T for Technological, L for Legal and E for Environmental. It allows you to structure your data in a meaningful manner, and present outcomes more convincingly. This section should also include details on industry structure, growth and market trends, market segments and target market selection and competitors' analysis (strengths and weaknesses).

VP and customer profile (two pages): This is the section where you elaborate the VP for your product/service and your target customer's profile. You should highlight the competitive advantage you have over your competitors.

Marketing plan (two–four pages): This section provides details of your sales and marketing mix. This includes launch strategy and details on how you intend to develop your brand, product and market development and also the market growth potential.

Management team (one–two pages): This section outlines the key people in the venture, their backgrounds and experience. Also include details on individuals in the background such as directors and any other shareholders.

Financing (one page): This section outlines the investment you need to launch your venture. External financers expect to see the owners' contribution and loan requirements. You should present a capital cost estimate here based on real quotations.

Financial projections (one-page summary plus appendices): Typically, financial projections for three years need to be provided, including an annual cash flow statement, income projections, balance sheet projections with details of key ratios as well as the assumptions on which your financial projections are based, particularly the bases for your sales projections.

Operations plan (two pages): This section outlines how your business will be run and how your product/service will be produced and delivered. The contents of your operations plan will vary, depending on the nature of your business (online/retail/manufacturing/service). This section should cover how you intend to scale your business in the future. The contents should include key operating activities, details on your partnerships, IP issues and scalability.

Implementation plan: To facilitate the tracking of implementation activities, a realistic implementation plan is also included in the business plan. At the start-up phase, such a plan is usually quite broad with a series of milestones, clear objectives and a corresponding timeline. The implementation plan can be readily captured within a 'Gantt chart'. Follow the general style and format provided in Table 13.1—based on a retail venture's implementation, making suitable modifications to capture your own venture's implementation requirements.

13.11. SUMMARY AND APPLICATION

Before you implement your idea, you must consider important issues like deciding on the manner in which you intend to protect your IP. The options range from applying for patents, copyrights to trade secrecy and non-disclosure agreements. Then, you need to decide on the legal format for your business weighing in the advantages and disadvantages of each format to find the most suitable and beneficial for you—the entrepreneur. Finally, you need to consider the taxation system of the country where your venture operates ensuring you comply with all regulations.

As a new venture, you can also consider franchising as a way of accessing resources and reducing risks associated with new 'green field' venture creation. Franchising can be an effective way to access expertise and skills from established franchisors. It offers several advantages for a new start up—including market penetration, brand recognition, a tried and tested business formula and already developed products and services which have sold elsewhere. Franchising can add value to your business by simplifying operations, leveraging your knowledge and capabilities, and reducing risk. However, there are also costs and revenue associated with such privileges in the form of an upfront franchise fees and a recurring royalty payment.

In terms of operations, you need to identify the list of key activities that need to be completed for running your new venture. These include activities both at the implementation and operational

TABLE 13.1 Implementation Plan 'Gantt Chart' Format

ACTIVITIES	MONTH 1				MONTH 2				MONTH 3			
	W1	W2	W3	W4	W1	W2	W3	W4	W1	W2	W3	W4
Pre-launch activities												
Signing a commercial lease agreement												
Obtain licenses												
Retail unit design												
Design briefing												
Design drawings												
Design approved												
Store fitted out												
Merchandise and stock planning												
Plan and order												
Shelfing												
Website design												
Staff recruitment and training												
Recruitment and training												
Setting up merchant accounts												
LAUNCH EVENT												

stages that derive from the business model (or mechanism to create new revenue) you have designed for your new venture. The list of activities will vary according to the type of business—three different broad categories have been featured in this chapter—internet-based, manufacturing and service-based. Once you have identified your key activities, a business plan can be developed for raising either debt or equity finance.

Exercise 13.1. List all the key activities that you need to perform for the success of your new venture. Think about implementation before launch of your venture and the day-to-day, key operational activities. List the resources required for the identified key activities. Next, prepare a business plan for your venture, thinking carefully about the risks associated with both implementation and operations.

Exercise 13.2. Consider the benefits of franchising to launch your new venture. Investigate, using search engines, what franchises are available for sale that are similar to your proposed new venture. Weigh the pros and cons of particular franchise opportunities. Contact the identified franchisors and collect relevant details about the supports offered and the associated costs. Decide whether franchising is a possible option you wish to explore and list the activities you would need to undertake to make it viable.

Thank you for reading—we wish you all the best in your entrepreneurial journey. If you have any thoughts or simply want to share your enterprise and entrepreneurship experiences, you are always welcome to write to us

—Ali, Punita and Iain

Bibliography

Auerbach, D. (2018). *FIP 60: David Auerbach interviews Samir Ibrahim of SunCulture*. Audio interview. Retrieved from https://findingimpact.com/fip-60-david-auerbach-interviews-samir-ibrahim-of-sunculture/

Bhattacharya, A. (2015). *5 great Elon Musk quotes on innovation*. Inc. Retrieved from https://www.inc.com/ananya-bhattacharya/5-elon-musk-quotes-about-innovation.html

Christensen, C. (1997). *The innovators dilemma* (1st ed.). USA: Harvard Business Review Press.

Christensen, C. M., Dillon, K., Hall, T., & Duncan, D. (2016). *Competing against luck: The story of innovation and customer choice*. New York, NY: Harper Business.

De Bono, E. (1985). *Six thinking hats: An essential approach to business management*. London: Little, Brown and Company.

Eberle, B. (1996). *Scamper: Games for imagination development*. Waco, TX: Prufrock Press.

Gascoigne, J. (2019). Idea to Paying Customers in 7 Weeks: How We Did It, Buffer.com. Retrieved from https://buffer.com/resources/idea-to-paying-customers-in-7-weeks-how-we-did-it

James, G. (2015). *How Steve Jobs trained his own brain*. Inc. Retrieved from https://www.inc.com/geoffrey-james/how-steve-jobs-trained-his-own-brain.html

Osterwalder, A., Pigneur, Y., & Clark, T. (2010). *Business model generation: A handbook for visionaries, game changers, and challengers*. Hoboken, NJ: John Wiley & Sons.

Read, S., Sarasvathy, S., Dew, N., & Wiltbank, R. (2017). *Effectual entrepreneurship* (2nd ed.). Oxford: Routledge.

Ries, E. (2014). *The lean Startup: How today's entrepreneurs use continuous innovation to create radically successful businesses*. San Francisco, CA: Crown Publishing.

Rizvi, A. (2017). *Entrepreneuring Pakistan: 27 stories of struggle, failure and success*. Karachi: CreateSpace Independent Publishing Platform.

Sarasvathy, S. (2009). *Effectuation: Elements of entrepreneurial expertise*. Northampton, MA: Edward Elgar Publishing.

Ulwick, A. (2005). *What customers want: Using outcome-driven innovation to create breakthrough products and services* (1st ed.). USA: McGraw-Hill Education.

Photo Credits

CHAPTER 1

Spotlight on Farhan Masood, 'Entrepreneur Extraordinaire' from Pakistan: Part 1
https://www.techinasia.com/inventor-recognised-brilliant-minds (Accessed on 7 January 2019)
Spotlight on Farhan Masood, 'Entrepreneur Extraordinaire' from Pakistan: Part 2
https://www.prnewswire.com/news-releases/microsoft-and-soloinsight-to-help-build-internet-of-people-together-300251699.html (Accessed on 7 January 2019)

CHAPTER 2

Spotlight on Professor Mouhammad Yunus, 'World's Banker to the Poor' from Bangladesh
http://archive.skoll.org/2013/12/18/3-key-characteristics-great-social-business-entrepreneurs/ and https://www.kazamagrameen.org/kgmi-network.php (Accessed on 7 January 2019)
NeoNurture, a Medical Device out of Car Spare Parts
https://www.designthatmatters.org/past-projects/ (Accessed on 7 January 2019)
Jack Ma: From English Teacher to the Warrior Spirited 'Super Entrepreneur'
https://www.pymnts.com/personnel/2018/alibaba-jack-ma-retire-philanthropy-education/ (Accessed on 7 January 2019)
An Example Storyboard
http://www.uxizhang.com/idm.html (Accessed on 07 Jan 2019)
Six Thinking Hats, by Edward de Bono
https://www.clipartmax.com/middle/m2i8Z5A0N4K9G6K9_six-thinking-hats-canvas-edward-de-bono-six-frames/ (Accessed on 7 January 2019)
SCAMPER, by Bob Eberle
https://www.slidegeeks.com/business/product/scamper-technique-tamplate-2-ppt-powerpoint-presentation-slides (Accessed on 7 January 2019)

CHAPTER 3

Spotlight on Dr Moses Kizza Musaazi, 'the Genius Fixer of Things' from Uganda
https://ugandaradionetwork.com/story/makerere-professor-who-invented-papyrus-sanitary-pad-is-dead and http://knickersfornewlife.org/makapads/ (Accessed on 17 January 2019)
Social Enterprise and Innovation Exemplars

https://www.legalwiz.in/blog/ode-women-entrepreneurship; http://www.m-kopa.com/m-kopa-solar-surpasses-60000-sales/ and http://www.thailandsocialinnovationplatform.org/project/klong-dinsor/ (Accessed on 17 January 2019)

Frugal Innovation Example: MittiCool Fridge by Mansukhbhai Prajapati

http://www.designwillsavetheworld.net/sustainability-and-design/20140609-MittiCool-clay-fridge-without-electricity-sustainable/ (Accessed on 17 January 2019)

CEMEX's (Mexico) GPS Tracked Cement Mixer Trucks

https://mexico-now.com/index.php/article/2806-cemex-to-supply-special-mix-of-concrete-for-mexico-city-new-airport (Accessed on 17 January 2019)

Natura's (Brazil) Skin Cream

https://www.octoprime.co/products/exclu-top-influenceuses-duo-de-cremes-visage-anti-signes-jour-nuit-30-natura-brasil-chronos/hat99 (Accessed on 17 January 2019)

A Pair of Glasses for Recording and Transmitting Video

https://kotaku.com/chinese-test-cheating-tools-look-like-something-out-of-1587970164 (Accessed on 14 May 2019)

Old Cell Phones Set Up as Cheating Devices

https://kotaku.com/chinese-test-cheating-tools-look-like-something-out-of-1587970164 (Accessed on 14 May 2019)

Haier's (China) Dual-Purpose Washing Machine

https://www.huffingtonpost.co.uk/2013/09/03/washing-machine-vegetables-china-_n_3860339.html (Accessed on 14 May 2019)

CHAPTER 4

Spotlight on Kadir Koymen, Founder of Edelkrone: Photography and Cinema Products from Turkey

https://ceotudent.com/baska-bir-sey-edelkrone (Accessed on 17 January 2019)

Dai Wei, CEO and Co-Founder of OFO: Chinese Bike Sharing Firm | Bird-in-Hand

https://www.slush.org/news/ofo-co-founder-ceo-dai-wei-yellow-bikes-worth-2-billion/ (Accessed on 17 January 2019)

Sachin and Binny Bansal, Founders of Flipkart.com: Indian E-commerce Giant | Lemonade Principle

https://www.indiatoday.in/magazine/cover-story/story/20150105-newsmakers-2014-sachin-and-binny-bansal-flipkart-806376–2014–12-25 (Accessed on 21 January 2019)

Gyanesh Pandey, CEO of Husk Power Systems: Indian Rural Electrification Pioneers | Crazy Quilt

https://www.thehindubusinessline.com/news/variety/bihars-husk-power/article20108183.ece1 (Accessed on 21 January 2019)

Daria Alekseeva, Founder of Charity Shop: Russian Social Enterprise | Pilot-in-the-Plane

http://mosurbanforum.com/speakers/1445 (Accessed on 21 January 2019)

Samir Ibrahim and Charles Nichols, Founders of SunCulture: Kenyan Agri-Tech Firm | Affordable Loss

https://expogr.com/detail_news.php?newsid=5248&pageid=2; https://impactalpha.com/sunculture-secures-backing-from-edf-group/ and https://www.nation.co.ke/lifestyle/money/Solar-powered-kit-brightens-farmer-trade/435440-2147928-s3qdp3z/index.html (Accessed on 14 May 2019)

CHAPTER 5

Spotlight on M-Pesa, 'a Money Transfer Service' from Kenya
https://www.cio.co.ke/safaricom-questioned-over-network-outage/; https://memeburn.com/2012/03/how-m-pesa-disrupts-entire-economies/ and https://www.bbc.co.uk/programmes/p04kxddv (Accessed on 21 January 2019)
Google Images Search Result
https://www.google.com/search?q=cycling+puncture+addis+ababa&source=lnms&tbm=isch&sa=X&ved=0ahUKEwiiq-Lgi4LiAhVdQhUIHZiuBQoQ_AUIDigB&biw=1536&bih=754 (Accessed on 14 May 2019)
Google Trends Comparison
https://trends.google.com/trends/explore?q=cycle&geo=ET (Accessed on 14 May 2019)
Online Forum Dedicated to Cycles and Cycling
https://www.cyclechat.net/ (Accessed on 14 May 2019)
Non-Participant Observation Example
https://hotels.ng/guides/destinations/hi-impact-planet-amusement-park/ (Accessed on 14 May 2019)

CHAPTER 6

Spotlight on Fax Machines
https://www.news.xerox.com/photo?id=586d2b412cfac25f877c63a2&fid=5023e3922937 1a4cae00038c (Accessed on 21 January 2019)
'Solutions' Change, Jobs Do not
Unsplash, https://unsplash.com/photos/VLGWE_SumrA (Accessed on 14 May 2019)
Engadget, https://www.engadget.com/2009/03/03/kodak-introduces-easyshare-z915-with-10x-zoomer/ (Accessed on 14 May 2019)
Samsung, https://www.samsung.com/us/news/newsRead.do?news_seq=19593 (Accessed on 14 May 2019)
DiDi Taxi App Part 1: A Customer 'Jobs' View of the Market Definition
http://fortune.com/2016/04/07/didi-kuaidi-valuation-25-billion/ and https://www.scmp.com/tech/apps-gaming/article/1844341/didi-kuaidi-chinas-top-taxi-hailing-app-launches-personal-chauffeur (Accessed on 21 January 2019)

CHAPTER 7

Spotlight on the 'Generator Economy' in War-torn Syria
https://www.gettyimages.co.uk/detail/news-photo/syrian-boys-sell-electric-generators-on-a-street-in-the-news-photo/166163649 (Accessed on 14 May 2019)
https://en.annahar.com/article/741737-more-than-a-year-later-syrias-aleppo-still-wrecked-by-war (Accessed on 14 May 2019)
https://www.nytimes.com/2016/02/23/world/middleeast/un-finds-deliberate-destruction-of-hospitals-in-syria.html (Accessed on 14 May 2019)
OFO Dockless Bikes from China Part 1: Value Gaps Identification
https://unsplash.com/photos/j8qMkXtT5hA (Accessed on 14 May 2019)

CHAPTER 8

Spotlight on DJI: The Future of Possible, 'Hi-Tech Drones' from China
https://www.dji.com/support/product (Accessed on 21 January 2019)
The Meituan Takeaway Mobile Application, China
http://www.thatsmags.com/shanghai/post/21104/how-to-order-delivery-on-chinese-food-apps (Accessed on 21 January 2019)
https://www.meituan.com/ (Accessed on 14 May 2019)
http://www.thatsmags.com/shanghai/post/21104/how-to-order-delivery-on-chinese-food-apps (Accessed on 21 January 2019)
A 'Sell-Before-You-Build' Example: Pebble Time on Kickstarter
https://www.kickstarter.com/projects/getpebble/pebble-e-paper-watch-for-iphone-and-android (Accessed on 21 January 2019)

CHAPTER 9

https://www.tink-africa.com/?offset=1490778236850 (Accessed on 22 January 2019)
Format of Formal Pitches as Seen on TV Shows
https://ismailimail.blog/2016/11/26/bamba-group-secure-250000-k-sh-25-million-on-kenyas-lions-den/ and https://www.altonivel.com.mx/empresas/emprendedor/la-joven-que-vende-galletas-de-chapulines-y-conquisto-a-shark-tank/ (Accessed on 22 January 2019)
Contrasting Presentation Styles
https://www.presentationzen.com/presentationzen/2005/11/it_was_one_of_t.html and https://www.davidtan.org/comparing-steve-jobs-and-bill-gates-presentations-style/ (Accessed on 22 February 2019)

CHAPTER 10

Spotlight on Dong Nguyen, the Creator of the Mobile Game Flappy Bird
https://www.cnet.com/news/dong-nguyen-on-the-return-of-flappy-bird/ and http://www.gameacademy.com/apple-google-rejecting-games-flappy/flappy-bird-dead-dong-nguyen-not/ (Accessed on 22 January 2019)
Public Relations Stunts
https://www.campaignlive.co.uk/article/giant-polar-bear-unleashed-london-sky-atlantic-stunt/1331134 (Accessed on 9 February 2019)
https://www.thedrum.com/opinion/2016/06/16/25-greatest-publicity-stunts-our-time (Accessed on 9 February 2019)
https://www.prexamples.com/2018/12/the-best-creative-pr-campaigns-publicity-stunts-and-brand-activations-of-2018/ (Accessed on 9 February 2019)
Kayani Bakery, Pune, India
tripadvisor™ and https://zoroastrians.net/2009/01/12/kyani-bakery/ (Accessed on 22 January 2019)
SELCO Solar Lights: Using Solar Power to Empower Rural Communities

https://www.youtube.com/channel/UCDu2UPy-fq1Ap7ufkDGUI9g/videos (Accessed on 17 May 2019)
Snapshots from YouTube and Facebook pages of SELCO foundation.
https://www.facebook.com/SELCO-INDIA-342064453443/ (Accessed on 18 January 2019)
MissMalini.com, India's Glamourous Digital Influencer
https://www.missmalini.com/; Snapshots from https://www.youtube.com/watch?v=tCw41uw4u7M (Accessed on 22 January 2019)
GMW Electric Smart Auto: Product Offerings
http://www.gayammotorworks.com/product/urban-et-3-wheeler/ (Accessed on 22 January 2019)
Bakeys, Edible Cutlery from India
https://www.business-standard.com/article/companies/bakeys-you-can-use-and-eat-this-innovative-cutlery-116062200024_1.html and http://www.bakeys.com (Accessed on 22 January 2019)
SELCO Solar Lights: Using Solar Power to Empower Rural Communities
https://www.youtube.com/channel/UCDu2UPy-fq1Ap7ufkDGUI9g/videos and https://www.facebook.com/SELCO-INDIA-342064453443/ (Accessed on 14 May 2019)

CHAPTER 11

Spotlight on Sumita Ghose, Indian Social Entrepreneur and Founder of Rangsutra
https://www.thebetterindia.com/80816/rangsutra-artisan-crafts-sumita-ghose/ and http://www.womenonwings.com/2016/01/adding-colors-to-lives-of-women-rangsutra/ (Accessed on 22 January 2019)
https://www.businesstoday.in/current/corporate/craft-company-rangsutra-to-launch-e-commerce-portal/story/281082.html and http://www.womenonwings.com/2016/04/facilitating-growth-at-rangsutra/ (Accessed on 22 January 2019)
Mast Kalandar, a Quick-Service Restaurant Chain
https://www.hindustantimes.com/business/techie-couple-cooks-up-a-storm-with-eatery-chain/story-QtaD2BuujWU3X9yeBB9qLK.html; https://www.asklaila.com/photo/Bangalore/Koramangala+6th+Block/Mast+Kalandar/0Ws94Ljt/1191685/; https://www.rakshaskitchen.com/mk-dabbawala-app-by-mast-kalandar/ and https://apkpure.com/mk-dabbawala-from-mastkalandar/com.presto.restaurant.mkdabbawala (Accessed on 22 January 2019)
Example Crowdfunding Platforms Operating in India
https://milaap.org/ (Accessed on 19 March 2019)
https://www.ketto.org/ (Accessed on 19 March 2019)
https://www.wishberry.in/#/home (Accessed on 19 March 2019)
Example Government Schemes in Developing Countries
Nigeria
https://www.nairaland.com/3319071/boi-yes-programme-cohort-2-facebook-group and http://dailypost.ng/2018/02/08/youwin-fg-releases-names-successful-candidates/ (Accessed on 22 January 2019)
India
https://startupindia.upgrad.com; https://www.innovationiseverywhere.com/make-in-india-meet-5-promising-internet-things-startups-bangalore/ and https://www.financialexpress.com/india-news/atal-innovation-mission-nurturing-young-minds/1222971/ (Accessed on 22 January 2019)
Vietnam
http://ipp.vn/en/ and http://natif.vn/en/about/history-1.html (Access on 22 January 2019)
An Angel Investor in Pakistan

http://www.cresventures.com/; https://www.facebook.com/sukoonpakistan/ and https://propakistani.pk/2016/03/23/perkup-raises-rs-15-million-in-seed-funding-round/ (Accessed on 22 January 2019)

Aavishkaar: A Social Venture Capital Fund Based in Mumbai, India

https://www.business-standard.com/article/companies/aavishkar-intellecap-s-vineet-rai-diary-of-an-impact-investor-118041900023_1.html and https://www.aavishkaar.in/ (Accessed on 20 March 2019)

CHAPTER 12

Spotlight on Rivigo, 'Making Logistics Human' from India

https://economictimes.indiatimes.com/small-biz/startups/features/a-roadside-chat-set-me-on-my-way-for-rivigo-moment-deepak-garg-ceo-rivigo/articleshow/62143469.cms?from=mdr; https://yourstory.com/2018/03/rivigo-billion-dollar-valuation-journey/ and https://www.rivigo.com/careers/the-rivigo-way-of-life (Accessed on 22 January 2019)

Karma Recycling, India: Venture's Name Reflects Its Core Value System

https://bizztor.com/in/karma-recycling/ and https://gadgets.ndtv.com/internet/features/electronic-junk-giving-you-nightmares-karma-recycling-can-help-777164 (Accessed on 22 January 2019)

M-KOPA Solar, Kenya: Bringing Electricity to East Africa

http://skollcentreblog.org/2017/09/08/interview-with-chad-larson-co-founder-and-finance-director-m-kopa/ and https://www.fsmonline.org/news/m-kopa-solar-honored/ (Accessed on 22 January 2019)

Adorn Online: Supporting and Nurturing the Work of Artisans

https://twitter.com/najiasiddiqui and https://adornonline.org/index.php/home/ourStory (Accessed on 22 January 2019)

Thrive Agric: Empowering Farmers in Nigeria

https://www.thriveagric.com/; https://medium.com/@thriveagric/a-thriving-hope-4c185f201d2 and https://medium.com/@wennovation/startup-spotlight-thrive-agric-48221c5c9dd0 (Accessed on 22 January 2019)

HealthifyMe, India: A Digital Weight Loss Platform

https://www.thenational.ae/lifestyle/food/healthifyme-app-tracks-nutrition-in-thousands-of-indian-dishes-1.657487 and https://www.healthifyme.com/ (Accessed on 18 January 2019)

Embrace Innovations, India: Improving Infant and Maternal Mortality

https://yourstory.com/2013/06/embracing-new-born-lives-in-a-warm-cuddle-embrace-innovations/ and https://yourstory.com/2015/07/embrace-innovations/ (Accessed on 22 January 2019)

Mirakle Couriers, the Silent Couriers of Mumbai

http://www.miraklecouriers.com/ (Accessed on 22 January 2019)

Sakha Cabs, India: Safe Transport Solutions for Women by Women

https://thenextbillion.global/globally-spotted-sakha-cabs-empowering-indian-taxi-service-by-women-for-women-a-driving-force-for-womens-rights-and-development-in-india/; https://www.governancenow.com/news/regular-story/-women-women-women and http://sakhaconsultingwings.com/ (Accessed on 22 January 2019)

Jayaashree Industries, India: Low-cost Sanitary Napkins for Women by Women

http://www.theweekendleader.com/Heroism/2359/not-by-profit.html; https://www.bbc.com/news/magazine-26260978 and https://oikos-international.org/wp-content/uploads/2015/06/2015_SE_free-case_Arunachalam_case.pdf (Accessed on 22 January 2019)

Vortex Engineering, India: Solar Powered ATMs

https://www.livemint.com/Politics/wPrxiJ5SrLDIStPtKUJ3pO/Cash-at-a-fraction-of-the-cost.html and https://solartribune.com/startup-launching-solar-atms-in-india-2014–04-29/vortex-engineering-solar-atm/ (Accessed on 22 January 2019)

Berman–Kalil Housing Concepts: South Africa, Innovative and Affordable Housing

https://www.homify.co.za/professionals/2805967/berman-kalil-housing-concepts and https://www.howwemadeitinafrica.com/south-african-company-making-shipping-containers-feel-like-a-real-house/ (Accessed on 22 January 2019)

WaterWalla, India: Improving Access to Clean Water

http://www.waterwalla.org/waterwalla-dharavi-pilot/and https://www.huffingtonpost.com/billrobinson/the-kairos-society-waterw_b_1321023.html (Accessed on 22 January 2019)

CHAPTER 13

Spotlight on ELEME, Gigantic Chinese Food Delivery Platform

https://www.retailnews.asia/war-in-the-food-delivery-market-on-its-way/eleme-3__trashed/ and http://www.timeoutshanghai.com/features/News-News/55510/Look-to-the-skies-Eleme-launches-food-delivery-drones-in-Shanghai.html (Accessed on 18 December 2018)

https://www.capitalwatch.com/article-1790–1.html (Accessed on 22 January 2019)

Kathi Junction, an Indian Quick-Service Restaurant Franchise

https://www.franchiseindia.com/content/Rolling-out-benefits-in-QSR-biz.1318; https://vegplatter.in/restaurant/kathi-junction-karnal/56/menu and http://thekashmirscenario.com/at-kathi-junction-apart-from-food-people-also-get-a-plate-of-love-an-interview-with-javid-parsa/ (Accessed on 22 January 2019)

GMW, an Indian EV Manufacturer

https://www.thenewsminute.com/article/duo-makes-smart-autos-efficient-diesel-ones-20-cost-59892; https://www.thenewsminute.com/article/hyd-based-startup-gayam-motor-works-supply-e-autos-ikea-its-delivery-fleet-86576 and snapshot from https://www.youtube.com/watch?v=SyTO6gNhd5c (Accessed on 22 January 2019)

https://energy.economictimes.indiatimes.com/news/power/acme-launches-indias-first-electric-vehicle-charging-station/58897254 (Accessed on 22 January 2019)

Index

B/326